Out
— of the —
Poverty Trap

Out
— of the —
Poverty Trap

A CONSERVATIVE STRATEGY
FOR WELFARE REFORM

Stuart Butler

Anna Kondratas

THE FREE PRESS
A Division of Macmillan, Inc.
NEW YORK

Collier Macmillan Publishers
LONDON

The Free Press
A Division of Macmillan, Inc.
866 Third Avenue, New York, N.Y. 10022

Collier Macmillan Canada, Inc.

Printed in the United States of America

printing number

1 2 3 4 5 6 7 8 9 10

Library of Congress Cataloging-in-Publication Data

Butler, Stuart M.
  Out of the poverty trap.

  Bibliography: p.
  Includes index.
    1. Public welfare—United States.   2. United
States—Social policy.   3. Welfare state.
I. Kondratas, Anna.   II. Title.
HV95.B88   1987   361′.973   87–14640
ISBN 0–02–905061–8

Contents

Acknowledgments

WE RECEIVED assistance from many organizations and individuals. In particular, we wish to thank the J.M. Foundation, Thomas and Shirley Roe, the Roe Foundation, and the Schultz Foundation for their generous support. The Heritage Foundation made it possible for us to undertake the project while carrying out our other duties. John Buttarazzi, Eileen Gardner, Stephen Moore, William Smith, and Gloria Vancko were of invaluable help in the research and preparation of the manuscript, and Burton Pines, Peter Germanis, Sar Levitan, Jack Svahn, and Pamela Taylor provided helpful comments and frank criticisms of sections of the earlier drafts. Needless to say, any remaining errors and questionable proposals are our responsibility.

STUART BUTLER
ANNA KONDRATAS

CHAPTER

1

Why the War on Poverty
Is Being Lost

IN THE SPRING OF 1985, many of the luminaries of the Lyndon Johnson Administration assembled in Austin, Texas, to reminisce and reflect upon the sweeping legislation they had conceived and enacted. Their presence turned what might have been a routine observance on the twentieth anniversary of the Great Society into a warm and nostalgic celebration of a remarkable episode in America's political history. After Bill Moyers, Sargent Shriver, Jack Valenti, and Joe Califano provided personal insight into their roles in that history, they boarded a bus with about a hundred others from the conference and headed for a Texas-style cookout at the LBJ ranch, hosted by the ever charming Lady Bird Johnson.

Even the few conservative academics present could hardly have been made to feel more welcome. The occasional barbed exchange at the conference itself was soon forgotten in a sea of good feeling down at the ranch. As the evening wore on, the Texas air rang with spirited—if less than accomplished—songs composed by Johnson's former staffers. Everyone laughed easily.

The Great Society veterans had every reason to be cheerful. Here they were in the fifth year of the Reagan presidency, and Johnson's legacy was showing every sign of withstanding the strongest attack ever mounted against it. True, a few programs had fallen victim to David Stockman's budget ax, and many others were squeezed, but the former Johnson staffers could feel understandably confident that the essential foundations of the Great

Society would outlast Ronald Reagan. With practically a full term ahead of it, the Reagan Administration onslaught was clearly stalled.

It would seem such confidence is still well founded. There is strong public support for the basic elements of the Great Society, and the Reagan Administration appears to have little stomach for an assault on the core of the welfare state, a political battle it would surely lose. Yet paradoxically, the greatest challenge to Johnson's legacy may actually lie ahead.

In the past, criticism of the Great Society usually centered on charges that its programs are inefficient, riddled with fraud, or of benefit primarily to those who administer to the poor rather than the poor themselves. While these arguments are still presented forcefully, the experience of twenty years of Great Society programs has given credence to a far more damaging line of attack: the claim that the system not only has failed to meet its objectives but, on balance, has in fact caused the underlying condition of America's poor to deteriorate.

Rumblings along such lines began to be heard in earnest in the 1970s. Early supporters of the Great Society started to write anxious articles for *The Public Interest* and other respected moderate journals, voicing concern at the disturbing inability of government to reach the lofty goals of the Great Society.[1] Increasingly after 1975, *Public Interest's* associate editor Mark Lilla notes, "A new, more aggressive line of argument was put forward: Whether well-intentioned or not, the attempt to expand government activity simultaneously in many social spheres had been a counterproductive mistake."[2] The remarkable thing about such writings was not so much what was being said—usually expressed in qualified, gentlemanly phrases—but who was saying it. The alarm was being sounded by liberal and moderate academics and policymakers—soon to be dubbed "neoconservatives" by the left (and defined by some conservatives as "liberals who have been mugged by reality").

The temperature of the debate began to rise noticeably when a number of black scholars and activists also began to challenge Great Society legislation, claiming that many of the antipoverty programs had discouraged blacks from improving their position, undermined the black family, and created a dispiriting dependency on welfare. That was bad enough, but then some of them even went on to question some of the basic tenets of the civil rights legislation, especially as it developed after the landmark Civil Rights Act of 1964. Thomas Sowell's book *Ethnic America*, for instance, argued that the degree of racial discrimination suffered by any immigrant group actually is a very poor guide to its ultimate economic and social success.[3] By implication, affirmative action and other steps meant to correct past and present discrimination were not the key to black progress. But Sowell marched farther into the minefield. Much of the leadership of the black community, he insisted, were interested not primarily in programs that would advance the cause of poor black Americans but in programs that would help them to join the white elite. Sowell did not win many friends in the NAACP.

In a less combative way, Harvard's Glenn Loury and others have also made the point that the black obsession with integration, combined with the intrusion of well-meaning government programs, has destroyed the spirit of self-reliance among blacks, making them more and more dependent on the white establishment. According to Loury, the Great Society approach to the problems of the black poor has been thoroughly discredited. The result of that misplaced strategy, he argues, has been to discourage positive attitudes toward education, family, and work among young blacks, hamstringing black progress.

If those challenges were shots across the bows of the Great Society, then Charles Murray's *Losing Ground* was a devastating broadside. Murray's book, published in 1984, examines each of the principal goals of the Great Society programs. His conclusion: Progress has certainly been made in some areas, but if we compare the trends already evident before the Johnson presidency with those since 1965, there is little reason to believe that the billions of dollars spent on the programs have made any significant improvement on what otherwise might have occurred.[4] Worse still, Murray maintains that spending on the Great Society has coincided with a slowdown or reversal of positive trends in many key respects. The percentage of Americans below the poverty line, for instance, fell steadily and rapidly from World War II until the late 1960s. Thereafter the decline tapered off. Moreover, he points out, if we add to the totals of officially poor Americans those who would be below the poverty line were if not for federal assistance—Murray calls them the "latent" poor—we discover that the percentage of

3

the population in poverty or dependent on government support began to rise in 1967, after falling since World War II.[5] Given that the central purpose of the Great Society was to lift poor Americans into self-sufficiency, Murray says, this "most damning" pattern strikes at the heart of the entire War on Poverty.

Murray claims that the distressing reversal in the fight against poverty, together with the crises in education, crime, and the condition of poor families, has occurred primarily because low-income youths have "become de-coupled from the mechanism whereby poor people in this country historically have worked their way out of poverty."[6] By providing them with a perverse set of incentives that encourage short-term behavior that is destructive in the long term, while masking those long-term consequences, the Great Society created a trap rather than a ladder of opportunity.

The ferocity with which Murray has been attacked is a good indication of just how seriously his charges are taken by the Great Society establishment. Whenever he attends a conference—he was at the reunion in Austin—he has to submit to a barrage of aggressive questions. And even if he himself is absent, his ideas often dominate a discussion on welfare, like some evil spirit that can be exorcized only by denunciation. Yet the counterattack has failed to shake Murray's basic thesis. True, there is plenty of room for uncertainty and disagreement over statistical details, but the thrust of his case remains intact: The Great Society, meant to eradicate the underclass, has instead expanded it.

Yet despite the effectiveness of challenges to the Great Society mounted by its many critics, no clear, comprehensive, and acceptable alternative has been presented. Murray devotes very little of his book to reform proposals. He does devote a few pages to a "thought experiment" in which the entire federal welfare and income-support system for working-age persons is scrapped, every law and court decision is reversed that awards differential treatment to any race, and an education voucher system is introduced. He speculates that a sweeping plan of that nature would be far more effectual in changing the behavior and condition of the poor positively than the host of expensive programs now in place. But he concedes that Congress is hardly likely to enact such a radical plan. Reform will eventually come, Murray concludes, "not because stingy people have won, but because generous people have stopped kidding themselves."[7]

Reform will certainly be delayed as long as it seems to be motivated by stinginess. The problem with Murray's thought experiment is that someone who has little sense of obligation to the poor could happily endorse most of it. That is the monkey on the back of all those who claim that we would actually make more progress in the War on Poverty if we were simply to bring all the troops home. The plain fact, confirmed in poll after poll, is that the American people care deeply about the poor and the underprivileged—even if they do not know how to solve the problem. And no matter how many hits are scored against the Great Society, Americans will continue to give broad support to its programs until an alternative approach is presented to them that combines the basic goals laid out by Lyndon Johnson with mechanisms that stand more of a chance of actually working.

The Reagan Administration has done little to bring that day about. Its attempts to change the Great Society—"reform" would be too generous a description—have been fatally ensnared in the campaign to reduce the federal budget deficit. The impression conveyed to the public is that the sole objective of Reagan welfare policy is to squeeze a few more dollars out of the poor to spend on defense. Had Ronald Reagan, like Lyndon Johnson, painted a clear picture of the society he was trying to construct, and how each policy brushstroke would contribute to that final picture, then he might have persuaded the country at large to stop kidding itself.

But no such picture exists. Early in his first term, Reagan did talk loftily of the spirit of volunteerism and the great potential of private sector initiative. But other than honoring some admittedly remarkable individuals and organizations, the rhetoric led to few tangible actions. Moreover, spokesmen for the voluntary sector undermined the President by complaining that they were being asked to carry a burden too large for them. To most Americans, the whole exercise had the appearance of a government trying to create a smokescreen to evade its responsibilities.

The Administration did little better in its attempt to reform federalism. Roosevelt and Johnson talked of a historic change in the nature of federalism, intended to build a stronger and more civilized nation in which national resources would be used to tackle previously intractable local problems. Reagan's New Federalism, on the other hand, had no clear shape to it for the

5

layman. It was too subtle, too obscure, with nothing to capture the imagination. When all was said and done, New Federalism seemed to most to be little more than rearranging the Great Society among various levels of government in order to save the federal treasury a few bucks.

To cap it all, while Reagan proposed reduction after reduction in federal spending on welfare programs, it was not until his fifth year in office that he even created a task force to examine how the system should be reformed—cut first and ask questions later. So it is hardly surprising that liberals in America are suspicious of conservative motives. Indeed, when one of the authors laid out some of his ideas at the meeting in Austin, he was greeted with a familiar question. "That all *sounds* very reasonable, Mr. Butler, but how do we really know you want to help the poor, not just take away the only crutch they have—even if it isn't a very good crutch?" The response—"I'll happily take a polygraph test!"—got some laughs, but it did not, of course, satisfy the questioner. Indeed, it would be hard for any response to do so until conservative criticisms of the welfare system are supported by a model of what they would put in its place. As long as the discussion occurs in the context of the federal budget, there will always be suspicion. Few Americans are enthusiastic about replacing the Great Society, for all its faults, with something that seems to be little more than a Low Budget Great Society—or even a Tight-Fisted Society.

Nevertheless, and despite the missed opportunities of the Reagan Administration, the conditions do seem right for a genuine and productive dialogue on welfare. The liberals have signaled their willingness to enter peace talks, provided the deficiencies of the Great Society are not used as an excuse to give up its goals. Conservative scholars are not yet being welcomed with open arms at liberal-dominated conferences on social welfare, but at least they are receiving invitations and getting a fair hearing. Democrats are now embracing conservative ideas that were once anathema to them, such as workfare, while rejecting, of course, any suggestion that they are conservative ideas. Ironically it was Ronald Reagan, in the early 1970s, who first gave prominence to workfare—drawing howls from liberals. And even some of Johnson's White House staff feel able to talk openly about the shortcomings of social policy. Less than a year after he traveled to Austin to eulogize his former boss, Bill Moyers was moved to make the CBS documentary *The Vanishing Family*, a depressingly vivid portrayal of the breakdown of the black family in America.

But there is still a vital missing dimension, making it impossible for liberals and conservatives to join forces in a structural reform of the Great Society: There is no agenda. Liberals and moderates may be willing to weld conservative ideas into the existing structure of welfare, but they will not propose a sweeping alternative to the Johnson legacy. The reason is simple enough. Suspicious of conservative motives, liberals fear that by frankly admitting the failures of the Great Society or proposing a radical restructuring of the programs, they will give conservatives the ammunition they need—not to reform the welfare state, but to destroy it.

Probably only conservative scholars can put forward a comprehensive agenda, and probably only liberals can enact it. Just as it took a diehard anticommunist like Richard Nixon to go to China, perhaps only a politician committed to the intent of the Great Society will be able to marshal the support necessary to change it drastically. But no liberal will risk making that difficult journey unless conservatives have first given their backing to proposals that offer an acceptable remedy to the failed promise of the Great Society. The last thing that liberals will do is stand up and admit the inherent deficiencies of the Great Society, only to have conservatives use that admission as a reason to savage welfare programs, leaving nothing in their place. Liberals will admit failures only if conservatives agree to an alternative way of reaching the essential goals of the War on Poverty. So far conservatives have failed to do so. They have either addressed only individual elements of the issue or, more often, concentrated on criticism rather than reform. Like Ronald Reagan, conservative scholars generally have presented no picture that the American people can judge in its entirety.

Before it is possible to paint such a picture, we must first explore briefly the foundation of the Great Society to determine where practice diverged from theory.

Why Things Went Wrong

The affluent America of the early 1960s had plenty to be ashamed of. More than half of its citizens over sixty-five had no

7

medical insurance, and one-third lived in poverty. Segregation was still rife in the South, and in many counties black Americans were effectively barred from registering to vote or gerrymandered out of political power. In their 1964 *Report to the President*, the Council of Economic Advisers described poverty in America as rampant and persistent. In 1962, nearly one in five Americans lived below the poverty line. Even though the rate was falling, the Council predicted that without decisive action it could still be stalled at 13 percent in 1980.[8]

The poverty problem had many roots, the panel of economists said. One was high unemployment in many communities. Single-parent families caused by divorce or desertion was also a factor. Another was the disability or death of the principal wage earner. Still another was low productivity, and hence low pay, due to inadequate education, health care, training, and motivation.

There are plenty of theories to explain why the response to that condition was the tidal wave of legislation known as the Great Society. But no matter how much weight scholars give to the intellectual climate created by such stirring books as Michael Harrington's *The Other America* or to the reform movement within government itself, few have denied that the key to everything was Lyndon Johnson, the big Texan with big ideas—a man who knew how to get things done in Washington. Johnson's uplifting vision of the Great Society was a call for energetic federal action in the confident belief that such a decisive tilt toward federal power constituted no threat to the American democratic system.

That was quite a transformation for Johnson. The Southern politician had denounced the civil rights provisions of Harry Truman's Fair Deal, declaring them to be "an effort to set up a police state in the guise of liberty" and asserting that "it is the province of the state to run its own elections." But now Johnson the President demanded sweeping federal civil legislation to thwart the efforts of Southern white politicians to limit the political participation of blacks. The man who had denounced Truman's comprehensive health insurance plan as "socialized medicine" now urged the passage of federally supported health care programs for the elderly and the poor.

The central theme of the Great Society, Johnson said, was to be a "national war on poverty. Our objective: total victory." The war was to be conducted on all fronts, using every federal policy weapon available: Money was to be made available to fight crime and urban decay, to improve basic health and nutrition, and to upgrade education and training. But significantly, the strategy of the War on Poverty would not envisage redistributing income so that the poor could be made more comfortable. Rather, the intention was to change the behavior of the poor by providing them with the education, skills, and motivation to become more productive. "Give a poor man only a handout and he stays poor," the 1966 Report of the Office of Economic Opportunity declared, "but give the same man a skill and he rises from poverty."[9]

Johnson's tireless political crusade for the Great Society's legislative agenda was a monument to his political skills, but it also sowed the seeds for intractable problems later. It was vintage Johnson. He wheeled and he dealed. Small favors that meant a lot back home were traded for key votes. Insufficiently enthusiastic lawmakers were brought down to the ranch for a dose of charm or pressure, whichever was more effective. Johnson could make an obscure congressman feel that his vote would change the course of history. Once he even brought tears to George Wallace's eyes by putting his hand on the Governor's knee and talking about the poor folks of Alabama.

Johnson's legislative successes were astounding. In 1964, Congress passed the landmark Civil Rights Act, food stamp legislation, the Economic Opportunity Act—the cornerstone of the War on Poverty—and programs for mass transportation. The legislation enacted in 1965 included Medicare and Medicaid, the Elementary and Secondary Education Act, The Higher Education Act, and the Public Works and Economic Development Act. By the end of 1966, the basic legislation to create the Great Society was firmly in place.

But crusades cannot wait for the details to be worked out, and decisive legislative victories invariably require a great deal of compromise. So it was with Johnson's Great Society. The attitude in the White House, a Johnson biographer, Doris Goodwin, observes, was: "Pass the bill now, worry about its effects and implementation later." Little time was spent on thinking through the implications of "creative federalism," the nebulous term Johnson used to describe far-reaching changes in the federal relationship, but much was devoted to striking bargains with governors and

Congress. "There seemed to be few among the principal officers of government who were trying to determine how the programs could be made actually to work. The standard of success was the passage of the law."[10]

Little concern was given to cost, either. Typical of Johnson's approach was his reaction to frustrating delays in the passage of the Medicare legislation. As a key Johnson aide, Joseph Califano, remembers:

> Sitting in Johnson's green hideaway office one day, White House and HEW lobbyists Larry O'Brien and Wilbur Cohen (later to become Secretary of HEW) responded to Johnson's demand that they move the Medicare bill out of committee. "It'll cost a half-billion dollars to make the changes in the reimbursement standards to get the bill out of the Senate Finance Committee," Cohen said.
>
> "Five hundred million. Is that all?" Johnson exclaimed with a wave of his big hand. "Do it. Move that damn bill out now, before we lose it."[11]

According to Lawrence Friedman, a Rutgers law professor, the Great Society involved a dangerous degree of compromise. The reason, he says, was that with the exception of the civil rights legislation, the Great Society legislation was driven by presidential determination, not a social movement pressuring Congress. Thus the laws were riddled with concessions to powerful lobbies. Sometimes Johnson made far-reaching concessions even after he had already won a stunning legislative victory in order to encourage the defeated lobby to play ball with the new program. After the passage of the Medicare and Medicaid bills, for instance, Johnson invited the lobbyists for the American Medical Association to the White House to clear the air. After amusing the lobbyists and his own officials with a selection of his best doctor jokes, Johnson assured the AMA that administration officials would listen closely to the organization's advice when it came to the details of rule-making. The officials certainly did, making concession after concession. Johnson gained the cooperation of the doctors in the new programs, but only by agreeing to rules that virtually guaranteed an explosion in program costs.[12] As Lawrence Friedman notes, such concessions constituted "a weakness at the very source. The war on poverty was brittle and vulnerable, to an unusual degree, even during the triumphant months of drafting and enactment."[13]

Federal spending on social programs has increased dramatically since the Great Society legislation. In 1960, less than $4 billion a year was spent on "income-conditioned" programs. By 1980 the figure had topped $70 billion.[14] Those figures include Aid to Families with Dependent Children (AFDC), Supplementary Security Income (SSI), low-income home energy assistance, the earned income tax credit, housing assistance, food assistance, Medicaid, training and education support, and social services. Billions more dollars are spent in economic development and urban programs.

Has it been money well spent? It would be hard to say yes, given the persistent problems of America. For supporters of the Great Society to argue otherwise, they must do two things. They must show that conditions have actually improved for those targeted by the Johnson programs. But that is not all: If conditions have indeed improved, they also have to show that the enormous expenditures unleashed by the Johnson programs significantly accelerated any positive trends already occurring in 1964. That is a tall order.

Proponents of the Great Society can certainly point to some apparent successes—even if the degree and cause of those successes can be questioned. There has been a marked decline in infant and elderly mortality rates, for instance, and a narrowing of the nutritional gap between the poor and other Americans. But other developments are more ambiguous. The last twenty years, for instance, have seen significant advances in black occupations and wages relative to those of whites. But the raw figures hide a disturbing underlying pattern. Blacks made great strides in entering white-collar jobs—up from only 14 percent of employed blacks in 1959 to 39 percent in 1980. But according to Michael Brown and Stephen Erie, about 55 percent of the increase in black professional, management, and technical employment between 1960 and 1976 was in the public sector. Social welfare positions accounted for half of the public jobs. So blacks have not exactly been joining the mainstream professional economy.[15]

Furthermore, a stark employment gap has developed within the black community. For the majority of blacks, access to the middle-class economy has allowed them to rise with the tide. But other blacks—especially urban youth—are falling farther and farther behind. In 1964, black unemployment among sixteen-year-old black males was 25.9 percent, 1.61 times the rate for white males of the same age. By 1980, after fifteen years of the War on Poverty, it was 37.7 percent, more than double the equivalent white rate. Rather than providing a ladder to allow poor black Americans to escape from the underclass, the Great Society has coincided with the condemnation of a whole generation of urban blacks to pauperism and hopelessness.

The War on Poverty is evidently going badly. The official poverty rate when Jimmy Carter left office was 13 percent. Yet Johnson's economic advisers warned in 1964 that *without* federal action it could be as high as 13 percent by 1980. Murray's measure of latent poverty suggests the situation is actually far worse than the official figures show—enormous federal expenditures are holding many just above the poverty line with little chance of escaping the poverty vortex.

The Great Society establishment is rapidly running out of excuses. It is no good trying to blame Vietnam or Richard Nixon, and the current pattern was firmly established long before Ronald Reagan came to Washington. Admittedly, many factors can affect programs at the margin and may even cause temporary reverses. But twenty years is hard to explain away. Rather than concentrating on supposedly callous politicians, unexpected economic influences, or minor cuts in rapidly rising federal spending, it is time liberals began to accept that there just may have been some serious flaws in Johnson's political handiwork.

At the time, of course, the potential problems inherent in the "solution" were not so obvious. But with two decades of experience—and with the benefit of hindsight—it is possible to identify the flaws that were built into the foundations of the Great Society. If Johnson's vision is to be realized, those deficiencies must be openly admitted and corrected.

Looking back after ten years, Lawrence Friedman noted that the underlying problems stemmed from the very design of the War on Poverty and the misplaced optimism of its founders:

> There were excessive hopes and promises, centering on faith in presidential charisma, faith in and by the intellectuals and experts gathered around him in the White House, faith in ability to surmount the rude irrationalities of politics.
>
> On the other hand, the central instruments of legislation were generally vague, lacking in specificity and even in policy. This meant that they were, or could be, almost all things to all people. The law (the Economic Opportunity Act) was highly discretionary, and in some sense, doomed from the start. There was no way to prevent much of the war from being

captured by local forces. Indeed, that was the point. The "local forces" might be established political machines, who would co-opt the programs; they might be the more ambitious among the suppressed, who would plunder them; they might be the militants, who would use them for social upheaval; or they might be bright people of good will who would use them to accomplish their ostensible goals.[16]

It is now clear that those and other inherent flaws have seriously undermined the effectiveness of the Great Society in a number of very specific ways.

1. By providing a perverse set of incentives and by entrenching the "rights" concept of w____ ___ ____ ____ _____ __ underclass.

Reasonable _____ is of
welfare and char_____ hills
the soul. It rais_____ liga-
tions of both the
During the t_____ tion
against the earli_____ eful
for whatever pu_____ orge
Orwell reserved_____ zing
instincts of the_____ *and*
London, publis_____ op-
pressive regime_____ eless
men in London_____ and
charity."[17]

The Great S_____ onal
staff administering them harbor a very _____ still
prevails in social welfare thinking: Not only is there nothing demeaning about receiving welfare, but anyone "in need," according to eligibility criteria, has a right to demand assistance from the government. They are entitled to it. Also, private charity, far from being a source of strength in a community, is seen in many ways as the indication of a weakness, a sign that a gap must be filled by private organizations because government is not willing or able to meet its obligations.

On the face of it, that attitude toward welfare and charity may seem like the mark of a civilized society. In some ways it is. But outcomes are more important than intent, and the outcome of making welfare more acceptable—and the obligation of government more extensive and automatic—has been to make *depen-*

dency on welfare more acceptable and thus more pervasive. It becomes a way of life, passed on from generation to generation. Moreover, as welfare has been transformed from a privilege into a right, it has become less acceptable for the providers of welfare to pass judgment on the conduct of those receiving help, which is thought to show a middle-class, paternalistic bias. A right, after all, is a right. It cannot be held hostage to good behavior. When everyone tells you it is your right to be on welfare and that there is nothing to be ashamed of, is it any surprise that people should be less inclined to leave the welfare system?

Whether or not the system's financial incentives encourage dependency, the "rights" view of welfare, whatever its humane intent, would probably have been enough by itself to undermine the War on Poverty. The structure of welfare eligibility and incentives has merely aggravated the problem. Assistance is based on need, rarely linked to efforts at self improvement. Failure is rewarded, and "deficiencies are the key to one's well-being."[18] When an unmarried teenage mother shuns the support of her family and home, she is more deficient and so receives more help. If the father of her child would rather live off her than provide for her, so be it, welfare checks will not stop arriving. If he marries her and gets a job reflecting whatever skills he may have, the assistance will be cut, of course.

The self-destructive nature of the new welfare philosophy and its incentives is most obvious in low-income black communities. Within those neighborhoods, the level of unemployment and the welfare dependency rate has reached staggering proportions, and family breakup constitutes a social and economic disaster. Between 1950 and 1963, the proportion of black illegitimate births rose slowly from 17 percent to 23 percent. By 1984 it had topped 59 percent. Among black women aged 15–19, no less than 89 percent of births were illegitimate that year. [19] That trend has had a marked connection with poverty. By 1984, female-headed families accounted for 68 percent of the black poor, and 75 percent of poor black children were concentrated in such families. [20] While the data do not suggest that welfare actually encourages illegitimate births, research does indicate strongly that welfare induces young unmarried mothers to set up an independent household, making it far less likely that they will ultimately escape dependency. [21]

According to an increasing number of black scholars, some attitudes arising from the civil rights movement have aggravated this crisis. Glenn Loury talks of the "enemy within," meaning such self-destructive influences as family instability and crime. That enemy goes virtually unchecked, he says, while black leaders insist on blaming everything on the "enemy without"—racism— and looking to whites and the government to correct all ills within the black community.[22] By confusing fault with responsibility, Loury insists, today's civil rights leadership encourages blacks to think of themselves as incapable of advancing without the assistance of the white establishment. Destructive conduct is accepted and blamed on past or present suffering. Economic self-sufficiency is ignored. Progress and equality are seen as contingent upon special, supposedly corrective, legal privileges and increased federal support.

The reinforcing combination of those influences, each an integral part of the ethos and policies of the Great Society, has served to drive a wedge between rich and poor America. Johnson's intention was to build a bridge. The malignancy of welfare dependency will never be overcome until those influences are corrected.

2. *The confused notion of "creative federalism," which underpinned the Great Society, led to micromanagement by the Washington government and too great a reliance on political, rather than economic, vehicles to allocate resources.*

The Great Society was an explicit attempt to use federal power to marshal national resources to address problems that some lower levels of government had failed to tackle. In some cases, most notably civil rights, the failure was due to sheer obstructionism by powerful local interests. In other instances it was seen as due to a lack of resources or commitment, or both. It was anticipated that the Great Society would deal with the problem by using federal muscle, where necessary, and providing federal help where it would be most effective.

The Civil Rights Act differed in key respects from the other legislative elements of the Great Society. Built upon a powerful social movement, it was essentially a collection of legal mandates placed upon state and local governments. The role of the federal government was to force action at lower levels. But the other components of the Great Society involved intricate combinations of federal, state, and local actions to tackle social problems. The arrangements put in place—Johnson's "creative federalism"—were a concoction based more on creative political compromise than on any innovative version of federalism. The glue that held those compromises together, other than Johnson's personal persuasion, was the promise of federal money and the federal obligation to tackle local problems. (By contrast, Reagan's "New Federalism" sought merely to swap obligations while reducing federal support. It is little wonder that President Reagan failed to persuade governors and mayors to accept the plan.)

Once passed into law, however, the strains within the structure began to show themselves in several ways. First, many Great Society programs did not merely provide federal money to individuals and governments, enabling them to achieve their own goals. Instead, federal officials became involved in the most intimate details of local action, from new towns and economic development to education and job training. That presented a dilemma: Either lay down tight national rules to ensure that federal and local officials hit the overall program goals, knowing that such rules will rarely fit local conditions or political factors, or allow wide discretion to field officials and local governments, recognizing that this risks a lack of control and cooperation by local interests. Usually some mixture of approaches was used, especially in the antipoverty programs. And that led to confusion, inefficiency, and unrealized objectives.

The second problem with Johnson's view of federalism concerned the method of deciding how resources should be allocated. The architects of many Great Society programs favored strictly political mechanisms to channel resources to those who needed them—political empowerment. They tended to avoid such devices as vouchers or direct cash assistance, which would give individuals economic clout and the incentive, as consumers, to make efficient choices for themselves. One important exception, of course, was the food stamp program. Families meeting the eligibility criteria were given vouchers of a certain value that could be used to purchase goods in most food stores. Each beneficiary could make his or her own purchasing decisions, within limits, and each had the incentive to use the stamps as wisely as possible.

Ironically, food assistance was one area where, although the Johnson Administration took a step in the direction of a "consumer" model, it could not bring itself to relinquish paternalist controls over the the poor, preferring instead to use vouchers instead of cash. Vouchers are most appropriate in those cases where the government has reasonable justification for believing that assistance given for one purpose might be used for some other, undesirable purpose. But the desire for adequate food is basic, and the problems of those who forgo food for liquor or drugs are rarely solved by vouchers; they simply trade them for cash. So the goal of assuring individuals adequate access to food could have been achieved more easily by cash support than by vouchers.

Moreover, even limited forms of the consumer model were not widely used in the Great Society programs. Those which may appear to have used a market method of allocation, such as Medicare and Medicaid, generally did not do so in practice. For example, in a classic case of Johnson compromise, the health care industry managed to win agreement in the debate over Medicare that no restraints would be placed on physician or hospital charges—they would merely have to be "reasonable." A market-like mechanism, such as a fixed-value Medicare voucher, which would have encouraged doctors and hospitals to compete for a price-sensitive patient, was rejected under pressure from the medical lobby. Instead, the industry was allowed to prescribe treatment, charge whatever it thought was appropriate, and then send the tab to Uncle Sam. Free of any price mechanism to moderate demand and cost, Medicare became a license for doctors and hospitals to print money.

Most other programs relied on an explicitly political model. Generally speaking, the idea was that some combination of federal and local agencies would decide how federal money should be spent. Usually the exact wording in the legislation was left vague to allow for maximum discretion and to leave difficult questions of jurisdiction until after the law was enacted. Sometimes provision was made for the direct participation of the poor in choices that would affect them, but only rarely.

The problem with that political structure of decision-making was that it often resulted in programs designed to advance the interests of key political blocs rather than individuals. The political power of a group can certainly be an effective means to secure benefits for some of its constituent members, but it is usually a very inefficient tool for dealing with limited or individual problems. A union, for instance, is not the best organization to bargain for a single worker. Moreover, as Johnson recognized, making sure that the the target population is well served by the political process usually means that many pockets have to be lined. That in turn often means there are never enough resources to deal with the original problem, since less deserving people must be rewarded. The strategy of assembling potent political coalitions may also mean, paradoxically, that dealing decisively with the problems of one group is avoided. In effect, politically sensitive groups become what one might call "political hostages." Public anxiety about the condition of those groups, or their own political power, is used to force changes that will affect a far wider group. Thus there is enormous opposition by liberals to education vouchers or any other device that might allow some parents to remove their children from bad public schools, in case that might leave others stranded with little hope of improvement. Better to keep the children of middle-class parents trapped in the system, they reason, since that will make those parents seek to improve the system for all.

Of course, the result of such a strategy can be that nobody's position is improved. The neoconservative scholar Irving Kristol tells of the occasion in 1968 when he was asked by President-elect Richard Nixon to join a task force on social policy. Kristol at one point recommended that the new resources made available should be used to end poverty among the elderly once and for all. The money was there, and the job could be done. But to his surprise, virtually every other member of the task force—many of them well known liberal social scientists—attacked the idea. Ending elderly poverty would be a mistake, they told Kristol, because that would leave other poor Americans defenseless. "The presence of old people among the poor, they explained, and especially their presence on television programs about poverty, was necessary in order to excite popular passion for the poor in general. So poverty among the elderly should be addressed as part of a larger antipoverty program." In its desire to win the war, the panel decided not to win a battle. "And that's why the elderly poor are still with us." Kristol did not attend any more meetings of the task force.[23]

The Economic Opportunity Act and its attendant Office of Economic Opportunity (OEO), initially directed by Sargent

Shriver, epitomized the way in which the political model can take on a life of its own. The objective of the legislation was the "coordination" of existing poverty programs with those established by the War on Poverty. In addition, the Director of OEO was empowered to make grants to nonprofit groups, dubbed Community Action Program (CAP) agencies, that were engaged in "community action" to deal with poverty and build up the capacity of individuals and groups to the point where they could deal with their problems without further assistance.

According to Paul Peterson and David Greenstone, of the Brookings Institution, community action began to have less and less to do with coordination, and "instead became an attack on political poverty, oriented toward increasing the political participation of previously excluded citizens, particularly black Americans."[24] The act required the design and coordination of poverty programs to be conducted with the "maximum feasible participation" of poor communities, and OEO insisted that one-third of the members of local policymaking bodies be local residents and members of the groups served. In theory, cities would have to compete for limited funds, and so Washington would have a lever to ensure efficient local coordination. But as Peterson and Greenstone point out, the federal government's leverage was significantly reduced by the need to win wide congressional support for the programs, which meant funds had to be distributed to virtually all communities. So increasingly, the CAP structure became a vehicle to exercise political power rather than a means to coordinate social services, and those taking the lead in the CAP agencies drew on the client population to advance their own political agenda and careers.

In fairness to the architects of the antipoverty programs, the strategy of building basically political structures to distribute social benefits had a good deal of logic to it. In the mid-1960s there was fierce resistance in many quarters to the notion that the federal government should play a leading role in securing the basic social needs of low-income Americans. Consequently, the Johnson White House saw the issue not so much as finding the most efficient mechanism to channel assistance to the poor or the elderly, but more as building a delivery system that would generate and sustain the political support needed to maintain the War on Poverty. Thus political structures took precedence over economic mechanisms. The problem that grew out of that strategy, which now must be corrected if the original goals of the Great Society are ever to be reached, is that those political structures took on a life of their own, condemning many of the Johnson programs to economic inefficiency and conflicting goals.

3. *By misjudging the political dynamics of the Great Society programs, the Johnson White House guaranteed that the programs would become steadily more costly, less efficient, and more difficult to reform.*

Lyndon Johnson once told Bill Moyers that passing the Great Society legislation was like writing with chalk on a blackboard. His Administration, he said, had simply cleaned up part of the existing blackboard and put some new writing on it. But after he was gone, others would add to what had been written and erase that which had not worked. In that way, he said, they would correct mistakes and improve the Great Society.

Johnson was half right. Others have indeed added to the blackboard. But erasing items has been a different matter. While some elements of the Great Society, such as the OEO, were later eliminated or substantially cut back, the bulk of the programs— whether effective or not—are still clearly on the blackboard. Erasing programs that were disappointing in their results or more expensive than envisaged has proved an extremely difficult exercise. Even the Reagan cuts have barely changed the shape of Johnson's legacy. "Improving" a program generally has consisted of leaving intact what was already there and then adding to it. The only way to prevent the blackboard from becoming overcrowded has been to keep extending it. And the blackboard is money.

The endurance of the Great Society programs is testimony to Johnson's remarkable political skills and to the strategy of building powerful political structures to pursue social goals. Johnson staffers looking back at their handiwork are no doubt pleased that they created strong and resilient constituencies, so that a conservative like Reagan cannot wipe the blackboard clean. But if they are honest about it, they will also have to admit that very often the programs have become an end in themselves, operating primarily in the interests of service providers rather than the intended beneficiaries.

The fundamental reason for the endurance of both good and

bad Great Society programs rests in the nature of the American political system. Whenever a program is enacted, a coalition soon develops around it, each element of which finds it in its interest to expand the program while defending it from attack. Understandably, officials administering a program tend to be committed to its purposes, and their careers are entwined with the program and its budget. If the program has clearly achieved its purposes, then it makes sense to them to use the successful instrument to solve other problems that those same officials have identified. More money will be necessary, of course. But what if the program has been disappointing in meeting its goals? Well, that merely shows that the problem is more extensive than had been imagined, and so more staff and resources are needed. Anyone who suggests otherwise simply does not really care about the problem.

Those outside the government who receive federal funds to provide services face similar incentives, whether they are legal service attorneys who litigate for the poor, doctors who treat the elderly, or nonprofit groups who train the indigent. Likewise, program beneficiaries have every reason to support increased funding and resist cutbacks. They may feel that money could be better allocated, but certainly they have no reason to want less money spent.

It is in the interest of each element of the coalition to ally with the others. Advocates for the poor depend for their employment on the existence of the poor and the discovery of new instances of poverty, just as the poor need their advocates. Recounting his days with the antipoverty program in Washington, Milton Kotler remembers that "there was rejoicing every time a new poverty group was found. I remember that [sic] discovery of poor Jews and Eskimos."[25]

Coalitions of that kind form around all programs at all levels of government. Defense spending is driven by such constituencies, as is spending on highways. It is hard to imagine a defense contractor who would oppose a defense buildup; he would not keep his job long once the stockholders learned of it. The liberals never miss a chance to bash the military–industrial complex, but they should recognize the existence of what the self-help advocate Robert Woodson calls the "social welfare–poverty complex." Social welfare professionals turn out to be disturbingly like their counterparts in the defense industry. Imagine a professional human services provider arguing that we need less spending on welfare or agreeing that his work would be better undertaken by a volunteer. It is not easy to picture. Whatever the program, there are groups of people who have a strong interest in seeing that program expand, even if it seems to deliver poor value for money. In the case of the Johnson programs, those coalitions have been particularly strong for three reasons.

The first is simply that programs at the federal level are more resistant to challenge than similar programs at the state or local level. Money from Washington is "cheaper," politically, than money from the statehouse or from city hall. That is because the farther one moves up the federal ladder, the wider the costs of programs are distributed, and the less the burden is on each taxpayer. Even though more people shoulder the cost of a federal program, it is the amount coming out of each pocket that tends to matter politically. Suppose the mayor of your city proposes building, at local taxpayers' expense, a costly project that seems likely to bring many economic benefits to a few developers and corporations but not much to the man or woman in the street. He is likely to face tough sledding with city voters, because each will have to pay a significant part of the cost without much direct benefit. But say the same mayor steps off the plane from Washington and announces that the federal government will pay for the project. He is likely to be treated as a hero. Even if city voters receive only a few crumbs, it is still something for nothing. And why does Washington fund such projects? The private interests who gain a great deal from projects lobby Congress hard and have memories that stretch all the way to election time. But the cost to each federal taxpayer is so tiny that it is rarely worth getting excited about. That combination of large, concentrated benefits and small, widely spread costs is the driving force behind the vast majority of federal programs, from social welfare to nuclear weapons.

The second reason why most of the Great Society programs have beaten off their attackers is that the essential altruism and public-spiritedness of Americans makes it hard for them to reject social spending. When a welfare program is in political jeopardy, the coalition finds it relatively easy to win public sympathy. Cold, hard efficiency studies count for little against a distraught welfare mother at a congressional hearing. Attacking antipoverty programs seems to most Americans to be equivalent to attacking the poor.

The third way in which the Great Society coalitions have protected themselves is by ensuring that constituencies within and outside government work together closely. The process was described by Daniel Patrick Moynihan back in 1965 as the "professionalization of reform," the process by which pressure for government action comes from within government agencies themselves, generated by technical experts who see their role as advancing government action to achieve reforms.[26] Armed with the data they themselves generate and working with coalition allies, social services professionals have been able to build momentum for first establishing and then expanding social programs.

The growth of Medicare and social insurance programs generally is a good example of the process. The experts brought into the Social Security Administration (SSA) after 1935 soon went to work to win support for widening the scope of social security. "The prevailing technique of policy analysis" (within SSA), Martha Derthick, a Brookings Institution political scientist, writes in her study of social security policymaking, "was to identify a social problem, such as lack of health care, and to develop the arguments and methods for dealing with it through social insurance."[27] SSA staff worked closely with organized labor and other pressure groups interested in grafting health care for the elderly onto the basic social security system. They channeled research data to supporters of programs and helped design legislative proposals.

Many techniques are available to the "professional reformer" intent on strengthening the coalition to which he belongs. One is to determine the research agenda. Each agency has considerable power to influence the academic and policymaking debate on an issue simply by designing research projects and channeling money to scholars likely to subscribe to the underlying philosophy of the agency staff. The Great Society has been a constant source of nourishment to a veritable industry of academics with a financial as well as an intellectual interest in defending Johnson's programs.

The courts have also proved an effective vehicle for sustaining and expanding programs. The civil rights laws, in particular, have been used skillfully by advocacy organizations to force extensions of programs that had limited support in Congress. If a political goal can be elevated to the status of a legal right, then a judge can often do more to advance an organization's objective in a five-minute ruling than the group can achieve through months of congressional lobbying. And once a right is established, cost usually becomes an irrelevant consideration. Special education programs for handicapped students, among many others, have made significant advances in that way.

The coalitions supporting federal social programs have also strengthened themselves by making the nonprofit sector increasingly dependent on federal money. The Johnson strategists were careful to incorporate nonprofit organizations into the Great Society structure, thereby giving private social welfare advocates and professionals a vested interest in the programs, while giving the false impression that social service had nothing to do with profit or personal gain. By 1980, according to an Urban Institute study, some 58 percent of the revenues of nonprofit social service organizations was coming directly or indirectly from the federal government.[28] So close is the relationship between government and the "voluntary" sector, the study's author, Lester Salamon, observes, that those nonprofits can best be described as "third party government."

The incestuous relationship between nonprofit professionals and the federal government has not merely enhanced the coalitions supporting federal programs of dubious merit, it has also served to freeze out indigenous community-based "competition" to those programs, to the detriment of the population supposedly being helped. Robert Woodson claims that the failure of many federal social programs can be traced in large part to the practice of "parachuting" government-designed programs and their accompanying professionals into poor neighborhoods. The nonprofit groups funded by these programs, he says, constitute

> . . . a seller's market in that professionals themselves decide when, to whom, and how to serve. The result too often is the paradox of careless care. . . . Since it is professionals who control the criteria of professional success and the definition of its category of clients and their needs, professional services can survive any malfeasance and continue in business, unlike a friendship, a family, or even a true market enterprise. Professionals themselves determine whether they have succeeded or failed and, if the latter, what the remedy should be.[29]

Moreover, Woodson argues, the government-funded service providers have the incentive to push up the operational costs of services and to press for tight "credentialing standards" and regulations to shut out lower-cost self-help alternatives. The result is not only less value for the dollar but also decisions that can actually exacerbate problems. The professionalization of foster care services, Woodson says, is a case in point, with approximately 70 percent of the $2 billion or so spent at all levels of government going on salaries and administrative costs. Meanwhile, institutions have become a permanent home for thousands of young people, simply because managers resist efforts to find the children permanent homes. They are more inclined to take a regular government check than to place the children with families and so lose a source of revenue.[30]

Advancing Beyond Welfarism

The social programs of the Great Society were the result of a remarkable and courageous effort, guided by a master politician, to use federal power to correct the many serious shortcomings of the world's most prosperous country. The lofty goals of that effort cannot be faulted, nor can it be denied that many of the programs benefit millions of deserving Americans. But even the more ardent supporters of the Great Society are beginning to admit that the War on Poverty has been going badly of late. The reason is that the political constraints of the 1960s forced unwise decisions in the basic design of many programs—flaws that have become increasing evident over the last twenty years in such forms as dependency and interest group politics. If the original ideals of the Great Society are to be achieved, some very fundamental reforms are necessary.

Johnson's crusade was predominantly political. By taking the political initiative, he thought he could build federal institutions that would provide sustenance and opportunity to the poor. As for the economics of the War on Poverty, well, that was of little concern to Johnson. If there was some problem, he would fix it later. And what about moral values or concepts of responsibility? That was a little ethereal to the man of action. Politics turns on power and rights, not on social values.

Some conservatives, of course, seem to be interested *only* in values: Preach to the poor, and get them to read the Bible every night, and they will soon find their way out of poverty. Other conservatives see the welfare problem as nothing more than an issue of economic incentives. Modify the regulations, or at the extreme simply do away with the programs, and the work ethic will be restored, leading to better results at a fraction of the price.

But the reform of welfare in America will require the integration of three elements, and government can play only a very limited role. Values and culture will be an essential part of any future victory over poverty. The "culture of poverty" cannot be eradicated solely by external action. It can be broken only by social changes within the communities that condone self-destructive behavior. A change in an individual's attitudes and sense of responsibility cannot be taught by government officials; it must come from the institutions of the community itself.

Similarly, economics does matter. It is no good for liberals to say that the task is too important to worry about the cost—they would hardly say that about defense. If the cost is too great, it can weaken the very engine of wealth creation that is the source of the help we extend to the poor. Moreover, there may be debate about the precise way in which economic incentives affect the poor, but it is hard to argue that only the rich and the middle class react to incentives. Economic incentives are not the only things that matter, but matter they certainly do.

Further, any solution must make for good politics. A solution to the welfare problem must pass an acceptability test administered by the American people. Conservatives do not always appear to remember that, so their proposals tend to flunk the test. But if conservatives are prepared to make some concessions here, while playing some hardball there, there is every reason to believe that they can both coax and prod the liberals to join in fundamental reform.

Forging that coalition for reform is a critically important task for the nation, and thus for conservatives. Besides the need to use our resources more effectively and efficiently in tackling the problem of poverty, a far more important reason for urgent and decisive action is that in America we seem to be on the verge of entrenching a poverty caste, a group of citizens who are blocked from moving up the ladder of prosperity. Such a permanent underclass may be an accepted feature of many Asian countries and— some might say—of certain European countries, but if it were to become a part of American society it would shatter the American dream of boundless opportunity for all citizens. Conservatives have another reason to concern themselves with the issue, besides a moral obligation. They need to show that the emergence of a poverty class in America is not due to a failure of capitalism, that it is due to a failure of government to extend capitalism to the poor.

Conservatives must also recognize that while their ideas may form the foundation of structural welfare reform, they may be denied the opportunity, and the political benefit, of actually implementing that reform. It may well be that only a liberal Administration will ever be able to implement such reforms, because only a political descendant of Johnson will be trusted by most Americans to change the writing on the Great Society blackboard. But perhaps only conservatives, free of the intellectual and political baggage of the Great Society, can propose the principles and mechanisms on which reform can be based. But then, as a little sign on Ronald Reagan's Oval Office desk rightly declares, "There is no limit to what a man can do or where he can go if he doesn't mind who gets the credit."

CHAPTER

2

The Foundations of a Conservative Welfare System

THE FIRST REQUIREMENT for winning any war is to identify the primary objective of the conflict and to keep it firmly in mind at all times. That objective should not be determined by generals. Although the generals must be responsible for identifying specific targets and developing strategies to gain them, they must defer to the plan established by the nation's leaders if the war is to be successful.

In many ways the Great Society diverged from that necessary rule. Although the goals of the War on Poverty reflected the principles and beliefs of the American people, the political exigencies of program development and administration led to programs and institutions of public charity that still cannot meet those goals. The operation of the system is now at variance with the values that gave it birth.

In particular, insufficient attention was paid to the detailed design of many of the Great Society's welfare programs. Sweeping declarations of "total victory" as a goal in the War on Poverty masked a fuzziness when it came to the specific objectives intended to embody the American view of welfare. Many of the continuing problems of the programs enacted in the 1960s stem from that initial confusion. As the French politician Georges Clemenceau recognized, "War is much too serious to be left to the military." But in Johnson's War on Poverty, the specifics of strategy were usually left to the officials who managed the programs.

All too often the preamble to each piece of legislation evoked lofty goals with which few Americans would disagree. But when the last political deal had been struck, and powerful constituencies and bureaucrats had finished writing the regulations, the fine print distorted those goals and departed from very basic attitudes held in the country.

If there is to be effective reform of the welfare system in America, it is more important to change the fine print than to revise every preamble. It is easy to understand why so many people were swept along by the Great Society. The broad objectives seemed worthy of a great nation. But the road to hell is paved with good intentions, and the political and economic dynamics of the War on Poverty resulted in programs that turned out to be very different in practice from what Johnson and his team envisioned. Again, if we are to devise a new approach that comes up to the rhetoric of the Great Society, we must go back to the fine print, and we must think through more carefully what tangible things, in practice, we should be trying to achieve. To do that, we must first reconsider exactly what Americans really mean by "welfare" and how they see their own role and that of other institutions in providing it. And we must be crystal clear about what we mean by "poverty." Not only is the notion itself very vague, but even if we can agree on its meaning, there are serious flaws in our ability to measure it. Only a clear understanding of those concepts can enable us to build the foundations of a successful approach to welfare policy.

The Road to Welfare, American Style

American attitudes toward public charity and welfare relief can be traced back to the traditions and laws of England, although in the New World they have gone through several new twists. Many of those debating the basic issues of welfare, such as dependency and social obligation, assume that they are breaking new ground—or at least that the debate started in modern times. But ever since passage of the Elizabethan Poor Law in 1598, the history of Anglo-American thought and policy on the subject of welfare reveals three inextricably intertwined themes: rendering humane public assistance to the needy; a concern that rendering assistance

29

without a work requirement fosters dependency; and an attempt to define the limits of public obligation in order to control out-flows from the public purse.

Needless to say, some of the terminology and most of the "solutions" of the Elizabethan welfare system seem unduly harsh by modern standards, yet both the problems and the policies of the time have a surprisingly modern tone. Tudor England, for instance, was racked both by inflation and by fundamental changes in the nature of the economy. Thanks in part to Henry VIII's bitter dispute with the Pope, which resulted in the destruction of England's extensive system of monasteries, the medieval "safety net" of church-provided help lay in shreds. Unemployed and destitute rural laborers flooded into the towns seeking jobs and assistance, often falling into the urban underclass. The Poor Law was an attempt to deal with the problem by creating a national welfare system. Despite numerous amendments, it remained the basis of England's welfare system until the 1830s. Under the sixteenth-century law, the local unit of society—the parish—became the political unit to deal with the poor. Overseers of the Poor were appointed, and a tax was levied on the parish to provide for welfare assistance.

Like today, it was well recognized that the poor are not a homogeneous group. People are poor for very different reasons, and it was well understood that sensible policy must take careful account of that fact. The Poor Law identified three types of poverty. The first was child poverty. The Elizabethan approach to dealing with the children of impoverished families was for the parish to arrange and finance apprenticeships so that poor children could begin to look after themselves and acquire the skills necessary to obtain useful employment in adult life. As for the second category, the able-bodied, they were to be given what amounted to public-sector jobs, so that the parish would obtain at least some return from providing them with living costs—a sort of Elizabethan workfare. Only the "lame, impotent, old, blind," and others genuinely unable to work were to be given pure welfare and shelter at the public expense. Policies and concepts of poverty have changed since those times, but much less than one might have expected in four hundred years. And the inherent political and economic dilemmas have stayed pretty much the same.

Those dilemmas are rooted in the political traditions and economic success of democratic capitalism. That astute observer of cultures Alexis de Tocqueville saw clearly that notions of poverty reflect the economic condition of the country concerned. As the French traveler noted in a description of England in the 1830s:

> In a country where the majority is ill-clothed, ill-housed, ill-fed, who thinks of giving clean clothes, healthy food, comfortable quarters to the poor? The majority of the English, having all these things, regard their absence as a terrible misfortune; society believes itself bound to come to the aid of those who lack them. . . . In England, the average standard of living a man can hope for in the course of his life is higher than in any other country of the world. This greatly facilitates the extension of pauperism in that kingdom.[1]

In other words, in a wealthy country absolute poverty may be substantially removed, yet many people will still feel poor when they compare themselves with those at the top of the economic pile. Somebody who might feel very rich in the South Bronx could feel very poor if he were suddenly transported to Beverly Hills. And such *relative* poverty usually makes people feel just as poor as does *absolute* poverty. A family in a depressed American city may have a well-built home with indoor plumbing, a telephone, a television, and even a reasonable income, and still feel very poor in comparison with others they see on the bus or on their color television sets. Many "middle-class" families in Third World countries would love to be that "poor." The idea of relative poverty also strikes home to those of us with the wherewithal to live comfortably. Obviously we feel concern, and sometimes guilt, when we see someone without the basics for a decent existence. But we also tend to think of people as poor merely because they fall well below the average standard of living in the country, perhaps even in our neighborhood.

Nevertheless, in America the sole fact of being poor, in either an absolute or a relative sense, traditionally has not been sufficient to lay claim to public funds. In fact, public assistance has been viewed as a potentially corrupting influence which could degrade the poor and burden the public. Welfare has never been seen, by most Americans, as a device to equalize incomes. Unlike the prevailing political philosophy in many other countries, which sees welfare as part of an overall strategy to even out incomes, Americans see welfare as a means of alleviating the worst aspects of poverty and giving the poor the opportunity to rise up the economic ladder.

Throughout the nineteenth and early twentieth centuries, American philanthropists and social critics wrestled with the implications of that philosophy. During the Progressive era, there was intense debate about the role of government and society, and about the responsibilities of the individual. Among the mainly middle-class professionals and intellectuals who constituted the backbone of the Progressive movement, there was a great awareness of the complexities of social issues. As the historian Richard Hofstadter put it, "the characteristic Progressive was often of two minds on many issues."[2] Many of the reformers, although concerned with social justice, saw their goal also as the restoration of individualism and restraint of what they perceived as the forces of collectivism.[3] Ironically, views that are perceived today as part of a dichotomy in liberal and conservative attitudes toward welfare were all very much a part of an integrated Progressive approach to treating poverty.

It has been widely recognized that one strand of Progressive thinking led to the welfare statism of the New Deal; many of today's liberals still consider themselves the standard-bearers of such "progressivism." But it is less generally appreciated that elements of modern conservatism also evolved from American Progressivism. For example, few would deny the prominent role in welfare practice and theory played by the philanthropist Josephine Lowell, who was typical of the enlightened reformers of the time. Liberals rush to identify themselves with the compassion of the Lowells, the Jane Addamses, and the Jacob Riises. Yet as Richard Hofstadter pointed out in the 1950s, the attitudes of contemporary liberals differ significantly from their heroes. The Progressive generation, Hofstadter explained, "looked to economic life as a field for the expression of character; modern liberals seem to think of it quite exclusively as a field in which certain results are to be expected."[4]

Indeed, Josephine Lowell began her book *Public Relief and Private Charity* with this contention: "It is not right to tax one part of the community for the benefit of another part; it is not right to take money by law from one man and give it to another, *unless for the benefit of both*."[5] Nonetheless, Lowell did not believe that public assistance was like a commercial transaction, devoid of social obligation or concern for others. She concluded the passage by reminding "those who object to public relief in all its forms . . . that human pity is imperative."

The notion that welfare or charity involves a responsibility in both the provider and the recipient has long been an entrenched characteristic of American thinking and attitudes. Until very recently the justification for providing welfare had rarely been couched in terms of engineering some concept of social equity or "welfare rights"; it reflected simple compassion and enlightened self-interest. And in turn, the person receiving help was held to have an obligation to use it, as far as possible, to improve his situation—not simply to make it less unpleasant. A safety net should be there to break a fall, but then the poor person was expected to start looking for a ladder and begin climbing upward again. That commitment to the ideals of self-sufficiency and self-improvement, as well as the injustice of income redistribution for its own sake, has characterized American attitudes through most of the country's history. In that regard, the American approach differs considerably from the more socialistic view of granting the poor "rights" to public funds, long a feature of European thinking.

It was not only the upper-class philanthropists like Lowell who shared those attitudes. Jacob Riis, an immigrant from Denmark and himself no stranger to poverty, spent much of his life attempting to clean up the New York slums. Yet he, too, was disquieted by the lack of attention public officials sometimes paid to incentives and self-improvement. He criticized one scheme, which relieved struggling parents of responsibility for their children, as making them, in effect, public wards. Even though the children would then be materially provided for, Riis felt that the program placed "a premium . . . upon child desertion in our community." Money spent unwisely, he maintained, does not eliminate poverty but creates dependency. "It is money scattered without judgment—not poverty—that makes the pauper. It is money scattered without judgment—not poverty—that marshals the greater part of this army" of paupers.[6] Few present-day conservatives would disagree. Moreover, Riis thought it wrong to remove "the stigma which fortunately attaches to *public* relief," because that would create an "incentive to parents to place their children upon the public for support." Welfare had to be morally unpleasant, because the objective was to encourage self-sufficiency. A soft heart should not to be combined with a soft head about human nature.

Also unlike the British, there has been a distinctly American resistance to assigning people to permanent social classes. Until very recently, the idea of an "underclass"—a caste that could never be expected to escape poverty—would have been unthinkable for most Americans. Thus, as one early Philadelphia commission put it, a system of permanent public relief may have been appropriate to Britain, where the lower classes were relegated to that class forever, but not to America. In short, the commission said, the British system of relief was "adopted for a country with privileged orders and not for one with equal rights and plenty of room for existence."[7]

In addition to their notions concerning social obligation, Americans traditionally have believed that when public assistance is called for, it should be the province of local institutions. To the extent that government should be the vehicle for welfare, then it should fall into the domain of local government—towns and counties. That view undoubtedly had its roots in the British legacy, where national laws mandated that parishes provide and finance public assistance to the poor. But in America a distinction also evolved between local community and local government.

There was a very good reason for that distinction. In many early American communities, of course, and especially during the movement west, there was often little that could even be called "government" in the all-encompassing sense in which the term was understood in Europe. In America all manner of *ad hoc* institutions had to be devised to achieve public purposes, including the provision of welfare. Sometimes it was a voluntary association, of which Tocqueville wrote with such admiration. At other times the church became the focal point of community efforts of a decidedly nonspiritual kind. Often it was a group of businessmen who decided to assess themselves a fee to pay for necessary services, which would benefit themselves as well as their neighbors. Until quite recently, few Americans would have automatically assumed that a community obligation—even a national obligation—necessarily meant a government obligation. The perceived efficacy of local control and design of relief is what made them the basis of the American welfare system until the New Deal. Even the Progressive philanthropists, as they developed their notions of the "science" of charity and laid down general rules for who should receive aid and of what kind, always stressed that each case must be judged on its own merits.

A reliance on local institutions and government, of course, does not guarantee that a community will have the means or the will to take care of those in need. That was one reason why Lyndon Johnson's poverty warriors were so determined to break down state and local resistance to greater involvement by the federal government. But in those communities where Americans lived up to their social responsibilies, local discretion meant greater flexibility and responsiveness to local needs. Americans believed that only those close to a problem had sufficient knowledge and incentive to deal with it effectively. How could some faraway government understand the emotional problems of Mrs. Jones's runaway boy or appreciate that Old Jack was just lazy and should be forced to fend for himself? Not surprisingly, attempts to standardize welfare programs even at the state level did not meet with much support. As a historian of welfare in Pennsylvania concluded in 1913, local resistance had overcome numerous attempts to standardize welfare strategies, so that "the lack of unity found everywhere in Pennsylvania's system will not be eliminated in the near future."[8]

The strong belief in localism was unshakable until the Depression, when social and economic distress overwhelmed many community institutions that previously had seemed able to cope with almost any disaster. The collapse of labor markets and the staggering degree of the economic and social calamity rendered the fiscal capacity of local governments and community organizations inadequate to meet social welfare needs. For the first time in their history, Americans began to turn to the federal government to help them deal with problems they had always felt were none of Washington's business.

Nevertheless, basic attitudes toward welfare, work, and self-sufficiency still did not change all that much. Social Security was for retired workers, to be paid for out of contributions made by those same workers—an "earned" benefit without the unpleasant odor of a handout or dependency. Welfare for the able-bodied was in the form of jobs programs to get them back on their feet. Even the fledgling Aid to Dependent Children program (ADC) was small in scope and originally aimed only at widows: They were not expected to be in the labor market anyway, and it was accepted that their lack of a means of support for their children was completely beyond their control. Just like local assistance, federal welfare thus continued to reflect prevalent American values in separating the helpless from the shiftless and those who deserve society's assistance from those capable of self-support.

Those prevailing attitudes about the purpose of welfare were not confined to officials administering programs or the taxpayers who paid for them. Americans receiving help tended to share similar views. There was a stigma to being on the dole. Welfare was nothing to be proud of; getting off the welfare rolls was something to be achieved as quickly as possible. As John Pearce, a Kentucky columnist, reminisced recently in the *Louisville Courier Journal* about the Depression:

> I suppose that during the Depression we were poor ourselves. . . . But we knew we weren't "poor folks" and would work our way out of it. Which we did. . . . Some people looked down on the men who took jobs on the WPA, created by President Roosevelt to keep people from starving, but most of us approved of it as a stopgap until the men could find real jobs. I don't think it ever occurred to any of us that the fledgling system of emergency jobs would turn into a welfare system that today supports millions who have neither prospect nor intention of earning their own living.[9]

While views may have changed regarding the specific role of government in providing welfare, there is still little indication that basic American attitudes have changed much concerning the purpose of help. For example, in a national poll conducted in 1985 for The Heritage Foundation by the Sindlinger Organization, the almost unanimous view of respondents was that job training and education components should be part of welfare to encourage independence. And fully 94 percent of Americans surveyed thought welfare should be temporary, like unemployment insurance.[10] While most Americans do not approve of the "stick" of benefit cuts to encourage independence, almost universally they view the purpose of the welfare system as *temporary* assistance, not income redistribution for its own sake.

Those attitudes toward the welfare system seem to be shared even by the poor. There is great concern among the beneficiaries of welfare that the design of the system often makes it difficult for them to reach the goal of self-sufficiency—despite the attempts of some conservatives to portray most able-bodied people on welfare as shiftless or cheats. A *Los Angeles Times* survey of poor Americans, for instance, found that more than 40 percent believe welfare benefits make them more dependent, and a clear majority of the poor feel both that young poor women have babies to get on welfare and that welfare encourages fathers to leave home. Whether that is actually true or not is beside the point: The survey indicates that poor people think the system works against them.[11] If one talks to those in poor neighborhoods who are trying to be independent, it soon becomes very clear that there is a deep-seated anger directed against a system that fosters dependency and undermines the work ethic—and against those who allow it to make themselves helpless. As Lincoln Barrett put it, when interviewed by the *Christian Science Monitor* during a series on rural poverty, a reason many remain poor is that they are "satisfied" on welfare: "If they'd rebel against it, they'd get out of it."[12]

Did something change, then, during the 1960s? Was there a radical transformation in the attitudes and philosophy of policymakers? Is that what led to a welfare system with incentives and effects that often seem to disregard the principles that guided welfare in America since colonial days? Strangely, if one examines the tone of the debate at the inception of the Great Society, there is little indication that the basics had changed. The War on Poverty was couched in familiar terms: helping individuals to improve their position and to escape from the dole, not simply making life easier for those on the bottom rung of the ladder. The goal was to better social conditions and to improve opportunities, not to substitute welfare for individual initiative. Lyndon Johnson was very clear on his objectives as he unveiled the great crusade against poverty. "Our war against poverty," the President declared, "seeks to give the desperate and the downtrodden the skills and the experience that they need to lift themselves from poverty."[13]

A remarkable aspect of the war was that it was not the result of any clamor from ordinary Americans for action against poverty. There was no popular groundswell in the 1960s to expand the welfare state or to change the purpose of assistance. In fact, it first began as a campaign exercise under the Kennedy Administration. According to Daniel Patrick Moynihan, a key player in the Great Society:

> The plain fact, the large and indispensable fact, is that the attempt to address the issue of poverty in the whole of the United States came in

37

the first instance from an informal committee of a half-dozen persons thinking up themes for President Kennedy's 1964 reelection campaign. At one point it appeared that the likeliest choice would be the emerging, challenging problems of the suburbs. Poverty held on, however. . . . But the electorate never asked for it; the *poor* never asked for it.[14]

It is difficult to escape the view that what happened in the 1960s, as Moynihan has suggested in his observations on the Great Society, was that those strategists ultimately lost control of the war. Johnson and his allies in the White House certainly had a vision of what they wanted to accomplish. But it is one thing to create and fund programs to eliminate poverty, and quite another to know how to make them work and to keep them on track. Increasingly, the architects of the Great Society welfare programs found themselves influenced by radical liberal wisdom about the condition of America and reliant on officials with a self-interested view of the federal role to write the details of programs and to execute them.

One of the underlying assumptions behind many of the government's efforts was the Michael Harrington thesis that the underlying social conditions prevailing in America created an underclass, and that it was the middle and upper classes who created those conditions.[15] According to that line of thought, society was somehow to blame for the condition of the poor, and only changing social conditions—basically construed as improving the material condition of the poor—would change the "culture of poverty." Never mind that much of Harrington's work, which had profoundly influenced the Kennedy coterie, was speculative exaggeration, and the rest imaginative interpretation. It is populist tracts that lead to revolutions, not scholarly and balanced analysis. Harrington and others launched the politics of moral outrage and middle-class guilt. Harrington's banner was taken up by those who designed the legislation to implement Johnson's vision and by those who administered the programs.

As programs developed and multiplied, the responsibility of the poor for their own future was relegated to a secondary role. In marked contrast to the prevailing view among the American people, the driving force behind the liberal welfare state was largely paternalistic, based on the views commonly held by caring, affluent liberals that the poor were different from other Americans, that blacks could not achieve economic emancipation on their own because of the legacy of slavery and segregation, and that the federal government was the only social institution with the resources and ability to elevate the underclass. In the absence of measurable goals, success began to be judged by the amount of money spent, the range of services provided, and the number of people "served," often without a clear idea of the effectiveness of the services provided. But then, as we all know, whether it be for defense or for welfare, the commitment of legislators to the goals of federal programs always tends to be measured by their willingness to spend other people's money.

Throughout the 1960s and 1970s, moreover, self-appointed advocates of the poor and program administrators increasingly began to argue that the poor should not be ashamed of being on the dole and that since Congress had passed assistance programs, the poor were "entitled" to benefits. While that might make for good political philosophy, it was a fundamental break with the whole ethos that had characterized American thinking about welfare. The "welfare rights" movement demanded handouts with dignity, and those economic "rights" became as sacred as political and civil rights. The poor were no longer to be required to feel a sense of gratitude or responsibility to the society that helped them. Nor were they expected to feel a stigma about being on welfare. The obligation implicit in welfare henceforth would operate only in one direction. Thus, Agriculture Department brochures in the mid-1970s were telling food stamp recipients that they were "in good company," that food stamps "should not be confused with charity"—indeed, in a remarkable twist of Great Society rhetoric, food stamps "are designed to help you help yourself."[16] The clear implication was that the poor could not manage without welfare, to which they were entitled as a right, and that the federal government was obliged to provide for them as long as they needed it, regardless of individual effort. That change in the tone of anti-poverty policy over the last two decades crept into the welfare structure almost imperceptibly, but its implications have been devastating for the poor.

In terms of a philosophy of welfare, the 1960s were thus a strange departure from the traditional American view. Not that tradition should be a political straitjacket, but ideas like mutual responsibility and the stigma of welfare were grounded in common sense: They were effective ways to push the able-bodied poor back into the mainstream of society. Unfortunately, the woolly thinking of the 1960s still lives with us in the design of many of today's welfare programs. If we are to achieve reform, liberals as well as conservatives must recognize that many of the sound overarching principles espoused by the creators of the Great Society were hijacked on the road to implementation. We must remind ourselves of those key principles as we try to make the welfare system effective in objectives shared by most Americans.

First, we must bear in mind that assisting those in need is a moral obligation and a mark of civilization. But it is an obligation that should be felt by individuals; moral obligations cannot be carried out on our behalf by a proxy. So when we say to an American, as we had begun to do, that his obligation ceases when he sends off his check to the IRS, we undermine one of the great strengths of American society. The liberal view that we can simply transfer our obligations to government by paying taxes is not just dubious morality—it weakens the effectiveness of society's response to social problems.

Second, while a civilized society takes care of the less fortunate in its midst, in a society as large and culturally varied as the United States a centralized and bureaucratic system is not the best way of helping the needy. That does not mean we must rely solely on the willingness or capacity of local communities to deal with local problems, but it does mean that we made a tragic mistake in failing to recognize the essential and vital importance of local institutions, such as family, church, and neighborhood organizations, in addressing social concerns. As we shall see in later chapters, the current welfare system has discouraged and weakened those institutions. We must strengthen them so that they can mobilize the resources and talents of communities to tackle social problems.

Third, the idea that low income creates a culture of its own is neither accurate nor useful. Poverty is as much a state of mind as a physical condition. Its causes are so deep and complex as to defy the well-intentioned efforts of sweeping federal programs. Unfortunately, as we shall see, welfare programs have encouraged individuals to focus on their weaknesses as a condition for aid. That has led to dependency and pessimism. So if we are to do anything to tackle poverty, we must seek to create broad conditions that will give individuals the incentive to seek their strengths and build on them.

And fourth, we must never forget that welfare is a two-way street. The "welfare rights" movement and the insistence on entitlements, which have been the guiding spirit of the welfare industry since the 1960s, vitiates the idea of personal responsibility for one's own condition and implies that the needy have no obligation in return for help. That strikes at the heart of sound policy and the entrenched views of most Americans. For a welfare system to succeed, there must be responsibilities on both sides. If we accept the notion that the provision of welfare should not be contingent on actions by the beneficiary to escape welfare, we are certain always to have the poor with us.

Defining and Measuring Poverty

It is impossible to deal effectively with any large-scale problem unless it can be defined and measured. That may seem obvious, but America has been engaged in a twenty-year War on Poverty with only a very fuzzy view of the target. Clearly a meaningful definition and accurate measurement of poverty are essential if we are to target our limited resources wisely and efficiently. But it is also important for a more subtle reason. The way we measure poverty has important implications for the politics of policymaking. The word "poverty" is laden with emotional connotations. The way Americans react to welfare proposals depends very much on their perception of how they affect poverty. That perception, in turn, is influenced by official measures of poverty. Is an action likely to cut "the poverty rate" or increase it? Thus welfare policy can be influenced significantly by the manner in which the poor and trends in poverty are described. A big obstacle to reforming welfare is the failure of our definition of poverty to describe accurately who needs public assistance and who does not.

Most of us recognize that the poverty of the Third World, with periodic famines and long-term mass homelessness, is different from poverty in the United States. Tocqueville's conclusions about poverty in England are just as valid today in America: Poverty is a relative concept. So just who is poor? Is it someone who faces starvation and homelessness, or simply someone who has much less than his neighbor? Is it someone whose best efforts cannot scrape together enough for the next meal, or someone who cannot manage his money prudently? Is it someone who is discriminated

41

against and exploited, or someone who ruins his own life through ignorance or lack of effort? In America, the answer is all of the above. But "all of the above" is not a single problem capable of a single solution.

Thus it is with deceptive precision that the numbers of the poor and the poverty rate in the United States are reported annually. It is deceptive because few people realize just how soft a statistic the poverty number really is. It does not measure need. It does not measure the absence of self-sufficiency. It does not distinguish between the the cost of living in Manhattan and that in Alabama. Incredibly, it does not even take into account accumulated wealth—so an elderly American can own a building on Fifth Avenue outright and still be considered poor. All it takes into account is regularly received reported annual cash income; families and individuals who appear to fall below a certain income threshold, adjusted for family size, are simply *defined* as poor by the government.

It is easy to forget that the very idea of an official national definition of poverty is a recent development. Before the mid-1960s, need standards for public assistance programs were determined by state and local governments, because that was where public responsibility for welfare lay, and those standards tended to reflect local factors. Even in the 1930s no national poverty standard was established. One reason was that many New Deal social programs were primarily targeted not at the poor as such but at the unemployment that led to poverty.

But with a federal War on Poverty declared, an operational *national* definition of poverty was absolutely necessary for the centralized strategy of the Great Society. State legislation and programs could be designed to accommodate local circumstances and prevailing notions of poverty within the state, but federal legislation and programs had to apply to the whole country, with broadly similar eligibility criteria across the nation. If there was to be a national assault on poverty, the federal government needed to know the dimensions of the poverty problem according to a national definition. Moreover, the definition had to be relatively simple. If subtle differences between localities were factored into the national definition, it would become incomprehensible to most program administrators and to the public at large. That, in turn, would lead to confusion, high overhead costs, and, perhaps more important, reduced public support. To maintain the political momentum, therefore, the Great Society strategists had to produce a definition of poverty that was easy to understand and to administer, whether or not it was an accurate reflection of popular notions of poverty. The war needed a clearly defined target.

The attempt to devise such a national definition opened a Pandora's Box of problems. Since poverty, like beauty, is to a large extent in the eye of the beholder, any poverty standard could be no better than quasi-scientific, regardless of how methodically it was developed. A poverty standard has to be a subjective device, since few can agree on the essentials of poverty, let alone the fine print. Thus the calculation depends very much on the judgment of those who set the standard.

Not surprisingly, propagandists for the Great Society saw poverty everywhere—poverty that could be solved only by a massive expansion of the federal role. According to Michael Harrington, in 1964 there were some 40 million to 50 million poor Americans, one-quarter of the entire population. And those individuals were not poor people who could get back on their feet with a little help, but Americans who were supposedly "immune to progress" and "maimed in body and in spirit."[17] However one might want to interpret low income, considering what we know of income mobility in the United States, it is impossible to accept Harrington's claim of rampant poverty as anything but dogma. Nevertheless, such assertions were challenged by very few at the time, and it was in the general climate created by such claims that the official U.S. definition of poverty was developed.

Such was the nature of the Great Society that the shape and extent of far-reaching programs turned on the work of obscure civil servants. The definition of poverty was central not just to federal spending on welfare, but to the American public's whole view of poverty and welfare. It has been the focus of debate ever since, the measure of success or failure of welfare policy. It determines a supposed rate of poverty in America, and the rise or fall of that rate has become a barometer of each administration's compassion for the poor.

The definition of poverty underpinning the War on Poverty, and subsequent amendments to it, was based primarily on the judgment of one person, Mollie Orshansky, then an analyst at the Social Security Administration. Between 1963 and 1965, she devised a set of poverty thresholds to measure changes in the number and demographic composition of low-income persons. Those experimental and semiofficial tools for judging progress in the War on Poverty became official in 1969, when the Census Bureau was entrusted with updating and revising them. According to Orshansky's definition, one-fifth of all Americans were poor in the mid-1960s.

How was that determined? Well, since subjective notions of poverty meant nothing to a computer, they were simply ignored. Essentially the method was to find the cost of items thought necessary for a household to avoid falling below an arbitrary level of absolute poverty, and then to estimate what total family income would provide the household with enough to spend on those items, given competing demands on the family's money. The original definition was calculated according to the prices of the items in the Department of Agriculture's 1961 basic food budget. That was multiplied by three to derive the income needed to reach the "poverty line." The multiplier was chosen because a 1955 food consumption survey showed that the average expenditure on food by all families in the sample (combining all income levels) was one-third of after-tax income. In 1969 the poverty thresholds were indexed to the Consumer Price Index—to the general level of inflation, in other words—rather than just the cost of food.

The thresholds have been criticized for a number of reasons. Even at the time the poverty definition was created, Orshansky's methodology was challenged. The economist Rose Friedman, among others, questioned the validity of using a multiplier based on the average of all families, when surveys indicated that low-income families typically spent a far greater proportion of their income on food and thus achieved a nutritionally adequate diet despite their income level.[18] More recent studies by the federal government itself and by private scholars have raised similar questions.[19]

The way the poverty definition was developed, moreover, presupposed that the poor do or should spend proportionally as much on clothing, shelter, travel, and presumably opera tickets as the middle class. Obviously that was absurd. You do not need a Ph.D. in statistics to realize that if a family suffers a cut in income, it will change its spending pattern to ensure that it can afford the necessities of life. But the poverty definition assumed that the pattern would not change, so it is hardly surprising that they concluded that many low-income families cannot possibly have enough food to eat, even if they have sufficient income to purchase the basics. Friedman estimated that the use of average budgets, rather than those reflecting the actual spending patterns of low-income families, would have overestimated poverty by 100 percent in 1962. Friedman calculated a 10 percent poverty rate, rather than Orshansky's 20 percent, using Orshansky's own base criteria. Routine acceptance of a methodology that leads to an artificially high estimate of poverty has obviously injected an enormous bias into the whole data series, affecting perceptions of the extent of poverty and the degree of anti-poverty measures needed.

Indexing the poverty threshold to the Consumer Price Index after 1969 injected a further upward bias in the level of poverty presumed to exist in the country. The CPI measures the increase in cost of a specific "basket" of goods and services over time. Indexing to the CPI thus ignores any substitution of one commodity for another by households to keep living costs down. If butter becomes too expensive, for example, a family might switch to margarine; at another time it might buy less beef and more chicken. Those actions and the significant impact they have on a family's condition are completely disregarded by the CPI. Indeed, until a 1983 revision of the housing component of the CPI, the cost of buying a new home was given five times as much weight in the CPI as rental costs. Thus the rapid inflation of home prices in the 1970s meant the CPI greatly exaggerated the actual increase in the cost of living for all low-income Americans who already owned a home (primarily the elderly) or who rented. That significantly distorted the poverty data. Indeed, John Weicher of the American Enterprise Institute estimates that by 1984 the housing component mistake alone implied an overcount of America's poor by about 4 million.

Moreover, no one actually counts the number of poor people. The estimate of the total number of Americans in poverty is derived from a statistical sampling of the population by the Census Bureau, and the income data in the survey are self-reported. The known underreporting to the Census of even legal income reportable to the tax authorities is one of the most serious deficiencies of the poverty data. The Census Bureau's own estimates indicate underreporting of aggregate income of about 10 percent, with welfare income underreported by as much as 24 percent.[20] Even if we ignore the completely unreported income generated in the multibillion-dollar underground economy—many of the "poor" actually have jobs and income that they do not report to a government agency—it is clear that the Census Bureau's data base ensures a miscalculation of the real level of poverty. Underreporting of income can have a significant effect on the calculation of poverty. The Panel Study of Income Dynamics at the University of Michigan, which has developed more complete income data than the Census Bureau's surveys, calculated the 1978 poverty rate at 6.8 percent, using the official definition, as against the official rate that year of 11.4 percent.[21]

There are other problems with the official poverty measure. Resources other than regularly received cash income are ignored, even though they may obviously have a considerable effect on the living standards of some families. Capital gains and one-time lump sum payments, such as life insurance, are not counted, nor are assets—even liquid financial resources. Nor are in-kind benefits such as food stamps and medical benefits, even though more than two-thirds of federal spending on the poor is in the form of in-kind benefits. That is particularly ridiculous. Imagine that you were unemployed and penniless, and then you found a job. But instead of giving you a paycheck, the employer paid you in kind by picking up your rent, delivering free groceries, taking care of your cleaning bills and so on. Obviously the IRS would not be happy, but clearly you would be much better off than before, even though you were still "penniless." Yet when the government provides a person with in-kind benefits, the official statistics show no reduction in poverty. Only cash matters. The federal government could give every poor person in America a free car, free housing and education, and free food for life, but as far as the official poverty definition is concerned, that would have had no impact whatsoever on poverty.

The highly flawed method of calculating poverty leads to many cases where people are defined as poor whom the average American would consider anything but poor. A retired couple owning a million-dollar house, a luxury car, and a bulging portfolio of stocks and bonds would be considered officially poor if their annual cash income were sufficiently low. A college student living apart from his parents and subsisting on scholarships and loans may be officially poor—indeed, the income rule at one time allowed the student sons and daughters of the rich to qualify for food stamps. And an author of books on welfare whose earnings fluctuated from year to year could be classed as poor in a year of low earnings, even if he or she sets aside money from good years to deal with lean years.

In one sense, of course, those people are indeed poor; they have little short-term discretionary spending ability. But society's obligations to them clearly differ from its obligations to an uneducated single mother of three who has no resources whatever and little hope for her children's future. Yet our definition of poverty does not distinguish between them. They are all "poor." Since the eligibility criteria for federal assistance programs are usually based on the poverty definition, but also take assets and other criteria into account, many of those individuals rightly do not qualify. But the existence of officially "poor" who are ineligible for benefits enables welfare advocates to point to a vast "unmet need" and buttresses their arguments for increased spending.

Our present measure of poverty does not, in short, reflect poverty as traditionally understood. It is not surprising, then, that almost 40 percent of "poor" households manage to get along with no government welfare benefits at all.[22] On the other hand, some 20 percent of Americans receive at least one means-tested benefit, far more than even the total number of imprecisely measured officially poor. That is because many federal poverty programs do not cut off eligibility until the beneficiary is well above the poverty line. To complicate matters further, it is quite possible for people above the official poverty line to be genuinely needy, since the poverty line is not adjusted for geographic cost-of-living differentials. For a family living in Manhattan without any assets, for instance, an income well above the official poverty level may be quite inadequate.

The official measure of poverty is seriously inadequate as a basis for welfare policy. Thus, America could establish a food stamp program to benefit "the poor" and then find, some years later, that enterprising but hardly disadvantaged college students are on the rolls. The students were not committing fraud; it is just that our poverty definition contains some grossly unwarranted assumptions about the relationship of poverty to low income. So trends in the official poverty population tell us little about the extent of poverty as that term is generally understood. Nor do they tell us much about the success or failure of welfare policy.

Not surprisingly, perhaps, there is only a loose connection between the official poverty rate and the eligibility criteria for most public welfare programs. The Office of Management and Budget issues poverty guidelines which are essentially simplifications of the Census Bureau thresholds, and some programs use a percentage of the OMB standard as the income eligibility level. For example, free school lunches are available to children from families with incomes below 130 percent of the guidelines. The two costliest programs, Aid to Families with Dependent Children and Medicaid, do not use federal poverty guidelines at all but are based on state standards of need. Officials and lawmakers, in other words, recognize that the official poverty rate is not a true measure of need. Americans below the official rate are not necessarily poor as generally understood, and those above the rate are not always free of poverty. Nevertheless, changes in the rate continue to be used as an indicator of the success or failure of welfare policy.

The U.S. Census Bureau has experimented with other methods of calculating the poverty rate, but they have not been incorporated into the official government measure. The official rate for 1985 was 14 percent, implying that 33.1 million Americans lived in poverty. But that counted only cash aid; it ignored food stamps, subsidized school lunches, assisted housing, Medicaid, and Medicare. The Census Bureau values those in-kind benefits at $56.2 billion for 1985, as against just $30.2 billion for cash benefits. The relevance of those in-kind benefits to the degree of poverty of a household is not always clear, however. Medical assistance is a particularly contentious item. If the father of a household is struck down by a serious illness, for instance, and receives medical treatment, paid for by Medicaid, with a value of $10,000, it would be unreasonable to argue that the family has been made better off by $10,000. On the other hand, non-poor families have to set aside part of their income for health costs or insurance and so Medicaid does imply a benefit to some degree. Trying to resolve such complications, the Census Bureau has computed the effect on the poverty rate of including various combinations of in-kind benefits. Depending on the particular combination, the bureau estimated that the 1985 poverty rate could actually be between 9.1 and 12.8

percent, implying a range of impoverished Americans of between 21.5 million and 30.4 million.

The questions hanging over the measurement of poverty are far from academic. A national approach to poverty requires a national measure of the problem, and that reveals a central dilemma of the War on Poverty: how to devise a poverty standard that meets the political and administrative test of simplicity, yet at the same time measures poverty when poverty is a notion that means very different things to different people. That failure should be recognized for what it is, an indication that *any* centralized approach to combating poverty faces severe operational limits before one even begins to discuss the details of a comprehensive national strategy. Like trying to run every skirmish in a war from central headquarters or every salesman's pitch from corporate headquarters, any attempt to establish a workable and comprehensible national concept and measure of poverty is bound to have serious shortcomings.

Although that basic flaw in a centralized attack on poverty cannot be avoided, defenders of such a strategy could at least reduce some of their problems if they would make one significant change in the basis of the poverty definition, namely substituting a national *consumption* standard for the national income standard of poverty. A consumption standard means that poverty would be defined as the income needed to buy a minimum quantity of specified goods and services. Those unable to acquire the "poverty market basket" would be considered poor. Such a consumption standard would be a step forward, but it still would not overcome many of the technical and conceptual problems with any attempt to establish a national standard for poverty. It would do nothing to uncover unreported income, for instance, nor would it necessarily provide a method to account for the assets of a family. It would simply add a little common sense to a very inadequate benchmark for a national policy.

The reason a consumption approach would be a step forward, though a small one, is that it would base definitions and eligibility criteria on a range of goods and services typically consumed by the poor (the cost of which might vary significantly from place to place), rather than nationwide income levels geared to a questionable food budget. That would at least remove some of the regional inequities of the current income standard. A consumption standard would also mean a poverty definition based on the actual goods and services that the poor could be said to need, rather than some fraction of the typical middle-class American's spending pattern. Moreover, as the broad social consensus about what constitutes a minimally decent living standard changed, the composition of the market basket could be adjusted, just as items are added or removed from time to time from the basket used to derive the consumer price index.

That would be a more comprehensible and reasonable national poverty standard than the national poverty income level, because it would reflect actual consumption patterns of the poor and the corresponding income level needed to escape poverty in different locations. Under the aegis of the Census Bureau, the states or localities would set the income thresholds necessary to achieve nonpoor status within their borders, based on the national consumption standard. That would not be dissimilar to the "fair market rent" concept currently used to calculate rent subsidies under federal housing programs. What happens in those programs is that the government finds the typical rent of acceptable housing in the particular location—which varies from place to place—and then calculates the appropriate rent subsidy to the family according to that rent. So different subsidies are awarded to families with the same income. It all depends on the local price of housing. A national consumption standard would simply apply the same approach to all the basics included under welfare. The American Public Welfare Association has recently endorsed a very similar concept as part of a sweeping welfare reform plan it has proposed.

Rethinking Our War Aims

If we look honestly at the systemic problems of the Great Society's War on Poverty, it is clear that our ability to mount a national campaign against poverty is very limited. The whole idea of poverty is a vague concept, meaning very different things to different people at different times, and to the extent we can pick an arbitrary definition, any effort to measure poverty on a national basis presents enormous practical and conceptual problems. It is just as plain that the flaws in the battle plan cannot simply be overcome by the use of massive federal financial firepower. Technical problems cannot be solved in that way, nor can the political and cultural factors contributing to poverty. As most liberals continually emphasize, America learned a hard lesson in Vietnam about firepower, strategy, and culture. Billions of dollars and state-of-the-art weaponry could not overcome a foe with few tangible resources. Now the liberals are learning the same lesson about welfare: Committing vast amounts of money is not the answer.

But recognizing one's own limitations, the Greek philosopher Socrates observed, is the first requirement of wisdom. Appreciating the limitations of a centralized government approach to welfare is the first step to improving our chances of making significant inroads into the poverty problem in the United States. That being the case, detailed welfare reform requires both a reassessment of our objectives in the campaign against poverty and a refinement of our overall strategy based on the capabilities of our weapons.

As we have seen, there is far more agreement about society's broad objectives regarding welfare than the political debate would suggest, even if there are endless disputes about tactics and specifics. That agreement revolves around a consensus that has been remarkably constant across time and place. Central to it is the principle that a civilized society is duty-bound to provide sufficient assistance to those who are infirm, disabled, or otherwise unable to support themselves to reach a minimum acceptable standard of living. Moreover, few Americans would dispute that the minimum acceptable standard is beyond the level of clothing, shelter, nutrition, and health necessary simply to keep that person alive. It reflects a subjective, changing notion of relative poverty that varies from time to time and from place to place. The problem comes in trying to devise a "national" welfare policy adaptable to such a decidedly nonnational idea of poverty.

A second element of the consensus concerns our approach to those who fall below the acceptable standard but who are "able-bodied"—difficult though that is to define. There is broad agreement that it is in the interest of society, as well as an obligation of society, to give such individuals temporary support if they fall on particularly hard times, while both prodding and encouraging them to start climbing the ladder out of poverty. Except for the most ardent proponents of "welfare rights," Americans believe that welfare involves an obligation on both sides. Society is obligated to help, but it is not required to create or accept a condition of dependency where the beneficiary chooses to remain on welfare rather than to strive to be independent. Providing welfare, in other words, should not be like giving a drug addict another fix so that at least he feels a little better for a short time.

Needless to say, there is intense debate over the degree of that mutual obligation and the policies needed to discharge it. The debate will and should continue indefinitely, as notions of obligation and standards change and as we learn more about the relative effectiveness of alternative policies. The economic capacity of the society itself is also obviously a factor in the debate, as is the proper balance between the stick and the carrot. But there is a broad consensus that providing the able-bodied poor with a sufficient degree of education and skills to achieve the acceptable living standard makes for good economics as well as good social philosophy. There is also wide agreement among both conservatives and liberals that all Americans are entitled to specified civil rights to allow them to exercise political power in an effort to secure welfare privileges and to pursue their interest generally—even if the extent of those rights arouses strong passions.

When we move beyond the consensus on those broad objectives of welfare to the specific strategies to be employed, disagreement quickly appears. If that tension is to be resolved, it is essential that we think carefully about the shortcomings of the War on Poverty and reconsider what would be realistic approaches given the nature of the American political system. That will require policies based on a number of important principles:

> *1. There is a big difference between "government" and "society" when it comes to addressing problems. We will solve poverty only if we recognize that a large part of the solution must come from stronger families, communities, and other social institutions. Government policy should aim to strengthen the institutions that are best equipped to tackle poverty, not to replace them with less effective programs and bureaucratic agencies.*

There is a crucial distinction, frequently overlooked, between the responsibility of society and the responsibility of government in social welfare. Each citizen is simultaneously a member of many social and political organizations—a family, a community, a state, a nation, and many others. Americans recognize clearly that different problems are best addressed by different institutions, and the responsibility of tackling poverty is shared by many elements of society. The 1985 Sindlinger poll conducted for the Heritage Foundation, for instance, found that most Americans believe the main responsibility for helping the poor rests with family and friends. Only one-third feel that government should take the lead. Three-quarters of all Americans believe that churches and community organizations have "some obligation" in aiding the poor.

It is vitally important that we recognize that government programs alone are not the solution. Stable families and strong communities are the building blocks of American society. When they crumble, society's ability to keep people out of poverty also crumbles. We shall never win Johnson's war until those institutions are reinvigorated. The culture of poverty can be overcome only by a more powerful social culture.

Despite the views of most Americans about the importance of certain social institutions, policymakers still turn almost automatically to federal programs to lead the attack on poverty. The federal government is clearly very bad at micromanaging the details of programs aimed at problems that involve local factors. Faraway officials are understandably not very good at appreciating why a particular youth is aimless or why a particular neighborhood is rundown. But there are powerful pressures, rooted in the political dynamics of the American system described earlier, causing approaches to such issues to be "nationalized."

That is particularly true in the case of welfare services. Local institutions often have the expertise and resources needed to tackle welfare requirements, yet the political dynamics of taxing and spending encourage local politicians to shift responsibility up to the federal level. In addition to the general political dynamics favoring centralization, Americans also tend to reason that although poverty and social problems have local characteristics, the fact that they occur nationwide surely means they fall within the domain of the federal government. Ironically, when Michael Harrington exhorted politicians to attack poverty, he recognized that Washington was not the best place to solve the welfare problems of an Atlanta or a Detroit. He called for a national effort at the federal level only by default, recognizing that "centralization can lead to an impersonal and bureaucratic program, one that will be lacking in the very human quality so essential in an approach to the poor."[23] He turned to central government only because he felt that cities lacked the fiscal capacity, and some (conservative) states the political will, to deal with the problem of poverty.

Yet Harrington also subscribed to Lyndon Johnson's view that poverty could be overcome only by creating a sense of national community, which would embody American ideals of publicspiritedness and included rich and poor, black and white. Integrating the poor into such a national community, according to both Johnson and Harrington, should be a basic goal of federal policy. Moreover, the national community itself, by elevating to a national level the American sense of community obligation, would mobilize the country's political and economic resources to break down the local barriers and economic deficiencies that allowed poverty to persist.

The idea of national community, the constitutional scholar William Schambra writes, has been "the essential underpinning for liberalism's extensive federal social service program."[24] Schambra also points out, however, that liberals have been noticeably unsuccessful in mobilizing Americans around their national community idea. While Americans clearly feel a strong sense of obligation and attachment to their neighbors within local institutions such as family and church, their intensity of commitment falls rapidly as the community grows larger and their "neighbors" more distant. Like an unstable chemical compound, a sense of national community easily breaks down. Ellen Goodman, a columnist, describing the schizophrenic attitude of Americans toward such national "mega-events" as the 1984 Olympics, Hands Across America, and the rededication of the Statue of Liberty, laments that,

> . . . the more splintered Americans are, the more separated in our private homes and ideologies, the more we yearn for shared community, shared enterprise, shared values. The mega-event fills that need, at least briefly. It gives us the hit of emotion, the momentary sense of belonging, without demanding much in return.
>
> We can check our egos at the door of a mega-event and pick them up again on the way out. We can link hands for hunger and go home for dinner. We can take a holiday from our individual lives to be members of a nation, and then take back a souvenir for our private collection.[25]

While the War on Poverty rested on the idea of a national community, Schambra observes, Johnson implicitly acknowledged that affinity to the notion is hard to create in Americans.

It is worth noting that Johnson settled on the expression *"war* on poverty" precisely because war is, above all, a time when the clamor of self-interest is quieted by mutuality and a widespread, public-spirited devotion to the national interest. War, Johnson explained, evokes "co-operation [and a] sense of brotherhood and unity." The "military image" of the war on poverty, he argued, would "rally the nation" and "sound a call to arms which will stir the people . . . to lend their talents to a massive effort to eradicate the evil."[26]

National community does not mean much to most people, whereas the more local version of community is a powerful force in America. As we shall see later, Americans traditionally have appreciated the importance of community institutions to their own interests as well as to the poor, and those institutions have been highly effective in dealing with the problems of the poor. Although the Great Society paid lip service to local community, the underlying strategy was to see community institutions as a political rather than a social force and to create political institutions in the community that would increase the pressure for federal action. Essentially the Johnson staffers gave up on poor communities as institutions. They assumed that the political and economic deficiencies of such neighborhoods meant they were beyond hope. So they were incorporated into one large community run from Washington, and the poor were taught to rely on institutions operated on their behalf by well-meaning outsiders. Had anyone tried to do that to middle-class communities, of course, they would have been denounced as trying to impose a centrally planned socialist regimen on Americans. It does not work in other countries, people would have said, and it will not work here. They would have said that ignoring local community and diversity was bound to lead to failure. But the War on Poverty was aimed at the poor, not at the middle class, and somehow it was assumed that in their case it would lead to success. So what we now have is capitalism for the rich (opportunity, competition, and choice) and a gray socialism for the poor (paternalism, centralization, and take-it-or-leave-it services).

An alternative approach, of course, would be to recognize that a policy of diversity and decentralization is a positive force rather than a recipe for fragmentation and weakness. In almost every aspect of life, Americans appreciate the importance of pluralism and the shortcomings of monopoly. Diversity and competition are seen as a vital ingredient in economics, in the media, and even in religion. But when it comes to public education or welfare, suddenly many of those same Americans become converts to the idea that only a monopoly serves the public interest. So they demand that welfare programs be the same throughout the nation and fear that allowing the poor to choose anything other than public education will cause society to crash in ruins. No middle-class American would accept such uniformity in his own life, but for some reason it is thought to be in the best interests of the poor.

If we are going to have a social welfare system that truly serves the poor, we must realize that having a safety net does not mean we are committed to rigidity and uniformity. What it should mean is that we have very clear goals, but that we give the maximum scope to individuals, community institutions, and government at all levels to experiment and find the best ways of reaching those goals in their particular area. That does not, however, warrant an assumption that states or communities have the means and the desire to tackle poverty and social problems. It means only that they should be the front-line troops in the war. The task of the federal government is not to plan and fight each battle or to provide ammunition to every division and regiment. Instead, it is to set the broadest goals of the war and to provide assistance only as needed, relying for ultimate success on the tactics of those closest to the fighting. In other words, rather than the top-down strategy that has characterized programs since the Great Society, with Washington as the driving force behind welfare policy, it is time we began instead to reexamine a bottom-up strategy, turning our efforts to strengthening such institutions as family, community, and state and local government, which should be in the forefront of welfare policy. That in turn requires a fundamental review of federalism in the United States, to secure the advantages of decentralization while assuring that lower-level institutions have the capacity and determination to take decisive action.

2. Government programs should not prop up the pathology of poverty. We should insist that the poor, like anyone else, must take responsibility for their actions and frame policies accordingly.

Whatever some leaders of the poor might claim, welfare is not the payment of reparations by the rich to the supposed victims of American capitalism. It is a helping hand to those in need for a variety of social and economic reasons. When we extend that hand, we have every right to say that we are not going to support activities that keep people in poverty. Very few Americans would knowingly give an addict the money to buy another hit, while most would give generously to help that person break his habit. But when it comes to poverty, many Americans seem to feel that they have the obligation to maintain a poor person but no right to demand a change of behavior. So when a young teenager decides to father a child out of wedlock, in all likelihood condemning the mother and child to poverty, we rush to provide welfare to all concerned. If the young mother thinks it might be more pleasant to live in her own apartment, we take care of that too.

Society should not condone such irresponsible behavior on the part of some individuals when it imposes enormous burdens on the rest of us. Welfare programs should not be "value-neutral" when it comes to self-destructive actions. We have every right to say to the teenage mother that we are not going to be held hostage by her innocent child. We can say that we will help the child because it is civilized to do so when the parents do not have adequate means, but we can also say that we are not going to allow the father to ignore his responsibilities or the mother to move out of her parents' home just because she would prefer that. Moreover, we have every right to demand that leaders of a community, such as its local politicians, teachers, and the church, make it clear that certain behavior will not be financed by the taxpayer. By not acting that way now, we simply encourage the poor to become a dependent underclass. There is nothing humane about doing that, any more than there is in paying for a drug addict's habit.

3. The current welfare system contains strong disincentives, which encourage dependency and act against those wishing to pull themselves out of poverty. We need to ensure that government, at the very least, does as little harm as possible and to explore changes in regulations and the tax code that will promote independence.

The welfare system might be adequate for those who are temporarily down on their luck because of an unexpected drop in income yet are basically in the mainstream of American life. But for those who are mired in poverty in the long term, the welfare system does little more than entrench them in that status. Not because that was the goal—quite the contrary. As Daniel Patrick Moynihan puts it, the government simply did not know what it was doing. Welfare reform would make considerable progress if the left and right hands simply worked in concert. Unfortunately the activities of the federal government are divided, as if by a wall, between revenue and expenditure, and only rarely are the public expenditure implications of a proposed tax change carefully considered. That is quite evident in the case of welfare and contributes to the powerful disincentives to self-help identified by Charles Murray and others. If the government is trying to help the poor with welfare policy with one hand, it ought to think about what it is doing to them with tax and regulatory policy with the other.

If we are to lift as many Americans as possible out of poverty, the government should not be taxing the income of the poor. It is absurd to give money to the poor and then take part of it away again in the form of taxes. Before World War II, approximately 90 percent of the population was below federal tax thresholds. Throughout the 1940s and 1950s, low-income citizens were not subject to federal income tax.[27] But during the 1960s and 1970s, inflation pushed more and more people over the tax threshold and taxes consumed larger and larger portions of their income. Steep rises in the Social Security tax added to the heavy tax burden, disproportionately hitting the working poor.

The combination of tax and welfare incentives has also helped to erode the family as a bulwark against poverty. The highest proportion of long-term welfare outlays go to families in which the mother had her first baby while in her teens, and in this sense teenage pregnancy cost state and federal government at least $16.7 billion in 1985.[28] But then, if a mother has little education and poor marriage prospects, it should hardly be surprising that she is a prime candidate for welfare dependency.

The tax structure creates particular disincentives in the case of large families, because welfare benefits increase with the number of children, while wages do not. So welfare becomes more and more attractive with each additional child. In a story run in 1985, the *Christian Science Monitor* focused on the typical Catch-22 welfare situation in the case of Zong Toua Hang, an unskilled Laotian refugee in California trying to support a family of seven. Hang discovered that if he worked too many hours each month, he would lose welfare eligibility. But to work his way off the welfare rolls, and make up the value of his family's welfare benefits, he would have had to earn about $1,000 a month, a virtual impossibility for a man of his skills.[29]

Unfortunately, good welfare policy is also thwarted in many instances by regulations intended to improve the efficiency of welfare expenditures. Reducing benefits when a poor person earns some income, for instance, can have the same effect as placing them in far higher "tax" brackets than those faced by the richest of Americans. This "tax" may not be imposed by the Internal Revenue Service, but the result is the same.[30] The aim, of course, is to target welfare assistance on the poor rather than to "waste" public money on those who have escaped poverty. That may seem efficient from a budget point of view, but anyone trying to work his way out of welfare gets hit with a financial sledgehammer, unless he decides to be dishonest and enters the underground economy—hardly a way to encourage self-help. Various "work incentive" schemes have been tried to phase out benefits more gradually, but they tend to have only a marginal effect on work effort.

Those and other work disincentives, such as regulatory restrictions on working at home, need to be examined very carefully, particularly as they affect dependency and the strength of the family as the basic economic unit in poor communities. Only by discouraging dependency and family breakup can we hope to meet the goal of encouraging the able-bodied poor to leave the welfare system rather than become entombed in it.

> 4. *The federal government, indeed any level of government, can only do so much. Rather than try to solve every problem and attempt to micromanage the poor, government should concentrate its efforts on getting the basics right. It should also be prepared to quit when it cannot get results.*

By trying to achieve victory simultaneously on all fronts, welfare policy has all too often resulted in costly, complex programs that provide overlapping benefits to some of the poor and little assistance to others. When shortcomings are detected, the usual response is either to increase funding in shotgun fashion, hoping that some of the money will hit the target and cure the problem, or to tighten up the eligibility and operation of the program, often making it even less flexible and sensitive to local circumstances.

So at the same time that the welfare system refuses to condemn behavior that is self-destructive, programs often deny the poor the opportunity to pursue the avenues to self-improvement that are available to the nonpoor. The system can also overlook the simple fact that small symbols of dignity are just as important to the poor as to anyone else.

Don Anderson, the executive director of the National Association for the Southern Poor and a veteran of the War on Poverty, complains bitterly of how both public and private officials routinely make decisions for the poor that suffocate dignity and self-reliance. He once took a foundation officer on a "tour" of rural poverty. They visited one family of fourteen living in a one-room shack without any plumbing. The staple of the family's diet was the beans they grew for themselves, and the family had to carry its water in from 2 miles down the road. When the visitor asked the mother what she would buy first if she had the money, the woman replied that it would be good clothes for the children to wear, because, she said, it is important that they be well dressed in school. The reply apparently stunned the visitor, who had simply assumed that the answer would be more food or better shelter.

To Anderson, the story illustrates a fundamental flaw of welfare policies designed far away from the people they are supposed to help. The only real progress against poverty, he says, comes when people are allowed to take control of their own lives. Creating the conditions for self-help is the public obligation. But almost by definition, Anderson says, self-help is stymied by middle-class preconceptions, services defined by others, and money that comes with a plethora of instructions telling the poor how they must use it.

Instead of trying to manage the lives of the poor with policies that seek to deal with every element of every problem, policymakers should recognize that there is more likelihood of success when the details of a strategy are developed by the institutions and levels of government closest to the scene, while distant institutions and government confine themselves to establishing a climate of rules and incentives to make sure that the job gets done. In the case of the federal government, establishing a tax and regulatory climate for strong economic growth and job creation establishes a sound base of resources for others to tackle the specifics of poverty. By concentrating on the "basics" of how to provide the poor with a sound education and skills, how to strengthen the fundamental institutions of family and community, and how to ensure that local institutions have adequate resources for their own initiatives, the federal government stands far more chance of securing victories against poverty than when it attempts to manage and lead every part of the campaign.

Besides avoiding the temptation to run every aspect of welfare, the federal government must also be prepared to admit on occasion that it cannot solve a problem. That is not easy for the politician or the official, but there can come a point with some poor but able-bodied Americans where initiative after initiative produces only failure. The usual response in those cases is to maintain that person, usually at great cost. So the persistent young offender is kept in an institution, and the welfare mother who cannot hold down a job stays permanently on the welfare rolls.

Few Americans would dream of sticking with costly failures in most aspects of their lives. When a businessman finds his product is not selling, he either changes it or withdraws it. When a repair shop seems unable to fix our car, we go somewhere else. Americans always seem determined to try a new approach when one keeps failing, except in the case of federal programs to combat poverty. When those fail we seem quite prepared to keep throwing good money after bad, unwilling to try something else. That does not help the poor. It is remarkable how we ignore so many organizations that seem able to solve problems that have stumped the best-funded government programs. Unfortunately they are not often given the chance to try. Why? Because politicians and officials may feel that it is an indication of incompetence if they admit failure, while the service providers have little financial incentive to turn away a client.

We should think more in terms of temporary welfare programs, controversial though that would be. If government cannot achieve a certain goal in a specified time, it should do no more than guarantee the most elementary items to the person involved. Other institutions in society should be expected to try another approach, while the government spends its resources where they seem to do some good.

> 5. *We can never know in advance the ideal policy to deal with any problem, and changing circumstances demand new strategies. Thus an effective welfare policy must have the ability to learn and adjust over time.*

Lyndon Johnson's War on Poverty grew out of a rigid approach to policymaking. By centralizing policy and thus preempting the power of many other institutions, Johnson ensured that there would be a unified approach to America's social problems. But that also reduced the amount of experimentation and innovation that could take place. The capacity of the system to compare different experiences and to learn from both mistakes and bold theories has therefore been far less than would have been possible with a decentralized approach.

It should not be surprising that with the greater discretion and obligations given by the Reagan Administration to states, municipalities, and nongovernmental institutions, new ideas in such areas as health care, work incentives, and service provision are now being tested at a remarkable pace beyond the Washington beltway. The limited degree of decentralization accomplished so far has energized the search for more effective welfare strategies. Remembering the time when welfare was almost totally in the hands of states and localities, many liberals understandably feared that decentralizing welfare would mean less help for the poor. But state government is very different now from what it was in the 1960s. Rather than avoiding decentralization and diversity, we should be trying to redesign welfare policy within a federalism framework that mixes the establishment of broad themes and obligations by the central government with the creative juices of localism.

CHAPTER

3

Reactivating Federalism

THE 1960S WERE no minor tilt or adjustment in the balance of American federalism. The proliferation of federal programs emanating from the Great Society, followed by revenue sharing and the grant-in-aid programs of the Nixon presidency, constituted a sweeping transformation in the nature of the federal system. While Ronald Reagan has sought, with some success, to restructure the relationship between Washington and the states, the federal arrangement established in the 1960s still prevails. Unfortunately for the welfare system, Johnson's strategy of centralizing federalism, despite its initial impact on the country's social problems, undermined America's ability to address those problems over the long haul in creative, economical ways. Until steps are taken to reinvigorate the federal system so that it becomes a partnership in practice as well as in theory, we shall continue to be severely restricted in our efforts to fight poverty.

It was not exactly surprising that the welfare reformers of the 1960s should look upon lower levels of government, particularly the states, with frustration and disdain. Even many state officials agreed readily that state government was moribund. North Carolina former Governor Terry Sanford admitted in his 1967 book, *Storm over the States*:

> The states are indecisive. The states are antiquated. The states are timid and ineffective. The states are not willing to face their problems. The states are not responsive. The states are not interested in the cities. These half dozen charges are true about all of the states some of the time and some of the states all of the time.[1]

The problem was most serious, of course, in the South, where state action often meant virtually no action when it came to the poor and minorities. In part, that was due to the general economic plight of the region. But more important, state and local government in the South was accurately viewed by the Johnson White House as the bastion of reaction and dereliction of duty. With state legislatures meeting briefly and infrequently, voting rights effectively denied to blacks in many jurisdictions, and politicians like Alabama's Governor George Wallace denouncing "pointy-headed" Washington reformers and preaching "segregation forever," there seemed little prospect of working effectively through state governments, even if the federal government were to provide funds to poorer states. As Denis Doyle and Terry Hartle, American Enterprise Institute scholars, explain, Johnson staffers "even had a name for their [own view of the states]—'The George Wallace Syndrome'—as in 'Do you want to give George Wallace that much power and authority over federal money?'"[2]

Rather than distribute federal funds to state and local governments and then keep their fingers crossed in the hope that men like George Wallace would see the light, Johnson's Creative Federalism provided both sticks and carrots to induce states to act in line with the vision of the Great Society. The civil rights legislation was one of the bigger sticks, enabling federal courts to force the South to open up its voting system to black Americans. The community action agencies added to the pressure by mobilizing the poor—or at least advocates for the poor—as a political instrument to leverage state and local funds to combat poverty.

Most important of all in forcing action by lower levels of government was the extensive array of federal grants that came with detailed requirements as to how the money should be spent and what matching funds were required. Not only were there regulations affecting the spending of specific grants, but increasingly Congress tacked "cross-cutting" requirements onto groups of federal aid programs, forcing governmental and private recipients of federal assistance to pursue and document their adherence to federal social goals, such as equal opportunity, citizen participation in decision-making, and the payment of "prevailing" wage rates. Although the federal mandates attached to those grants made them a poisoned chalice to more reactionary politicians, their bribery power was considerable, driving a wedge between politicians and voters. Constituents with little interest in the balance of state–federal relations demanded that their representatives take and spend the money, poison and all.

The amount of that money has grown steadily since the Johnson presidency. In 1965, just under $10 billion was distributed to the states. By 1980 the figure had topped $60 billion, about 20 percent of which was passed through to local governments; in addition, the federal government distributed more than $20 billion in aid directly to local government. The Great Society programs also led to an expansion in the range of earmarked federal assistance. Until 1965, federal grants were confined largely to income security and transportation. With the Johnson programs, however, billions of new dollars went to support education, training, social services, health care, and economic development. Later, such items as environmental and energy assistance and revenue sharing were added to the list of big-ticket grants.[3] By 1979, some 498 federal programs aided state and local governments in everything from providing health care for the indigent to controlling rats and jellyfish.

The availability of federal money has had a profound effect on state and local government—as the Great Society architects intended. The earmarking of most of the money for specific activities had the result of changing the priorities of states and localities to fit federal objectives, with ever increasing numbers of officials administering federal programs. Various intergovernmental bodies, such as Federal Regional Councils, sprang up to coordinate and spend federal grant money. Moreover, the matching requirement in many federal grants, designed to ensure that federal dollars did not simply reduce dollars spent by lower-level governments, helped to stimulate a sharp rise in total government spending. Between 1959 and 1979, federal–state–local outlays rose from 15.9 to 25.9 percent of GNP.[4]

The federal mandates accompanying the substantial increase in federal funds available to state and local government have tightly restricted the actions and decisions of officials. Local discretion has been seen as an invitation to discrimination. Federal regulations have increased generally, with the *Federal Register* expanding from less than 10,000 pages in 1950 to more than 85,000 by 1980. And by 1980, about 90 percent of the federal regulations and publication requirements affecting state and local governments were in the form of conditions attached to federal aid.[5] Such regulations have been enforced more stringently over time.

Federal regulations attached to grants were a powerful weapon with which Johnson could force recalcitrant jurisdictions and institutions to abide by the Great Society's agenda. After anguishing for months, for instance, over whether segregated Southern hospitals would turn down Medicare patients rather than integrate, Johnson gambled that the prospect of increased business would induce them to accept a no-segregation rule attached to federal Medicare reimbursement. He was right.

Needless to say, many state and local officials have challenged the federal intrusion on constitutional grounds, arguing that it constitutes an infringement of the Tenth Amendment, which reserves powers to the states. But the courts have tended to side with the centralizers and regulators, not with the states. Nowadays it is commonplace for state and local bodies to be sued successfully by citizens for failing to abide by federal rules. Indeed, according to Carl Stenberg, a former assistant director at the Advisory Commission on Intergovernmental Relations, "during the 1970s, the highly intergovernmental area of litigation relating to federal grants-in-aid mushroomed. Federal grant law, called by one jurist a 'slumbering giant,' awoke to the point where there are now [in 1980] more than 500 decisions directly related to receipt and use of federal assistance."[6]

The Great Society strategists were highly successful in their campaign to force the states and localities to execute an agenda designed by a national government in Washington, and Johnson's Creative Federalism still forms the heart of the intergovernmental system. Yet it also appears that they bit off more than they could chew. Johnson's highly centralized version of federalism required something that is practically impossible under American democracy: comprehensive and coordinated policy planning at the top, and the enthusiastic commitment of lower levels of government to implement policies over which they have little control. As Paul Peterson of the Brookings Institution points out, the pre-Johnson version of federalism had thrived, from a management point of view, because

[n]ational and local administrators had worked together on highway construction, vocational education, aid for federally-impacted schools, and mathematics and science programs. In all these programs federal

and local governments had a common interest in seeing these projects prosper and expand. When the creators of the Great Society asked the federal system to carry out a host of redistributive programs—in health care, education, housing and numerous other policy areas—they placed that system under considerable stress.[7]

That stress is apparent in a number of ways. In the first place, the tail wags the dog in that the various constituencies that gain directly from federal programs—including state and local politicians as well as private interests—find that the political dynamics favor them over the proponents of a national interest. Thus the level of federal spending on social and economic development programs has risen far faster than the amount of money reaching the areas and individuals most Americans would consider needy. Study after study indicates that it is political clout and influence that determine the distribution of federal grants, not poverty and distress. A study of disbursement patterns by the economists Randall Holcombe and Asghar Zardkoohi, for instance, found no statistically significant correlation at all between discretionary grants and standard determinants of poverty. On the other hand, "the data showed the grants to be allocated based upon political power. Per capita grants were higher in those states with more seniority in the Senate, with a larger percentage of majority party members in the House, and with members on the influential House and Senate committees."[8] Similarly, a 1977 Congressional Budget Office study of federal economic development programs found that counties in the top fifth of per capita income received considerably more assistance per resident than those in the bottom fifth.[9]

The surprising distribution pattern of federal aid, whereby the rich get richer, is called "fruitcake federalism" by Aaron Wildavsky, professor of political science at Berkeley. Culinary analogies, in fact, are the traditional means used to describe federalism—one would be forgiven for assuming that constitutional theorists spend their weekends reading Julia Child cookbooks. The early view of federalism, with various levels of government having the exclusive domain over particular functions, is often characterized as a "layer cake," while the various cooperative arrangements preceding the Great Society are known collectively as a "marble cake." Federalism today, Wildavsky says, means that interest groups and lower levels of government come to Washington and use their political leverage to extract the maximum quantity of delicacies from a Congress not exactly known for its powers of self-restraint. "At budget time," Wildavsky laments, "it is always Christmas. The season is festive with anticipation. There are plums to be had for the picking. The closer one approaches the brandy-soaked cake, the more intoxicated one becomes with the rising fumes. One is sober enough to pick out the goodies but too drunk to notice how much one is eating."[10]

Centralized federalism has also reduced the level of innovation in policymaking and program sensitivity to local needs, as explained earlier. The suffocation of local innovation and activism has been a disturbing yet unavoidable by-product of the Great Society's determination to prevent state and local holdouts from thwarting the agenda set in Washington. Such restrictions placed on state and local officials tend to be of particular concern to the younger and more professional officials often found these days in governors' mansions and city halls. The consequences of running programs by remote control from Washington was a prominent theme in the recent Report of the Committee on Federalism and National Purpose, a blue-ribbon panel of academics and both active and retired officials from all levels of the federal system. The committee, co-chaired by Senator Daniel Evans and Virginia's former Governor Charles Robb, complains that in the case of social service and community development programs, good management requires the ability to tailor projects and services to address local circumstances. But, says the report,

> [b]y placing significant financial and policy responsibility for these programs with the federal government, the intergovernmental system skews priorities, creates delay and often raises cost through complex bureaucratic procedures. Decisions are made at the federal level where officials are least acquainted with local circumstances and least accountable to local constituencies that will feel the effects of those decisions. Too much reliance on shared programs may also have a chilling effect on state and local activism: officials at these levels may at times hold back on addressing public problems because they presume that initiatives, funds and guidelines will be forthcoming from Washington.[11]

Those problems and deficiencies of today's centralized form of federalism are not all that surprising when one realizes that centralized federalism is basically the policymaking equivalent of centralized economic planning. It is ironic indeed that a country that appreciates so well the profound flaws in trying to run a centrally planned economy has been so willing to embrace a system of federalism built on the same shaky foundations.

Most Americans understand that no matter how much talent is brought in to design and administer a national economic plan, a decentralized economy will outperform it. A centralized economy may be able to mobilize resources and maintain popular support when there are only a small number of clear goals to be reached, such as sustaining a war. But when the goals become more numerous and complex, popular support soon evaporates, and the planning process quickly breaks down; shortages appear in some areas, surpluses elsewhere, and total production suffers. Moreover, as the planners try to keep the grand design on track, they are forced to issue tighter guidelines and instructions to plant managers, fearing that independent action will frustrate the overall plan. Managers soon learn that it is in their interest to act according to the letter of the law, while using their political and bureaucratic connections to obtain special consideration whenever possible. Innovation suffers, and the interests of the consumer fall to the bottom of the pile.

We have experienced a similar outcome in the War on Poverty. Johnson issued a call to arms with what seemed to be a clear and simple goal—victory over poverty. Centrally designed plans were developed, and lower levels of the federal system were forced to become federal spear-carriers rather than policy entrepreneurs. But once the public came to understand that the war would take much longer than expected, and that there were complex tradeoffs to consider, the goals became fuzzier and the public more critical. Over the years, as relatively simple plans failed to conquer poverty, planning became more complicated and the rules tighter. And officials and interest groups began to give increasing thought to their own condition.

Correcting the policymaking deficiency does not mean going to some form of *laissez-faire* federalism in which each level of the system pursues its own goals and we just hope that poverty and other problems will somehow be taken care of. That would risk a return to the political and social inequities that were quite properly the target of the Johnson forces. What it does mean, however, is that just as we have a market economy that functions well because it encourages innovation and entrepreneurship within a legal and tax framework that reflects society's goals, so we should move toward a system of innovative federalism that stimulates policy entrepreneurship within broad national goals—in short, the exact opposite of Johnson's centralized federalism.

Strengthening the Roots of Federalism

In almost every aspect of their lives, Americans believe strongly in the idea of "bottom up" progress. Large government economic projects can make some difference here and there, for instance, but few would dispute that the foundation of America's economic expansion—and the thing that differentiates the economy of this country from those of other countries—is the fact that enterprise and innovation are a grassroots phenomenon. The person next door, the one who decides to go into business with a couple of friends, is the driving force for progress and economic improvement. We know that government can create a good or a bad climate for him to work in, but he is the key to success or failure. We know it is essential that all kinds of people try out all kinds of ideas, if the nation as a whole is to prosper. Diversity means we do not put all our eggs in one basket. It means we have a better chance of finding the right product or the right answer to a problem.

The strange thing is that in recent years we have overlooked the importance of grassroots creativity in social welfare policy. Johnson apparently persuaded the nation that creativity was a purely middle-class characteristic. Although millions of poor immigrants built the country, somehow the poor of the 1960s could make progress only if they were placed in the womb of the federal government. The social welfare system put in place in the 1960s stands traditional American thinking on its head. While a "bottom up" strategy works for the rest of us, for the poor we now have a "top down" approach. The federal government takes the lead, and other levels of government and institutions have to fit into Washington's blueprint. And it has failed—for the very reasons that we have avoided the same approach in every other aspect of our social and economic 'ife.

The secret to making real progress against poverty and distress is to realize that it will come from a "bottom up" and not a "top down" process. America possesses a vast array of both private and public institutions and organizations that can move into action if they are allowed to. What the federal government has to do is create a climate hospitable to those institutions, enable them to learn from each other's successes and failures, and ensure that sufficient resources reach needy individuals and institutions for them to make reasonable progress. We have become trapped in a social welfare philosophy that assumes that diversity is a mark of chaos and inadequacy—a mistake that few of us would make when talking about the economy. Rather than try to stamp out diversity in an effort to find the unitary solution to welfare and social problems, we should be nurturing diversity, recognizing that it is the key to success and progress in all fields.

Such a model of policymaking sees the federal government's role rather differently from that envisioned in the Great Society mind set, which still dominates social welfare policy in Washington. Instead of a government that epitomizes society and acts as the leader in social change, the model sees government simply as one agent among many that a society has to pursue the consensus goals of its citizens. Progress is swiftest when Washington tries to strengthen other institutions while loosening its reins upon them, not when it tries to replace or restrict them.

America, of course, boasts a range of nongovernmental institutions unlike that of any other country. Those institutions are critical to the fabric of American society. In particular, there are those institutions that the sociologists Peter Berger and Richard Neuhaus refer to as "mediating structures . . . those institutions standing between the individual in his private life and the large institutions of public life."[12] Among them are family, church, neighborhood, and voluntary association. As Berger and Neuhaus point out, the strength and stability of such institutions is essential for individuals to exist in society. It is hard to imagine how we could function without those institutions; life would be very empty indeed. And we all belong to some such institution beyond our families, be it the Rotarians or the PTA, the Polish Club or a church choir. Those institutions add a richness and completeness to our lives that cannot be created by any department of government. They act as anchors, allowing the individual to flourish in the knowledge that he is linked firmly to others and can count on their help.

Two of the mediating structures stand out as critical to relieving the scourge of poverty in America: community and family. The erosion of those two fundamental institutions lies at the heart of our seeming inability to end what has become a culture of poverty and hopelessness among certain groups of able-bodied Americans. While strong communities and families are by no means a guarantee of social stability and improvement—many Americans living in close-knit families within stable communities remain very poor—there is ample evidence to suggest that stabilizing those institutions is a precondition to success in tackling poverty. Unfortunately, well-meaning policies over the last twenty years have only undermined those essential building blocks. Strengthening those two fundamental institutions is absolutely necessary if we are to counter the culture of poverty that causes able-bodied Americans to be trapped in the underclass.

But the mediating structures do more than play a key social role within the community itself. They are also a potential source of services to combat poverty and social distress—a source that policymakers have tended to ignore. It is as though we were assuming that only the Fortune 500 companies could provide the goods and services we need, and that small, local enterprises could provide little of value. But just imagine what it would be like if suddenly everything from the local bakery to the gas station suddenly disappeared, and we had only IBM, GM, and their brethren to deal with. That is exactly the kind of effect we reach for in social welfare policy. We think in terms of mega-structures and overlook the enormous possibilities of the rich array of both formal and informal organizations in poor as well as rich communities, organizations that are intimately bound up with people and sensitive to their needs. If we are turn the tide against poverty, this grassroots level is where we must start.

Beyond the very basic institutions of family and community, there is an enormous web of private organizations of various sizes intended to pursue a multitude of purposes. A group of mothers agrees to share babysitting duties so that they can all engage in part-time work; members of a church congregation organize food and shelter for the homeless; retired executives donate their time to staff a business trainin center for inner-city entrepreneurs; former youth gang leaders establish a safe haven for other gang members seeking something more in life than street violence. The list is enormous. According to Neal Peirce, co-author of *The Book of America: Inside Fifty States Today*, the range and sophistication of those organizations are growing:[13]

> In my own reporting for the last decade I have witnessed an incredible outpouring of grassroots initiatives. Community economic development corporations, neighborhood citizen security patrols, tenant-managed public housing, gardening and energy conservation and do-it-yourself, sweat equity housing rehabilitation experiments—all are part of the picture. Neighborhood organizations are forming alliances that permit themselves to become fully recognized partners in the political and social life of their cities. From confrontational starts, they themselves often evolve into consensus-building forums.[13]

Quite separate from the function of those organizations as agents in giving a new sense of stability and purpose to the poor, they also provide tangible services to the poor. In many ways it is not surprising that a liberal welfare state would see them as political organizations demanding services from government, rather than as providers of services to the poor. But conservatives have also fallen into that trap. They have been very reluctant to stimulate the growth of such organizations. Like many liberals, conservatives tend to see them as primarily political institutions; but whereas liberals view grassroots groups as allies, conservatives tend to remember the activist days of the 1960s and see them as a threat. That is a fundamental mistake. Genuinely grassroots groups are basically economic and social organizations, not political instruments.

The way to bring those organizations "on line" as service providers, adding immeasurably to the services we can deliver to the poor, is to do something that will make most conservatives flinch: empower the poor and the organizations that serve them. Empowering the poor in this context means making it possible for them to act like consumers, controlling their own resources and making their own choices. It means enabling community organizations to play a much larger role in catering to those consumers. Thus it is not a question of "consulting" with community institutions when programs are being designed by officials or making it easier for them to exert political pressure on the political process, as the Office of Economic Opportunity sought to do. Nor is it a question of funding them so that they can be co-opted to work on behalf of government. Empowerment means giving the poor real consumer power. By doing that, we would strengthen the service institutions that best serve the poor.

But Berger and Neuhaus sound a warning note, especially important in light of the way in which government contracts have affected the nonprofit sector. The best way to empower organizations is to empower those who make use of their services, not the institutions directly. Otherwise there is

> . . . the real danger that such structures might be "co-opted" by the government in a too eager embrace that would destroy the very distinctiveness of their function. The prospect of government control of the family, for example, is clearly the exact opposite of our intention. The goal in utilizing mediating structures is to expand government services without producing government oppressiveness.[14]

Empowering institutions directly can be helpful, in other words, but we must be very careful who is paying the piper. If the government stepped in to fund our local baker or gas station and we could obtain subsidized bread and gasoline, we might cheer at first, but what kind of service could we expect three months later?

How can we empower organizations and turn the poor into consumers? In the first place, we can change federal mandates and rules at all levels of government that have the effect of shutting out *ad hoc* institutions that may be able to play a key role in providing social welfare services. In that way the poor would be able to exercise real choice, because a much greater range of providers would become available to them. At the federal level, the cross-cutting requirements attached to grants are often so rigid that the cost and complexity of complying with them prevents financial support from reaching the very groups that are closest to those in need and most trusted by them. In addition, many state and local regulations, ranging from teacher certification and day care licensing to zoning, have the effect of restricting the activities of grassroots organizations. Often those rules, many of which are said to be to protect the poor, are very harmful to their interests and actually result from the efforts of professional service providers to shut out competition.

Restrictions emanating from jealous interest groups are particularly damaging in the cause of education. The Washington-based National Center for Neighborhood Enterprise, for instance, has discovered hundreds of independent neighborhood schools, mainly serving inner-city minority children. They operate on a shoestring and were established in the main to compensate for the miserable education available in the local public schools. For the most part those schools depend for their financing on very modest tuition charges and on neighborhood fundraising. They are highly successful in providing children with the basic education skills that seem to be off the curriculum at many public schools. Yet they also face enormous obstacles in the form of building codes, credentialing requirements, and other regulations enforced at the behest of public school teachers, who feel threatened by the success of the independent schools.

Even when performance standards and other requirements genuinely attempt to assure that services to the poor are of high quality, the perfect often ends up being the enemy of the good. Take day care, which is a vital service for single parents wishing to work and so avoid welfare. Most jurisdictions have a host of rules affecting the supervision of children. Places used for the care of more than a certain number of children must have specified facilities and must be appropriately zoned. In larger centers, supervisors must have specified child care credentials. The idea, of course, is to make sure that working mothers can be confident that their children are well cared for—although, as several recent court cases demonstrate, regulating day care institutions is no guarantee against outrageous child abuse.

The problem is that the rules often mean no certified day care is available in many poor neighborhoods that need it most: People in the neighborhood do not have the paper qualifications, and in any case the cost of meeting the facility standards is prohibitive. Moreover, professional day care providers find it financially unattractive to serve the poorer communities. So what happens? Either mothers in poor families find themselves trapped at home, and on welfare, rather than working to support their children, or they resort to illegal day care—so they are not protected by any rules. That is no small problem. Surveys carried out in Washington, D.C., by analysts at the American Enterprise Institute, for instance, suggest that as much as 80 percent of the day care provided in that city is illegal and hence unregulated. That does not mean day care providers are free of all informal regulation. One mother explained to the authors: "We don't have any rules written down on paper, but the people who look after the kids in this neighborhood know there is one rule that counts: 'You hurt my kid—you are in *big* trouble.' "

There has been some progress in recent years in streamlining regulation, and the Reagan Administration has reduced the burden of federal requirements attached to many federal grants. Nevertheless, a great deal more needs to be done. Much more red tape has to be consigned to the trash bin. In the fight against poverty, paper qualifications and textbook procedures are simply not a good indicator of potential success. Simplification of regulation makes sure that the competition of ideas and approaches is more intense, and it reduces the cost of trying to solve social problems, making it easier for organizations with limited means to have an impact.

The second way to empower the institutions, within the existing grants framework, is to contract *with* the poor for social services to be provided in their own communities, rather than have government deliver them directly or contract with outside organizations to provide services *to* the poor. But we should remember the cautionary words of Berger and Neuhaus. This can be a dangerous game, inviting government takeover, suffocating the best qualities of the group concerned. The best way to avoid that is to make sure the group under contract does not have a monopoly. Like other Americans, poor people must be as free as possible to shop around.

Budget pressures on municipalities are already encouraging contracting out to neighborhood organizations by causing officials to look for lower-cost alternatives to traditional service delivery methods. As the *New York Times* noted in a 1983 article on city services, city managers across the country increasingly are ignoring union opposition and turning to community organizations to provide shelter for the poor, youth counseling, drug treatment, and many other social services. "Such delegations of authority, unheard of in the past," the *Times* reported, "are writing the latest chapter in the fast evolving role of neighborhood groups in the 'privatization' of local governments. Part of this trend is that neighborhood groups are becoming more formally organized and entrepreneurial."[15]

Contracting with organizations within poor communities does not mean that the poor receive cheap but shoddy services. Quite the opposite, in most cases. Generally the services provided by indigenous groups are better attuned to local circumstances and the needs of the poor, and often they involve highly creative solutions to problems. The reasons are simple enough: Local groups have a far more intimate understanding of the pulse of the neighborhood and a better idea as to what will work and what will not. While outside contractors have little or no contact with their clients after the service is provided, contractors who live in the community have to face their neighbors every day—indeed, in many cases they themselves are on the receiving end of those services. One reason tenant management of public housing has proved so successful is that the managers live in the projects. Maintenance calls are answered very promptly at the Kenilworth-Parkside project in Washington, D.C., a tenant manager, Kimi Gray, says, because the "engineer and the managers all live here. So when the heat goes out, we all get cold, too."

In case after case, the neighborhood contractors have proved to be pacesetters. For instance, based on the remarkable successes of David and Falaka Fattah in turning around young gang members in their West Philadelphia neighborhood, the juvenile courts now send some of their worst cases for care at the Fattahs' group home. In a survey of recidivism in the city, the Philadelphia Psychiatric Center found the rearrest rate of ex-offenders sent to the Fattahs was just 3 percent, as against up to 87 percent at some far more costly "correctional" facilities.[16] Similarly, a community-based adoption agency for low-income blacks in Detroit, Homes for Black Children, placed far more children with responsible black families than all thirteen of Detroit's placement agencies combined. The pathbreaking techniques of the group are now being copied by the city's professional agencies.[17]

A third way to empower local institutions is to give vouchers to the poor instead of paying organizations to deliver services to needy people. That avoids the potential co-opting problem raised by Berger and Neuhaus. A voucher is a certificate of a certain face value that can be used like cash, but only for specified goods and services. The poor person can choose among the providers available and simply exchange his voucher for the services. Providers of specialized services can be licensed or otherwise required to meet certain criteria—bearing in mind, of course, the problems discussed previously that can arise from such regulation. The service provider then takes the voucher to whichever level of government has issued it and turns it in for its cash value. The voucher thus turns the recipient from a dependent client into a powerful consumer, enabling him or her—rather than the government—to decide who is going to supply the service.

Besides their obvious attraction as a way of giving the poor the dignity of choice, vouchers also change the dynamics of services to the poor in a profound way. By putting the power of decision-making into the hands of the poor, vouchers force each service organization to demonstrate to welfare recipients that it can provide a good product. Friends in Washington or city hall are not much use if the poor must be approached as customers who can make choices, rather than dependent clients who must take what they are given.

By placing control in the hands of the service consumer, vouchers encourage the expansion of the sources of supply favored by the poor. Given the tendency of the poor to turn to local institutions for help when they have the chance to do so, Peter Berger is almost certainly correct in his prediction: "Most people, if given a choice, will 'cash in' their vouchers at this or that mediating structure, either already in existence or newly set up to provide a particular service."[18]

Vouchers are not a new idea, even if they are underutilized as a funding device. The GI Bill was essentially a voucher program. The government did not contract with Anystate U. or Downtown College to provide an education for returning military personnel. Instead it allowed the GIs to make the choice and then picked up the tab for tuition. The food stamp program, created as part of the War on Poverty, is actually a classic voucher system.

What other services could be made more sensitive to the needs of the poor through a voucher approach? Probably a great many. Education is the most obvious and also the most hotly debated. The National Education Association has so far stymied efforts at the federal level to implement a large-scale education voucher program, claiming that it would threaten the quality of education in many public schools. Vouchers certainly would do that, of course, but in a positive and not a negative way. Since the pressure for education vouchers and tax credits has been primarily from the middle classes, opponents may seem to have a point that a universal voucher program might lead to middle-class flight, leaving inner-city schools as dumping grounds and educational wastelands. That is highly questionable, but a voucher only for parents of the poor—particularly, as the Reagan Administration has been championing, for Chapter I compensatory education for the disadvantaged—would give low-income parents real clout and would stimulate innovative local approaches to education. That would give them real economic power. Not suprisingly, the highly successful inner-city independent schools, and the parents who scrimp and save to support them, are fervent supporters of education vouchers.

In addition to education vouchers, housing vouchers have enormous potential. Instead of segregating the poor into public housing ghettos or high-priced special private projects built with federal support, housing vouchers involve giving poor families a rent certificate equal to the prevailing cost of reasonable housing in the area, and then letting the family shop around in the open market, choosing where it wants to live. If quality of housing is high on the family's list of priorities, it can supplement the voucher with extra dollars taken from elsewhere in its budget and seek better accommodation or a better neighborhood. But that is the family's choice, not the government's. The federal government has already experimented with housing vouchers, finding that they keep housing costs down while increasing freedom of choice, and Congress has permitted the Reagan Administration to implement a limited national program. Still, the full potential of housing vouchers has scarcely been explored.

Plenty of other voucher possibilities exist. There have been moves to introduce a modified voucher concept for Medicare, and discussion of vouchers for Medicaid, as a means of stimulating innovation in health care delivery systems. Among existing uses of vouchers for welfare-related activities, the National Center for Neighborhood Enterprise, under a contract from the federal Office of Juvenile Justice and Delinquency, provides "technical assistance vouchers" to neighborhood organizations dealing with troubled youth. The vouchers can be used by those groups to purchase specialized services to aid their work. Vouchers have also been suggested for vocational training, day care, and many other services.

Not that there are no limitations or problems with the voucher idea. Vouchers are more effective in some circumstances than in others. One limitation is the amount of information and specialized knowledge possessed by the recipient. Medical vouchers, for instance, require greater sophistication on the part of the user than vouchers for basic, everyday items such as food or housing. But we should not take that too far. In the case of Medicare, prepaid Health Maintenance Organizations are essentially voucher-based. Moreover, the paternalists in America, together with the provider interest groups that feel threatened by poor people's consumer power, are forever insisting that the poor cannot make rational choices on a vast range of issues. Besides demonstrating utter disdain for the common sense of the poor, this line of argument overlooks the simple point that people do not make wise choices until they are first allowed to learn by making bad choices. Moreover, the "experts" who tell the poor what services they need do not have an impressive track record in curing the problems of the poor.

A second problem is fraud. Food stamps are notorious for it. The reason is that a typical welfare family undertakes so many transactions a month with the food stamps that keeping track of who is actually using them has been virtually impossible. Eligible people who do not use their full entitlement simply sell their stamps to middlemen at a discount. Even greater fraud potential occurs at the retailer level. At times the buying and selling of stamps has reached epidemic proportions in some cities. But fraud is by no means unique to vouchers. It is rampant in many welfare programs, such as Medicaid. Moreover, it is far less of a concern with other types of voucher. A housing or education voucher, for instance, involves just one transaction a month or semester, and the overhead cost of verification would thus be very small. But even in the case of vouchers with multiple transactions, technology may soon eliminate much fraud. "Smart" welfare cards that can be used like credit cards have already been developed and tested. Eventually, the card of an eligible food stamp recipient, for instance, might be credited by the government each month, and deductions made electronically at food stores. The card could contain a picture for identification purposes, and the food store could maintain an account with the government, which would be credited electronically each time a purchase is made. There would be no stamps to buy and sell on the black market, and transactions could be monitored for patterns suggesting fraud.

A third problem with vouchers—but again by no means unique to them—concerns eligibility criteria. If vouchers are available for goods and services, there is also a tendency for people to make creative use of the eligibility criteria. In addition to inequities, there is always going to be political pressure from groups of individuals who are just outside the eligibility criteria to be included under a voucher program. And when the vouchers are fully funded by Washington, state and local politicians have the incentive to gain popularity by supporting "eligibility inflation." In the food stamp program, for instance, the state pays for a large part of the administrative overhead, but Uncle Sam picks up the entire cost of the stamps themselves. So states have little reason to contain the cost of the program. If they put extra money into combating fraud or tightening eligibility, they lose twice: They carry the administrative costs but receive none of the program savings, and they have to face the angry beneficiaries and the welfare lobbyists.

One way to limit the pressure for expanding eligibility beyond reasonable levels might be to set only the broad minimum requirements at the national level and to provide a block grant to the states based on the total expenditure that would imply. The states could be required to meet a certain proportion of that expenditure, and they, rather than Washington, would be responsible for the detailed eligibility rules. That approach would accomplish two important goals. It would force the states to live with any expansion of the rules that state legislatures agreed to: They would have every right to widen eligibility, but they would have to find the extra money. In addition, it would encourage an element of diversity, and so promote innovation in the use of the particular voucher.

Such approaches would begin to nourish the grassroots of America's welfare system. By activating local organizations without suffocating their self-interested inventiveness, the ability of the federal system to experiment and to provide services more in tune with local circumstances would be significantly enhanced. Yet that would be only one part of the reform equation. Needed too are a number of steps to combine the benefits from decentralization *inside* government with mechanisms to assure that lower levels of government are willing and able to reach the consensus goals of welfare policy—in short, to turn the federal system from a lumbering, top-heavy giant into a powerful force for supporting local initiative.

The Resurgent States

While local institutions are the essential first line of defense in providing services to the poor, nobody could reasonably argue that they are sufficient for the whole task, with or without financial help from government. Just as small, local businesses are not sufficient to make an economy, neither are community organizations sufficient to make a social welfare policy. Before the Great Society, the states were the main institutions of government that supplemented and helped to finance the various public, private, and voluntary institutions that served the poor. It was the states, for instance, that experimented with a host of social insurance programs in the 1920s, many of which found their way into the New Deal. But in the 1960s the states were passed over, for all intents and purposes, when it came to devising a national War on Poverty.

They have stayed in the background ever since, even though they are once again on the cutting edge of innovation. The states are the missing link in the policy chain. They provide an essential bridge between the federal government and the myriad public and private institutions at the local level. They can marshal enormous resources, and yet they are also close to the people, unlike the federal government. They are the ideal level of government to explore creative approaches and to manage the public side of social welfare policy.

Of course, when the Johnson White House considered how the power of the federal system might be brought to bear on poverty, it is hardly surprising that they saw the states as obstacles rather than as allies. Aside from the blatant obstructionism of a George Wallace, the states in the early 1960s were the backwaters of the federal system. Reflecting the nineteenth-century distrust of state government, most were incapable of decisive action on anything, bound by extremely restrictive constitutions that were long on "shall nots" and short on "shalls." All but a dozen or so state legislatures were limited to very short biennial sessions. State executives were kept very much in check: Many states limited governors to a single two-year term, and few permitted the kind of organization and professionalism needed to operate sophisticated programs. Turning state officials into adjunct federal bureaucrats seemed about the best that could be done.

But things have changed dramatically at the state level over the last twenty years. When such states as Arkansas, West Virginia, and South Carolina are moving decisively to tackle health problems among the indigent, there is reason to suspect things have changed. When civil rights leaders shed a tear as George Wallace announces his retirement and Selma declares Martin Luther King Day a holiday, you *know* things have changed.

There has been a distinct change in attitudes among state and local officials in the last twenty years, especially in the South where official racism aggravated poverty among blacks. Part of it, of course, has been forced on the region by the Voting Rights Act, the Civil Rights Act, and various other federal actions. But the South has also evolved socially, eroding "do-nothing" attitudes and support for segregation and paternalism.

Yet the transformation in state government across the country has far more to do with management and constitutional reforms than with reactionaries finally seeing the light. In recent years, those reforms have led to a complete about-face by scholars, observers, and the public in their opinions of the quality and potential of state government. State government was very popular in the South of the 1960s, of course, but public impressions of state government throughout the nation have improved steadily since the 1960s. By the time Ronald Reagan entered the White House, a Gallup poll found that Americans believed, 67 to 15 percent, that state government is more understanding of community needs than is the federal government, and 67 to 18 percent that it is a more efficient manager of social programs; by a margin of 56 to 28 percent they said they favored a concentration of power at the state level rather than the federal level.[19] Moreover, when it came down to comparing state legislatures with the U.S. Congress, by the end of the 1970s the public had come to believe by similar margins that state legislatures are closer to the people and better at overseeing the day-to-day business of government.[20]

According to the Advisory Commission on Intergovernmental Relations, "The transformation of the states, occurring in a relatively short period of time, has no parallel in American history."[21] John Herbers of the *New York Times* reports that "some observers say that American federalism seems to have gone full circle, returning to the days before the Great Depression, when some states were experimenting with social insurance programs and the protection of labor unions, acting, in effect, as laboratories for later national policy."[22]

The journalist Neal Peirce sees the voting rights and civil rights legislation as a significant factor in the change in public attitudes, and he notes that the federal requirements on states served to build up a state bureaucracy that became more expert in social welfare programs. In addition, Peirce says "on the organizational level, the states acted as if they had read the prescriptive list of changes drawn up by public administration specialists and good government groups and enacted them into law."[23] Forty-three states now make provision for annual sessions of the legislature, for instance, as against only eighteen in 1960, and seven states have full-time or nearly full-time legislators. In most states the power of the governor has increased significantly through such changes as broadened appointment rights, longer terms of office, and the introduction of cabinet forms of government. In addition, about three out of every four state bureaucrats are now covered by some form of merit system.

Virginia typifies the resurgence of state government. Just a generation ago the government in Richmond was a shadow of its days of glory early in the life of the Republic. But now the legislature meets annually, and its committees meet all year round. It also has its own equivalent of the federal General Accounting Office to provide independent program evaluation. Among many other reforms, staff support for legislators has been substantially improved. Governors and former Governors of Virginia, like Charles Robb, are viewed as adroit statesmen and skilled administrators. In 1985 the state elected its first black to statewide office.

The radical improvement in the capacity and sophistication of state government explains why many opponents of decentralization turned out to have been unduly concerned when the Reagan Administration won congressional approval in 1981 to consolidate almost 200 grant-in-aid programs into nine "block" grants with reduced funding and streamlined federal rules. Reagan had argued that the states had the capacity and the will to take back the federal functions which had been usurped by Washington, and that the greater management flexibility afforded the states under the block grant system would bring about efficiency gains more than compensating for reduced federal support. Critics of the strategy had said the outcome would be very different: With less federal support and without detailed federal mandates to force the states to spend money in prescribed ways, the states would quickly reveal their true nature, shedding social responsibilities and ignoring the needs of vulnerable groups.

Yet devolution to the states did not herald the end of programs to assist the poor. Far from it. Indeed, most advocates for the poor were pleasantly surprised to discover that state governments took action, despite the constraints of the recession, to continue—and in some cases expand—service programs. "The states were far more progressive than we expected," says Maybelle Bennett, research director at the Coalition on Block Grants and Human Needs, formed to protect social programs.[24] The legal director of the American Civil Liberties Union, Burt Neuborne, notes that in the 1960s the ACLU was heavily engaged in fighting "the rednecks of local government." But now, he says, "We find ourselves consistently cooperating with local officials to protect minorities and other people adversely affected by national policies."[25]

The states did not abandon the poor. What they did do, George Peterson of the Urban Institute says, was reassess their priorities, using the flexibility provided under the block grant structure to replace federally designed programs that imposed high management costs with less expensive programs better tailored to local needs and resources. Thus in Texas, Peterson notes, the daily cost of the state's day care program fell from $10.87 per child to $8.15 under the new Social Services Block Grant by reducing staff–pupil ratios and staff training requirements, thereby increasing the number of children served. Similarly, the State of Michigan substituted home-based day care for institutional day care, also boosting the numbers served. In each case, the states argued, switching to an "economy" service level still allowed them to meet citizen demands quite satisfactorily.[26]

Although the states often got off to a slow, "even timid" start in many cases, Peterson says, gradually they began to reorganize and experiment and to emphasize the delivery of services to high-need or at-risk groups. In addition, the states began to combine monies from different block grant programs to support an overall strategy:

> The majority of states, once freed from federal restrictions, cut back on household transfer payments to cover utility bills. Instead, they directed more funds into weatherization and insulation programs meant to pro-

duce savings in energy consumption. These programs had the further advantage that they could be combined with monies from the Community Development and Community Services Block Grants to provide jobs for neighborhood residents.

On the other hand, states "used the block grants' flexibility to weed out programs that apparently were being kept alive only by federal 'force feeding.' None of the states, for example, provided general replacement funds for the community action agencies."[27] The U.S. General Accounting Office found similar patterns in its survey of thirteen states, published in 1985.[28] Those states transferred $125 million in funds among block grants during 1982 and 1983—chiefly from the low-income energy assistance grant, which received increased financing from Congress, to the social services programs, which Congress had cut. In addition, they stepped up the use of state funds, particularly for health and social service programs. State support rose during the period studied by about 9 percent in preventive health and health services and about 24 percent for maternal and child health. The GAO found that in health and social service programs, the switching of funds and increased state outlays led to increased expenditures in about three-fourths of cases.

The GAO also detected distinct changes in funding patterns, as states established their own priorities. Under the Social Services Block Grant, for instance, there was a switch in spending emphasis toward adult and child protective services, employment, education and training, and home-based services. On the other hand, most states introduced tighter poverty criteria for those service providers operating under the Community Services Block Grant. Combined with Congress's reduction in the total funding level, that meant about 90 percent of all service providers in the thirteen states had to face cuts in their support. Most of those providers turned to alternative sources of funding and to a greater use of volunteers.

That is not to say, of course, that states generally stepped in to replace federal social service spending dollar for dollar. They did not. But the response to the 1981 devolution by the federal government was very different from what would have been expected twenty years earlier. Within the budget constraints they faced during a particularly harsh economic recession, the states turned to management efficiencies, innovative uses of existing funds, increased state funding, and changes in spending priorities in order to provide support more effectively to those in need. They acted just as any business would. Faced with the loss of a long-time supplier and a turbulent market, they reacted to the crisis by changing the way they did business and by cutting costs.

But simply analyzing the responses in cash terms, as many critics of decentralization are inclined to do, is misleading, because it underestimates the level of service to the poor. Few of us would assume that quality is measured solely by price: Just as we have learned that it is unwise to assess the value of a weapons system simply by looking at its price tag, the volume and quality of assistance to the poor cannot be measured solely in terms of total outlays. Thus increased efficiency and innovation, plus the improved targeting of funds made possible by the flexibility allowed under the block grants, allowed the states to use dollars more effectively. The quality of social services to the poor was often significantly improved, not reduced, when high-priced professional service providers were replaced by volunteers and community organizations.

Nevertheless, the responses of the states also revealed patterns in the political dynamics of social policy that must be addressed in any general move to base reform of the welfare system on decentralization within the federal structure. Both Peterson in his studies and Princeton's Richard Nathan in his wide-ranging study of state responses to Reagan's budget cuts observed that while states did indeed take action to preserve or expand many services to the poor, different types of programs received very different responses. In particular, Peterson noted, programs with small recipient populations aroused less state interest that those with larger populations. While that might seem alarming at first sight, we should remember that it is exactly those small populations that can best be served by volunteers and local government; indeed, they are best able to deal with what can turn out to be very individual requirements.

Cuts in major entitlement programs, such as AFDC or food stamps, however, also were not replaced by states as readily as other welfare programs. One reason was that in many cases reductions in spending resulted from changes in eligibility criteria that the states agreed with. There are several other reasons for the pattern, according to Nathan. For one thing, budgets for entitlements are no easier to control at the state level than at the federal level, so states have hesitated to commit themselves to such open-ended programs, preferring instead to look for other means of assistance. In addition, state and local governments tend to avoid income redistribution programs, fearing that if they raise taxes on the minority of richer residents to provide reasonable levels of income support, when nearby jurisdictions do not, there will be an outmigration of richer residents to lower-taxed jurisdictions, and an inmigration of poor seeking relatively better benefits. Even though richer taxpayers may grumble at income redistribution via the federal tax system, Nathan points out, they would have to emigrate to avoid the tax.[29]

Even more fundamental, according to Nathan, is the simple rule: "The more discrete and visible a federally-aided program is, and the greater the political salience of the problem it addresses, the more likely it is to receive state and local support." Moreover, he says:

> Part of the reason for the political appeal of certain kinds of social service programs as opposed to others is a reflection of the organization and character of the providers. This point is very important for social programs. The larger the stake providers have in a given social service, the more likely it is to win support in periods of retrenchment like the current one.[30]

Skilled professional health care and social service providers, Nathan points out, tend to have "well-organized and politically strong 'trade' associations, and this is one reason that such programs fared relatively well under the Reagan block grants and budget cuts."

But provider-driven programs often distort good welfare policy in a democracy by overemphasizing the interests of the providers. The negative effects of provider-lobbying, however, are reduced as programs are decentralized. For one thing, if a program is transferred to the state level it means that provider trade associations have to set up shop in fifty state capitals, not just in Washington.

There also tends to be more voter resistance to unreasonable demands as one descends the federal ladder. When programs are discussed at the national level, the likely tax impact one way or the other is minimal for the average voter, so he tends to acquiesce in spending. It is hard to get him fired up to support a campaign to cancel a program. In addition, the discussion at the national level is remote: The voter generally has to rely on secondhand information, usually via media inclined to give programs the benefit of the doubt, rather than any firsthand evidence of how well his tax dollars are being put to work. That tends to help the organized social service lobby, which finds it comparatively easy to create a favorable national impression about a welfare program, whether or not it is actually successful. The closer taxing and spending are to the people, however, the harder it is for proponents of programs to win easy approval for spending, since each taxpayer feels the bite more directly, and he can better assess the costs and benefits of more localized programs.

Such public choice dynamics help to explain a number of different experiences with similar proposals at different levels of government. The privatization of services and facilities, for instance, has moved far faster at the state level—and faster still among municipalities—than at the federal level. The principal reason is that public employee opposition can be mobilized far more effectively to block privatization at the federal level than at lower levels, where voters can see the benefits more directly. Similarly, while the education voucher concept has made almost no headway at all in Congress, where the teacher unions can exercise considerable clout, Minnesota and other states have managed to overcome union resistance and pass versions of the concept. It has been the same story in many other areas, from teacher competency testing to health care delivery; the states have been able to overcome vested interests and adopt creative solutions to problems, while the federal government has scarcely been able to move for fear of offending key interest groups.

There has clearly been a renaissance of state government during the last twenty years, which has far-reaching implications for the way we can utilize the federal system to fight a more successful battle against poverty and social problems. States can and should play a key role in the social welfare system. Yet they have shortcomings as well as distinct advantages, and a new approach to welfare policy must accommodate that. On the asset side of the balance sheet, the states can mobilize enormous resources and evidently have a greater will to do so than most Americans would have assumed just a decade or so ago. Thanks in large part to the legislation and court decisions of the 1960s, which democratized state legislatures, they are more sensitive to all their residents and have won the confidence of the public. Ironically, many conservatives who now point to the effectiveness of state government opposed the very changes in federal law that enabled the states to blossom into strong and sensitive components of the federal system. Conservatives should give liberals credit where credit is due, just as many liberals should learn to have confidence in state government.

The states are also large enough units of government to manage complex programs and to provide the direct assistance that local governments and nongovernment organizations need to tackle poverty and distress in their communities. Yet states are also small enough to be entrepreneurial and able to tailor programs with a better eye for subtle variations in local circumstances. Moreover, fifty heads trying to solve a problem in their own ways are far more likely than one head to come up with a good answer.

On the liability side, the states are like any lower level of government: They are less inclined to support income transfer programs than service programs. There is also the thorny issue of clashes between state priorities and the broad national consensus on what is the minimum acceptable level of support for certain groups—much less of an issue now, of course, than when Lyndon Johnson occupied the White House. And there is a problem of fiscal capacity: Some states may be quite willing to reach certain standards and goals, but they simply have too many poor people and too few resources of their own.

The secret of good social welfare policy is to find ways to minimize the liabilities of the states through carefully constructed intergovernmental policies, while allowing the states to use their unique assets to address the central problems of poverty.

Empowering Federalism to Attack Poverty

Bearing in mind that government is only one of the instruments the nation has with which to address poverty and social distress, several steps should be taken to change the relationships between the levels of the federal government. Broad national goals could then be achieved through a system of federalism that would ensure the achievement of acceptable standards while encouraging vigorous policy innovation.

> *1. To stimulate innovation throughout the federal system, each level of government should utilize intergovernmental agreements to obtain equivalence rather than uniformity in the welfare programs of subsidiary governments. Waivers should be granted to states wishing to pursue alternative strategies to reach goals, and federal "welfare opportunity zones" should be created to foster welfare policy experiments.*

Uniformity smothers innovation and flexibility. Yet Americans tend to feel that although the states may be in a better position to administer programs, in the case of welfare there are national standards that should be upheld across the nation. The way to accommodate both factors would be for Congress to set performance goals and standards for the states—rather than issue federal mandates requiring specific actions—in broad areas of policy such as basic health care, nutrition, and housing. The states would be allowed to reach those performance standards however they wished, subject to federal approval of the approach. States should adopt a similar approach to welfare programs at the local level. That would provide each level of government with wide flexibility, which would encourage economy and innovation.

The Reagan Administration has already moved in that direction in a number of areas of policy. In the operation of surface mines, for instance, states are now required to have in place programs that are "no less effective than federal rules," rather than programs that are "no less stringent than federal rules." In the case of air quality regulation, the Administration set generic standards that state plans must meet, removing the need for case-by-case federal review when plans fit the guidelines. "This step," George Peterson says, "has freed the states to exercise more initiative in putting together market-based plans, like the sale and purchase of emission rights, which let firms meet air quality standards in a least-cost manner."[31] In the case of social welfare, the Department of Health and Human Services under Ronald Reagan has instituted "fast-track" waivers to permit the Secretary, under his discretionary powers, to modify, suspend, or waive certain rules. Most important of all, legislation passed in 1981 permitted states to request waivers from rules governing Medicaid so that they could explore alternative health care delivery systems. The states welcomed their new flexibility, and since

1981 there has been an explosion of management and delivery innovation.

To push forward at the edge of welfare policy development, the federal government should also invite the states to advance proposals for experimental approaches to welfare problems that might have national implications. Such proposals could involve the whole state or just a part of the state. Legislation should be enacted to the effect that if the proposal were to be agreeable to the federal government, the appropriate federal agencies could waive or amend the regulations as needed to allow the experiment to take place. No new federal money should be made available for such an experimental program; thus the experience of Urban Development Action Grants, where projects already planned are redesigned simply to tap into extra federal money, would be avoided. But it should be permissible for funds available under existing programs to be used in new ways in such experiments. The federal government and the states should take steps to make the results of such experiments available as widely as possible. Similar arrangements should be made between states and local governments.

In addition, the federal government should take the lead in proposing experiments to the states, to be conducted in "welfare opportunity zones." Washington would conduct welfare policy experiments that might have national or state applications. The zones would be limited in scale and duration. If they proved successful, they would become the model for permanent state or federal strategies.

The Reagan Administration proposed such a strategy in its study on welfare reform, issued in late 1986. The study declared that the federal government did not and could not have the answer to America's welfare problems, and that only by encouraging experimentation by states and communities are solutions likely to be discovered.

To create such zones, the federal government would negotiate a plan of action with the state and local governments involved, including the waiving or amendment of state and local regulations to permit the experiment to proceed. That would be a similar arrangement to the enterprise zone model proposed as a new strategy for inner-city revitalization by the Reagan Administration, but frustrated by congressional inaction. In that model, the federal government was to reduce specific taxes and agree to regulatory relief, provided the state and locality put forward an acceptable "course of action," such as tax and regulatory relief. Although congressional approval has not yet been forthcoming, a majority of the states have gone forward with their own versions of the enterprise zone concept.

A policy change of this kind fits the existing dynamics of federalism and the welfare debate. States are already experimenting in many aspects of social welfare policy and have long been urging the federal government to modify regulations that impede such efforts. In addition, the Reagan Administration recognizes that the welfare problem is so complex that some sweeping new "Reaganite War on Poverty" blueprint, albeit based on conservative principles, is unlikely to work, because progress probably will be achieved only by a process of step-by-step experimentation. That is why the White House officials charged with overhauling the welfare system chose to undertake discussions with governors and community leaders on how states and the federal government can encourage state and local experimentation. The favorable responses those moves have elicited from the state level suggest that there would be a solid base of support for decentralization.

2. *A switch to a "consumer is king" model of service provision, making use of the voucher concept, would encourage alternative methods of service provision. Localities, states, and the federal government should examine their licensing and regulatory systems to give the poor greater access to such alternative providers.*

The voucher mechanism is a powerful instrument to empower the poor and to harness the efforts of self-help organizations, mediating structures, and innovative service providers in the battle against poverty and social problems. Unlike cash, a voucher ensures that assistance is used for the purposes intended, but permits the recipient to exercise wide choice. In many areas, including housing, food assistance, education, training, and delinquency prevention, vouchers have already proved successful. In stark contrast to the political model enshrined in Johnson's community action program, this consumer model would give the people— rather than their self-appointed representatives and advocates—a real say in the design of service programs.

As it reviews grant regulations and considers waiver proposals from the states, the federal government should systematically encourage wider use of vouchers and similar measures to put economic decision-making power into the hands of service recipients. Localities, states, and the federal government should also make it easier for alternative service organizations to bid for voucher dollars by reviewing licensing and other regulations that inhibit such providers.

To reduce the strong tendency for "eligibility inflation," so common when criteria for benefit programs are established at the federal level, the detailed eligibility rules and financial arrangements for any voucher program should be the province of the state government. The federal government should establish only broad minimum requirements. To the degree that the federal government provides support for such programs, the level of federal aid formula should be based on the minimum federal requirements. Thus if states wish to expand eligibility, it would be up to them to provide the additional funding.

The wider use of vouchers is more likely to be achieved through campaigns begun at the state level. It is there that the inclination to experiment is greatest and where political victories against established provider groups stand the most chance of success. In addition, mobilizing disparate alternative providers and beneficiaries is easier first at the state level. Initially the best course of action for the federal government would be to recognize such providers more explicitly in regulations attached to grants.

> 3. *To ensure that low income Americans receive basic income support from the states, federal mandates attached to grants should continue in use. The states, however, should be permitted to adjust eligibility criteria more widely within federal guidelines.*

Welfare policies must avoid the rigidity and disincentive to innovate that accompanies uniformity. Yet the American public has made it clear that it expects a certain basic standard of living to be available to all. That is a legitimate expectation of a civilized society. But it also raises a dilemma. Recognizing the political reluctance of many states to provide adequate income support programs, we might be inclined to suppose that the federal government should lay down tight requirements on the states or even contemplate full federal funding. However, if we are to avoid dependency and disincentives for self-improvement, while encouraging economy and policy innovation, we must give states the flexibility and incentive to modify basic programs to make them more effective. Very careful use of mandates may enable us to escape the dilemma.

Federal mandates are now a common feature of America's system of intergovernmental relations. Since 1937, when the Supreme Court issued a number of decisions expanding the definition of the Constitution's commerce clause and the Fourteenth Amendment, the federal government has significantly increased its regulation of the states, as well as businesses and other institutions that previously had been considered solely within the jurisdiction of states. The regulation of the states has taken two general forms: requirements on the states to meet or exceed specified objectives and "voluntary" mandates attached to federal grant programs.

Federal mandates continue to be a source of intense legal and political debate. The extent to which explicit regulation of the states may or may not violate the federalism principles enshrined in the Constitution is a particularly thorny issue. In 1976 the Supreme Court, in *National League of Cities v. Usery*, blocked federal attempts to interfere with functions that threaten "to directly displace the states' freedom to structure integral operations in areas of traditional governmental functions." But that position has been steadily eroding ever since. In 1981, for instance, the Court established a three-pronged test for determining if a federal statute or rule is unconstitutional: It must regulate "states as states"; it must address matters that are clearly "attributes of state sovereignty"; and compliance by the state must "directly impair" the ability of the state to structure "integral operations in areas of traditional governmental functions."[32] An even bigger obstacle confronting opponents of federal mandates appeared in the form of the Supreme Court's 1985 ruling in *Garcia* v. *San Antonio Metropolitan Transportation Authority*, where the Court essentially removed itself as the arbiter in conflicts over the limits of authority within the federal system, leaving the task instead to Congress. Nevertheless, the legal debate is still keen, and if the Supreme Court continues its slow shift toward a more conservative interpretation of the Constitution, the balance of power within the federal system could easily move back in the direction of the states.

"Voluntary" mandates have aroused less judicial concern, since they are attached to "take-it-or-leave-it" grants. But even those rules arouse passion in state houses and among many conservatives disturbed by federal encroachment. Besides constitutional objections, critics at the state level also complain bitterly that to take taxes from citizens within a state and then offer to give the money back with strings attached hardly constitutes voluntary action. Moreover, the states say, the federal government is unduly inclined to issue rules or pass statutes that require state actions— and then simply leave the states to figure out how to pay for them.

Those are very real concerns. If a national standard is to be achieved in all states, there has to be a measure of coercion upon those states that resist meeting it. Yet placing the federal government in a position to force actions and expenditures by lower levels of government, at no cost to itself, is an open invitation to excessive centralization. On the other hand, if the federal government were to take over the entire funding of such programs as AFDC and Medicaid, as many governors have urged, there would be little incentive for the states to seek more efficient ways of providing such support. Moreover, it is hard to see why high-income states should be relieved of the burden of providing a substantial portion of the funding for supporting the poor within their borders.

The least offensive and least dangerous course of action would be for the federal government to mandate states to guarantee a degree of assistance to the poor wherever they reside, based on the consumption standard discussed earlier, while allowing maximum flexibility to states to meet the standard and providing financial assistance to low-income states. Given the difficulties of measuring poverty and "need," discussed earlier, the states should be required to meet broad goals, such as ensuring adequate housing and medical care, rather than specific levels of cash support. The mandate would require the state to achieve these broad goals, to be determined by Congress in consultation with the nation's governors. But the exact eligibility criteria and the management and design of each state's programs to reach that goal would be the subject of federal–state agreement in each case. In that way, states would have the incentive to explore creative ways of reducing dependency and costs.

It is important that the degree of support given to the states be kept low, in order to give states a keen financial incentive to keep total expenditures down through management innovations. With the current 100 percent federal support of food stamps, for instance, states have no incentive to spend time and money seeking ways to reduce fraud and poor targeting, other than the threat of federal sanctions. Ideally, the percentage of support provided by the federal government should be inversely related to the per capita income of the state and linked to the statewide cost of the benefits to be provided. Poorer states would then receive a greater degree of help, as they do currently with such programs as Medicaid.

The idea of resorting to federal mandates, of course, is anathema to many conservatives, even when they might approve of the goal sought. Conservatives see mandates both as an onerous burden on the states and as an open invitation for future liberal administrations to interfere with the democratic decisions of state government. That danger is very real, which suggests that mandates should be treated with caution. But conservatives still should not flinch from using federal mandates to help bring about welfare reform. The fact is that state interests are effectively represented in Congress in a manner that makes it very difficult for the federal government to impose requirements or programs on the states that they vigorously oppose. States have worked closely together to defeat legislation that they see as a significant threat, such as the New Federalism proposal. There is, in other words, a real check on the use of mandates; so it is unlikely that a future Congress would be able to use mandates to enforce totally unreasonable welfare demands on the states.

It is actually more likely that states would accept burdensome mandates proposed by liberals and opposed by conservatives, because they would tend to be attached to new spending programs. That is why it is so important to keep the proportion of federal financial support accompanying any program as low as possible. It is also a good reason to resist the argument, often put forward by states, that if the federal government issues a requirement on state houses, it should also pay the full costs incurred by states when implementing it. While that might at first glance seem a reasonable demand, it should be remembered that governments at all levels impose costs on individuals, corporations, and organizations without compensating them. Given the choice between the federal government's placing spending requirements on powerful institutions, such as states, and spending the money itself to achieve local or regional goals, conservatives should prefer the former, because there is likely to be far more resistance to unnecessary spending than when Uncle Sam hands out the cash.

Trying to persuade states to accept mandates with reduced federal support would be no easy task, of course. States are always willing to discuss reductions in federal rules, and some have even proposed taking over the obligation to finance and provide some federal social welfare programs. But they have strongly resisted the full devolution of such programs as food stamps, Medicaid, or AFDC. To stand a chance of acceptance, the unpleasant-tasting pill would have to be sugar-coated with a very attractive package: a deep tax cut and a system of "Fiscal Equity Grants."

> 4. *To address the problem of states that have inadequate resources to reach acceptable welfare standards, while avoiding too much federal support to richer states, the federal government should substantially reduce most grants-in-aid, using the savings to finance a system of "Fiscal Capacity Grants" and a general tax cut.*

Simply providing limited federal support, while requiring states to reach certain income assistance standards and make available essential services, obviously would leave some poorer states financially strapped. The typical response of Congress to such a situation is to embrace the "fair share-ism" syndrome and legislate grants that are available to communities in all states, in the hope that enough of the grant shotgun blast will reach the poorest states and communities. As we have seen, the net effect has been to tax the rich states most and then to give most federal support to those same rich states. It is time to cut out the middleman. It is also time to look for ways to target federal assistance more effectively on the states that need it.

Proposals have been put forward that might be a step in the right direction. Richard Nathan, for instance, favors a "safety net" not for states but for poor communities. He proposes that part of every cut in a domestic grant program be placed in a "safety-net grant fund." The money would then be distributed to local governments "for general purposes, on a basis that focuses on the most urgent community needs."[33] The money, he says, should be channeled through the states, with the stipulation that the state must distribute the money according to criteria laid down when the fund was established. Nathan suggests that the criteria should be developed by a commission of federal, state, and local officials, together with experts in public finance.

On the face of it, Nathan's proposal is sound. It would shift the balance of grants away from richer communities and states and toward poorer ones. Still, it is very likely that Nathan's commission would soon become the center of a political brawl, as states tried to write the criteria in such a way as to return as much as possible of the money they lost in the general cutback. Moreover, Nathan's proposal would be geared for services within a local jurisdiction rather than for welfare programs operated by the state.

A similar idea has been put forward by the Committee on Federalism and National Purpose. The committee favors what amounts to a safety net for states in the form of a system of fiscal capacity grants:

> To help the least affluent areas provide essential public services at a minimum level of adequacy, the federal government should provide a system of fiscal capacity grants to states. These grants could be used by state governments for any purposes. In essence, they would be general purpose revenue supplements. But they should be provided *only* to the dozen or so states with the least resources and the greatest need for public services.[34]

The committee suggests we should look at what is known as the "tax capacity" of each state. That is the amount of tax that would be raised if a hypothetical standard tax code were applied. The tax capacity would be compared with the assessed level of need in the state. The required grant would then be calculated on the basis of those two figures. If the need in each state was calculated on the basis of the consumption standard discussed earlier, such a grant would target those states facing the greatest difficulties meeting federal mandates.

Given the strong representation of state and local officials on the committee, it is perhaps not surprising that the panel was attracted to a new federal grant or that it favored 90 percent federal funding responsibility for a minimum level of AFDC and Medicaid benefits. But the committee also agreed that many social service and other programs should be devolved to the states, with the states obliged to finance them.

Rather than fund such a grant from new federal taxes, as some governors and many liberals would be inclined to prefer, it should be financed by reductions in the total level of grants-in-aid to the states, which, together with direct aid to localities, now amount to about $100 billion a year. According to the Committee on Federalism, if the revenues of the twelve states with the lowest fiscal capacity were brought up to within 10 percent of the median for all states, only $3 billion would be required. Thus an even more generous fiscal equity grant system could be established while making only a small dent in the existing level of federal–state grants. In turn, if the degree of general federal support to the states were to be cut substantially, the grant reforms could—and should—be combined with a sizable federal tax reduction.

That may sound like a warmed-over version of President Reagan's 1982 New Federalism proposal, which elicited a collective thumbs down from the states and died a painful death before it even reached Congress. But consider the key differences. The New Federalism initiative saw the federal government completely taking over the Medicaid program, and the states in return taking full responsibility for AFDC, food stamps, and a host of other federally supported programs. A $28 billion federal trust fund was to be set up and then phased out over ten years; the states, to the degree they chose, would raise their own taxes to compensate for the diminishing fund.

The proposal was as radical as it was doomed. The states and their taxpayers had little to gain, and state officials saw themselves facing angry voters demanding a continuation of services but rejecting tax increases to pay for them as the trust fund evaporated—in short, a politician's nightmare. Moreover, poorer states saw themselves as particularly hard hit, since they would have been forced to take over a relatively high proportion of welfare programs with a relatively low tax capacity to support them.

The proposed fiscal grant and tax cut combination has rather different politics. It would improve the position of the poorest states by targeting aid to them. Unlike New Federalism, which offered state voters only the prospect of a state tax increase, with no relief of federal taxes, a federal tax cut would be a part of the package, with obvious attractions to voters. Moreover, since a general income tax reduction would mean more to residents of richer states, they would receive more "compensation" for the cuts in federal aid they would face under a fiscal equity grant system. The best way to cut the federal tax would be to increase the personal exemption and those for dependents. That would still cut everybody's taxes, but it would give the greatest benefit to the working poor who are struggling to stay off welfare.

Reforming the federal structure according to these four proposals would be a significant first step on the road to resolving the deep problems of poverty and social distress in America. But reforming federalism will not, of itself, lead to a solution. It simply provides the essential precondition by substantially improving the ability of the political system to *find* solutions and by channeling the nation's resources more effectively to where they are needed. To deal with the underlying causes of our problems, we need to look at ways in which a more potent system of federalism can help us to rebuild the basic social institutions of America, and how it can assist us in reforming our policies in the principal areas of welfare.

4

Rebuilding America's Communities

FIRST IMPRESSIONS CAN BE very misleading. Not long after he emigrated to the United States in the mid 1970s, one of the authors happened to take a train journey upstate from New York City. After passing the fashionable upper East Side the train crossed the East River and entered the South Bronx. The following ten or fifteen minutes made the same impression on the author as on millions of others whose exposure to that neighborhood is limited to a passing train ride or images on a television screen. "How could anyone live in a place like that?" Burned-out buildings everywhere. Piles of bricks and rubble where once there was a city block. The absolute desolation is reminiscent of many European cities after World War II. No wonder many people say that the only way to revive the South Bronx would be to destroy everything there and start all over again.

About a year later, the author returned to the South Bronx. Instead of taking an elevated train ride above the neighborhood, he was driven through it by a young architect with the Pratt Institute of Brooklyn. This time he received quite a different impression. Instead of focusing on the desolation, the architect talked enthusiastically about his work with a number of area community organizations. The Pratt Institute had been helping those groups to remodel buildings that had been abandoned by their owners. The organizations had occupied the buildings to prevent vandalism or arson, and then had negotiated with the city to allow them to turn the buildings into cooperatives. In many cases the buildings were eventually bought by former tenants, who put "sweat equity" into the restoration—long hours of back-breaking work under the direction of a few volunteer craftsmen and Pratt architects.

Those organizations proved to be remarkable oases amid the desolation. Turning the corner of a block of decay and depression revealed a few blocks of feverish activity and determined optimism. In the oasis occupied by the Banana Kelley group, rehabilitation work was very much in evidence. Those on the street seemed to have somewhere to go, and the whole atmosphere of the site suggested a place that had seen some very bad times but was now on the way up. The group's offices conjured up a combination of revivalist meeting room, political headquarters, newsroom, social center, and advice bureau. People swarmed in and out, both orders and advice were being given, a newsletter was being run off on an old but apparently reliable Xerox copier, and a campaign was under way to persuade City Hall to permit the group to begin work on another block. This oasis intended to roll back the desert, not to be engulfed by it. Banana Kelley's motto—indeed, its rallying cry—summed up the tone of the activity: "Don't Move—Improve!"

The rest of the tour with the Pratt Institute architect, and more recent trips to the South Bronx, uncovered similar patterns elsewhere. In some cases the organizations are large, like the Bronx Frontier Development Corporation, which has revived many once-abandoned blocks. It has even created an inner-city horticulture farm amid the piles of bricks and garbage, which supplies fresh produce to Manhattan. But sometimes they are very small, like the eccentric "Professor" Hetty Fox's one-woman Neo-Presearch Foundation, which has occupied and revived just a few houses on Lyman Place, a block near the legendary "Fort Apache" police precinct. Fox used to teach black studies at a college in California. In 1970 she decided to move back to her parents' home on Lyman Place and to do something to improve the block. She organized families to move into abandoned houses on the block and to throw out the drug pushers and prostitutes. She created a cultural center, where she teaches everything from belly dancing—she is an accomplished dancer and drummer—to African history and chess. When the street needs some work she pesters the city until the bureaucrats realize that it is easier to give her what she wants. She operates the entire "organization" on a few thousand dollars in contributions and free meals from her parents.

Recent studies of the South Bronx, which suggest that the area is beginning to turn around, pay enormous tribute to those sometimes strange but highly effective organizations. Unlike the millions spent on "official" projects, which in so many cases seemed to have little if any permanent effect, the community-inspired self-help activities evidently laid the groundwork that first stabilized the area, then became a springboard for recovery.[1]

The author was as surprised as everyone else at the success of those groups when he first visited the Bronx, but his study of American history reminded him that what has been happening in the Bronx is really not that unusual in America. In Europe there has always been a strong tendency for people to turn to "the State," as the embodiment of society itself, whenever something needed to be done. But Americans are far more inclined to turn to various institutions that can best be described as "community," rather than government, whenever challenges or opportunities arise.

Community has been central to the growth of America and to the ability of ordinary people in this country to exploit opportunities and to overcome daunting barriers. Banding together in a group elevates the individual and gives him more confidence to tackle the unknown. Americans have always recognized that when they band together in a group, be it a church, a neighborhood association, or a brotherhood, they can achieve goals that as individuals are beyond their grasp. Few Americans were able to build a barn by themselves, but as a community working together they could build dozens.

For Americans, then, the idea of community is not some ethereal abstraction. It is a fundamental part of everyday life, an extension of the most basic group—the family. It means much more than a physical neighborhood. It is the church congregation that comes together to give comfort and financial assistance when a factory closes and men and women are thrown out of work. It is the group of tenants, like those in the Bronx, who try to improve their neighborhood. Or, if there are no positive institutions to provide brotherhood and support, it can be the street gang. People are drawn to groups that constitute a community. A strong community means strong individuals. But when a community is weak, individuals are also weak and alienated.

Unfortunately for poorer Americans, particularly black Americans, the sense of community that once gave encouragement and support to people in low-income neighborhoods has become seriously weakened in recent years. The reasons are complex and disputed, but there can be little doubt that the erosion of America's poor communities stems in large part from the explicit attempt of the Great Society reformers to fold them into the larger "national" community. The assumption was that the deficiencies and disadvantages of low-income communities and depressed neighborhoods—places like the South Bronx as well as small towns in rural Mississippi—were so overwhelming that only action from the outside could save them. That view, enshrined in 1960s liberalism and espoused by Johnson, produced program after program that tore apart what was left of the social fabric of America's poor neighborhoods, destroying fragile but critically important institutions, lowering horizons, and turning the hapless into the helpless.

The same idea is trotted out time and again today: There is absolutely nothing of value in the institutions of depressed, poor communities, it is said, so why not bus the people somewhere else, where they can absorb other people's values? That assumption was and remains a fundamental mistake, based on the outsiders' impression of a neighborhood. It causes policymakers to overlook what is actually there, if difficult to see, and it ignores the most basic lessons of American history. And it has led to failure after failure.

Unless the institution of community becomes better understood by policymakers and programs are redesigned to encourage the poor to draw upon their strengths rather than focus on their weaknesses, no amount of federal money will win the War on Poverty. We understand well enough that local institutions in middle-class communities are critically important to mobilize the resources of the neighborhood to address its problems. It is about time public policy recognized that those institutions are even more important in poor neighborhoods. The thesis underpinning so much federal action since the Great Society, and some before it, is simply wrong. Almost all poor neighborhoods have positive institutions that can be built upon, if officials are prepared to believe that they just might be there. If they can exist in the Bronx, they can exist anywhere.

Community institutions, in fact, have proved an effective bulwark against many threats, including resentment and racism. During the vast nineteenth-century migration to America, poor immigrants turned to strong ethnic community associations to protect themselves from discrimination and to pool their meager resources so that each might prosper. Chinese workers arriving in San Francisco during the 1870s, for instance, could expect abuse and harassment from white laborers. Several West Coast China-towns were even put to the torch. Everywhere Chinese were excluded from desirable business activities. "For the Chinese in the United States," the historian Ivan Light writes, "obtaining a livelihood was a question of scraping the bottom of the barrel after the whites had helped themselves."[2]

The Chinese did not respond to such discrimination by succumbing to poverty or turning to government for aid. Instead, like earlier immigrants, they turned inward, building strong community institutions so that they did not need to depend on their hostile neighbors. The Chinese formed themselves into associations based on district of origin. Similar organizations were formed among other groups of Asian immigrants. The Japanese *kenjinkai*, for instance,

> . . . played a leading role in overseeing the social and economic welfare of the immigrants. The Kenjinkai published newspapers, offered legal advice to members, sponsored the tanomoshi, and served as employment agencies. Prefectural contacts were critical sources of influence in business and politics. Kenjinkai provided direct welfare assistance to destitute or needy members, buried the indigent, and paid medical bills.[3]

Perhaps most important for the long-run economic success of the Asian immigrants, they also formed rotating credit associations, so that savings in the community could be pooled to provide capital for its budding entrepreneurs. The institutions of the community in that way made up for the lack of support from bank sources available to other businesses.

Needless to say, the Asian communities draw some of their strength from philosophical and historical factors that are unique to them and obviously cannot be reproduced in other neighborhoods. Nevertheless, there seem to be characteristics that in varying degrees are common to virtually all strong, self-supporting communities, from the earliest New England settlements to the transient wagon train communities, to the family and regional associations of San Francisco's Chinatown. By recognizing those characteristics, we can learn what to look for in "hopeless" neighborhoods like the South Bronx. Once we can appreciate those sometimes dormant strengths in neighborhoods that the War on Poverty wrote off as "disadvantaged" and "deficient," we can begin to design policies to build on those foundations.

Three characteristics are particularly important. One is the notion of a two-way obligation, with a code of behavior and morality that ties everyone together for the common good—and hence the individual good. The institutions of the community are there to help the individual in time of need, but the individual is also bound by obligations to the common good. On the great trek across the plains, members of those transient and temporary communities actually signed community contracts specifying their obligations. In the immigrant Asian communities, the absolute need to uphold the honor of the group strengthened internal solidarity. The social and moral pressure was critically important in enabling the institutions of the associations, such as the credit system, to flourish:

> The ability of Chinese and Japanese revolving credit associations routinely to provide credit without requiring collateral depended, in the last analysis, on the strong, informal, and moralistic social relations of lenders and borrowers. These purely social relations served as an alternative form of security against the pure risks of lending. The rotating credit associations also required members to have confidence in the honesty of any individual member's close circle who stood moral surety for him. . . . Building and maintaining social trust required more or less continuous attention to the punctilio of decorum, honor, and especially of family reputation.[4]

The second key point to understand about stable communities is that they contain a network of power and interdependency that is usually neither official nor obvious to the casual observer. Leaders of effective community organizations in the Bronx are not designated by the mayor, nor did they get their credentials from Harvard. They are there because success counts and because they have the confidence of the community itself. If they did not have local support they would be able to do nothing. Similarly, the essential fabric that holds these and other communities together has nothing to do with buildings, but much to do with networks of what one urban writer has called the "public characters" in a neighborhood.[5] When one thinks for a moment about poor neighborhoods that are nonetheless stable, it is obvious just how important those networks are, from the minister who preaches hard work and honesty from the pulpit, to the barber whose shop acts as both a social center and a watchtower for the street, to the busybody who notices that old Mrs. Jones did not take her usual walk this morning and sets out to investigate. Nobody has an official title. Nobody is a "community official." But each plays a key role in the organic community. And we should note that such networks are rarely possible without diversity in the economic and architectural fabric of the neighborhood, allowing a range of public characters to exist. Without the barbershop nestling amid the apartment houses, or the street life that comes with many different activities, the bonds of community are weak.

The third key characteristic is that it is local people who make the important decisions, not some faraway politician or bureaucrat. When the wagon trains trundled over the plains and forded the rivers of the West, nobody was there to make sure they acted in some way that was prescribed in Washington. Thanks to their remoteness, they were masters of their own destiny. So they had the freedom to experiment and to learn. Had they been forced to abide by some handbook assembled back east, few would have survived. Similarly, no distant expert told Hetty Fox or the other community leaders in the Bronx how they should go about saving a block. They were on their own. Thanks to that benign neglect, they were able to try things that no official would permit. Just as on the American frontier, local control is essential if poor communities are not to become decaying communities.

Even a cursory glance at American history shows that strong communities have been the bedrock of American society, particularly for the urban poor. Observers and historians from Tocqueville to Oscar Handlin have emphasized the critical importance of community to the early settlers, the pioneers moving west, and the millions of immigrants arriving in a strange land. Communities have provided a ladder by which the strengths of the group could be pooled to support individuals' efforts to improve their situation. They have also provided a social safety net by which the group discharged its moral obligation to aid the needy. Needless to say, there were often large holes in the safety net and rungs missing from the ladder, but the history of American communities is a remarkable story of social advancement.

So what has gone wrong? Why do we so often think of poor neighborhoods today as little more than wastelands?

How the Great Society Weakened Poor Communities

Nobody would ever argue that America's poor communities were somehow in great shape until Lyndon Johnson came on the scene, and then things fell apart. That would be absurd. In the cities especially, a number of changes since the turn of the century had begun to put enormous strains on neighborhoods, eroding the critically important street-level relationships. There was considerable migration, which disrupted some neighborhoods, of course, but that was nothing new. Far more important were political changes in American cities, which encouraged centralization at the expense of subtle local networks. The urban analyst Robert Yin argues that there were three principal factors: the establishment of political order in the great cities, which meant that power shifted from neighborhoods to city halls; the professionalization of urban service providers, such as police and teachers, which meant that local *ad hoc* initiative was increasingly replaced by central management; and technological innovation in transportation, communications, and other services, which encouraged centralization. Those political changes certainly helped city leaders to ensure that garbage was picked up and the trains ran on time. In that sense the growing strength of city halls meant stronger cities. But there was another side to the coin. Centralization loosened the bonds that hold neighborhoods together. By the 1960s, Yin writes,

> . . . urban bureaucracies were overly centralized, inflexible, and removed from the neighborhoods. . . . Over and above the debilitating effects of centralization on the server–served relationship, the population turnover in most cities by the 1960s threatened destruction of the street-level bargaining, mutual trust, and social symmetry that characterized the immigrant city. Policemen, teachers, firemen, and other public employees tended to be white and working class, and not to be residents of the port-of-entry neighborhoods where the new immigrants arrived.[6]

But the poverty warriors assumed that if poor neighborhoods were crumbling, it had to be because of the deficiencies of the neighborhoods themselves and, more important, of the residents of those neighborhoods. Despite the fact that many of the immigrants who built the country were poor and illiterate, it was assumed in the 1960s both that poverty and illiteracy led directly to bad neighborhoods and that bad neighborhoods produced poor and illiterate people. The Johnson White House perceived the process as a vicious circle, which could be broken only by integrating those neighborhoods into the wider "national" community. So, rather than look for hidden strengths within poor neighborhoods and create a climate in which people could draw on those strengths, Great Society strategists attempted to use federal programs to build new institutions and thereby to reconstruct local communities.

That turned out to be a fundamental mistake. In several very specific ways, the tactics of the War on Poverty, enshrined in programs that continue today, accelerated the erosion of the building blocks of community, making victory against poverty all the more difficult.

One reason why well-meaning intervention has often hastened decline is simply that national programs force local bureaucracies to pay closer attention to federal thinking and regulations, and even less to their own neighborhoods. Of course the War on Poverty did establish "community" agencies, under the Community Action Program, in an effort to invigorate local organizations. According to Johnson's view of a unified national community, they were intended to speed social change, so that the fruits of America's political and economic progress would be shared more equitably. But created and supported by Washington, they were creatures of Washington. Local residents certainly were to be included in local policymaking bodies, chosen "wherever feasible" according to democratic procedures. But power groups often unrepresentative of the communities, or even unconnected to them, quickly dominated the bodies. Although blacks were supposed to be the main beneficiaries of the pressures to mobilize poor communities, Daniel Patrick Moynihan noted, "the various planning groups were made up exclusively of middle-class whites."[7]

It is hardly surprising that the Great Society view of community did not sit well with either radical supporters of genuine community empowerment or those committed to more traditional views of neighborhood. Nor did the notion of a "national community" do anything to forestall the urban riots that were to come. Many New Left leaders denounced the Johnson view of community enshrined in federal action as an attempt by distant bureaucracies and megastructures to manipulate the poor. Others resented the inherent paternalism of the whole approach. Black power leaders like Stokely Carmichael and William Hamilton attacked Johnson for advancing a program based "on the assumption that there is nothing of value in the black community and that little of value could be created among black people." Many white ethnic spokesmen and leaders were equally unimpressed. Michael Novak urged a retreat from centralism to strategies based on "the organic networks of communal life: family, ethnic group, and voluntary association in primary groups." George Wallace, in more pungent and sinister terms, joined in the denunciation.[8]

The second way in which the legacy of the Great Society has debilitated communities, ironically, is by providing them with free, professional, "expert" assistance. Indeed, the federal government has saturated them with outside experts. John McKnight, who worked in several urban neighborhoods during the 1960s and is now Associate Director of the Center for Urban Affairs in Chicago, recalls that in one neighborhood, professional service providers representing no less than forty-two different specializations descended on the population, including daily living skills advisers, urban curriculum developers, environmental reform workers, and home budget management trainers. Each conducted "needs surveys" to pinpoint the supposed deficiencies of the area.[9]

Whatever struggling community-based institutions might exist in such neighborhoods are often suffocated by such infestations of experts. The poor have been urged to come for help and to explain their shortcomings and disadvantages to the service provider. The more problems they or their professional helpers can discover, the more assistance they can obtain. Seeing the glass as half-empty is rewarded. Seeing it as half-full is not. With such an emphasis on deficiencies in the client, is it any wonder that increased dependency followed in the wake of the Great Society and that community institutions preaching mutual aid and self-help were discarded?

The professionalization and federalization of community services has also led to the co-opting or freezing-out of traditional but competing institutions. In some cases the professionals no doubt are motivated simply by a desire to keep amateurish "quacks" out of the way. But there is another reason. Professional service providers are very similar in their instincts to other professionals: They do not like competition. In particular, they do not like competition from lower-priced alternatives to themselves who turn out to be just as effective, if not more so.

By pressing for the registration or certification of individuals wishing to provide services to their neighbors, human service professionals have forced countless organizations and individuals either to cease their activities or to continue on terms established by the professional lobby itself. "Through organizations and lobbies," the sociologists Peter Berger and Richard Neuhaus explain, "professionals increasingly persuade the state to legislate standards and certifications that hit voluntary associations hard, especially those given to employing volunteers."[10] Mothers who have raised several children are deemed unfit to care for their neighbors' children while the parents are at work, because they lack diplomas in early child care. So either the community loses control of its children or single parents stay at home on welfare. Neighborhood groups lacking training in legal issues cannot be expected to resolve landlord–tenant disputes, the argument goes, so those questions must be taken over by eager legal services lawyers intent on changing "the system." The earmarking of federal money only for duly constituted and certified groups means that increasingly it is the federal government that calls the tune for community organizations.

By 1980, nearly 60 percent of the income of America's social service groups came directly or indirectly from the federal government. The influence of Washington is now so great that it is little wonder that the Urban Institute scholar Lester Salamon describes such groups as "third party government."[11] Thanks to such co-opting of local inititiative, the ability of poor communities to tackle their own problems has been seriously reduced.

Third, communities have also been eroded in a very direct way by the physical development and housing policies of the federal government. Despite talk of rebuilding communities, Great Society programs and later initiatives have generally perpetuated the myth that neighborhoods are mere collections of people and buildings and that by erecting "better" buildings and rearranging the people, the neighborhood can be improved. While urban renewal—often accurately described as "Negro removal" by its foes—shifted more toward revitalization rather than demolition later in the 1960s, the federal bulldozers remained active. The intangible bonds that hold communities together were shattered as planners mistook diversity and shabbiness for chaos and decay. Old communities, hanging on thanks to common bonds and informal institutions that architects and engineers could not see, were torn apart by new highways to speed suburbanites to the central cities. Poor people were carefully classified and segregated according to income and deficiencies. Then they were placed in nice new buildings, free of those street-corner barbershops and other meeting places that allow people to keep an eye on the block, indeed free of all the economic and social "clutter" that actually gives life to a neighborhood. Without those essential ingredients, buildings promptly deteriorated, eventually limping along as symbols of desolation and hopelessness.

In some instances, those projects have turned into social catastrophes. One of them, in St. Louis, has entered the folklore of spectacular public housing disasters. Completed in 1957 and widely praised for its design, the Pruitt-Igoe development housed 10,000 low-income people from the rural South in forty-three high-rise buildings. The great majority of tenants were pleased with their units, but no opportunity was provided for them to express their views on how the project should be run, nor was there any attempt by the city to work with residents to help them develop a genuine community. That turned out to be a serious mistake. Nobody knew anyone else, and life in the urban high-rise was nothing like life in the rural South. So the social fabric of the project began to crumble. Soon after that the physical fabric also began to deteriorate. Within a very few years the project had become an urban jungle of vandalism and violence. By 1969 some 40 percent of maintenance time and 30 percent of materials were devoted to repairing the results of vandalism: That year the project consumed 16,000 window shades and 20,000 panes of glass.[12] By

1974 Pruitt-Igoe was completely abandoned, and the city demolished it in 1976.

Even attempts by the Johnson Administration to tailor development to the goal of community revitalization through the neighborhood development program and Model Cities bore little fruit, primarily because of delays and micromanagement from Washington. More recent strategies, such as Jimmy Carter's Urban Development Action Grant (UDAG) program, avoided much of that problem by streamlining and simplifying procedures. UDAG is meant to supply just enough federal support to enable marginally economic development projects to go ahead. But streamlining red tape in Washington has not solved the remoteness problem. It just means that mayors and developers have found it easier to extract money to subsidize projects that are far from marginal. Increasingly, the UDAG program has become more of a subsidy for commercial developers than a vehicle for revitalizing poor communities.

The fourth reason why some programs designed to revive neighborhoods have actually hastened their deterioration stems from confusion about the proper role of business in low-income communities. Inner-city working-class districts in America's cities once buzzed with basement workshops and street-corner retailers. Inexpensive old buildings and backyard garages enabled entrepreneurs to start firms near major markets with minimal capital and overhead costs. Such small enterprises are important to the social life and economic health of any neighborhood. They bring people into the street and provide a band of local leaders who are invariably the first to take action when something needs to be done. But if they are important in middle-class communities, they are critical to the life of inner-city communities. They add to the "public characters" of the neighborhood and provide an economic and employment base. Indeed, small, volatile firms of fewer than twenty employees are responsible for about two-thirds of all net new jobs.[13] Yet until very recently, economic development policies not only failed to recognize the importance of small enterprises to stable communities but actively discouraged the street-corner vendor and garage repair shop.

The assumption among most development officials was that such small enterprises surely could have little impact on the economy of a neighborhood; in any case, they were probably breaking virtually every zoning and tax rule in the book. So zoning and building codes were designed to rid residential neighborhoods of small business activity, while cities tried to lure large firms with generous tax concessions and other expensive inducements—often meaning higher taxes for struggling, indigenous entrepreneurs. In some cases cities were even prepared to sacrifice existing stable neighborhoods to accommodate a large firm. For instance, the city of Detroit literally destroyed the strong ethnic neighborhood of Poletown to make way for a Cadillac plant, spreading the inhabitants throughout the rest of the city and turning many once-stable families into welfare problems.

Those development strategies have rarely saved neighborhoods. More often than not they have wrecked them, creating few jobs for local people while undermining the social and economic base of the community. By segregating residential and business use of buildings, for instance, cities have made it harder for many single mothers to stay off welfare by working at home. By making it costly and sometimes even illegal for a young man to try his hand at legitimate enterprise in his community, wrong-headed development policies have driven countless entrepreneurs into crime. After all, why should someone waste long hours dealing with petty bureaucrats down at City Hall just so that he can make a little money running an honest business, when he can make real money pushing drugs?

In varying degrees, virtually all poor communities have been affected by the unpleasant side effects of policies intended to help them. But in the case of America's poor black communities, the consequences have been disastrous. When most other groups came to America, they brought with them traditions and customs that helped them to build tight communities to withstand hardship and discrimination. In the case of black Americans, however, slave-owners recognized that by ruthlessly crushing self-sufficiency and requiring slaves to be totally dependent on their owners for all the staples of life, the plantation could do without high walls or barred windows and still be a prison.[14] The whole culture of community and independence was weakened by the slavery experience. So when freedom came, most black community institutions—with the important exception of churches—were far more fragile than those of most other groups. They have remained relatively fragile. So when government programs weaken community institutions, the effect on blacks is devastating.

One might have thought that black leaders would therefore be particularly critical of these aspects of federal programs. Black power leaders, as well as some other radical black leaders, certainly have been. But the same is not true of most of the official leadership. In fact, several black conservative writers charge that today's black leadership unwittingly perpetuates dependency and the weakness of black community institutions. Those new black leaders speak for one side of a division that stretches deep into black history and culture. It is a division that symbolizes two views of black progress: those who see progress through self-help, where blacks react to discrimination and poverty as other minorities have done—by building on their own institutions and strengths—and those who believe that the only way forward is to use political pressure and an appeal to basic rights to enable blacks to gain admittance to the political and social establishment monopolized by whites. The logic of the second approach, Harvard's Glenn Loury argues, "seemed to be that unless whites are willing to mix with blacks, black children will suffer self-image problems. Thus black development and self-respect was made out to be inherently impossible without the cooperation of whites. . . . Once the civil rights struggle moved from ending de facto segregation to forced racial mixing, blacks often seemed to be rejecting the very possibility of beneficial association with themselves."[15]

Unfortunately, the grand coalition of the Southern President and the civil rights movement, which declared a successful war against legalized segregation, also adopted the view that only by turning their backs on their own communities and joining the white community could blacks ever achieve social and economic salvation. In keeping with that view, and in tune with the professional service outsiders who cater to the black population, the official leadership of the black community seems determined to portray the glass as half-empty. Instead of encouraging blacks to pool their considerable resources of capital, as the Chinese did, the leadership tells blacks that they are incapable of starting a business without special government set-asides or free government capital. Instead of teaching teenage girls the word "no," the leadership puts up with self-destructive behavior and calls for more government support for unmarried teenage mothers. Given the view of

116

black Americans evidently held by their leaders, it is hardly surprising that trends that weaken the fabric of community in other groups have almost destroyed it among blacks.

So by stressing the disadvantages and deficiencies of poor American neighborhoods and weakening community institutions, the programs launched under the Great Society have encouraged the poor to look outward for help to compensate for their own shortcomings, rather than inward to themselves and their community for assistance to build on their strengths. And let us face it! If any of us were told over and over again that we possessed nothing but deficiencies, and that the more of those deficiencies we listed the more help we would receive, how many of us would continue to think we could ever make it on our own? So why should the poor react any differently?

Why There Is Cause for Hope

Can we revive the idea of community in poor neighborhoods, so that poor people can begin to mobilize their own resources more effectively? Fortunately, the answer seems to be yes. Like blades of grass growing up through the asphalt, community institutions have a habit of springing up in the most unlikely places. But government cannot create the spirit of community. Whenever it tries to do so, the result is invariably artificial, and usually disappointing. What it can do is try to create the conditions in which community institutions can flourish, and it can be prepared to rely on them to provide basic services in a poor neighborhood. How can it do that? The Reagan Administration has tried two ways: a direct approach, which has not been very successful, and an indirect approach that has produced some results.

Ever since he first came to the White House, Ronald Reagan has emphasized the importance of community and its institutions in tackling social problems in America. But while Reagan evidently has a broad view of the importance and role of community, he seems to have no clear idea of how to get there from here. Shortly after entering office in 1981, he tried the direct approach: Get the private sector to take on responsibilities previously reserved for government, and foster "public–private partnerships" in which the public and private sectors work together for the common good. It all sounded fine—the kind of idea that brings applause at the annual country club dinner. So the Administration set up a blue-ribbon Task Force on Private Sector Initiatives with the objective of stimulating voluntarism and a sense of community.

Yet it should have been obvious to anyone sitting in on the panel's inaugural meeting that it was not going to win any wars against poverty. The task force consisted almost entirely of corporate executives and officials of large private foundations. In many ways it was even farther removed from the nuts and bolts of community than were the planning groups of Johnson's Community Action Program. After agreeing that voluntarism was a Good Thing, the task force essentially confined itself to giving awards to groups that others might emulate. Its sole contribution to the goal of strengthening communities was to press for a move away from the notion that only public ventures can secure social goals and that objectives could often best be reached by some mixture of public and private efforts.

That turned out to be no great leap forward. Moreover, the business industrialists clearly had not prepared themselves for the inevitable counteroffensive from the welfare industrialists. It was not long before the task force allowed itself to be trapped into the position that "public–private" simply meant corporations paying for public programs. The task force even endorsed the idea that corporations should impose a kind of tax on themselves, equal to 2 percent of their profits, to help fund programs recommended by lobbyists for the human services professionals.

Ironically, the greatest stimulus given to the formation of genuine community institutions had nothing to do with the task force. It was administered by David Stockman. Far from being an offer to help, it took the form of a refusal to help. While the extent of federal cutbacks has been exaggerated, primarily as a ploy to force reinstatement of funding, budget reductions enacted early in the Administration's first term did have two important consequences. First, the federal pullback weakened the welfare industry that had grown up around the Great Society programs by putting it on a financial diet. Needless to say, the industry screamed loudly, but municipalities, faced with a contraction of federally financed services, had to start looking for alternatives, like it or not. Second, and more important, the federal government sent a clear message to poor neighborhoods themselves. They could no longer simply count on Uncle Sam. In essence, the budget cuts provoked a crisis, and if there is one thing that gets the adrenalin flowing, it is a crisis. Standing on the edge of a cliff with a bull rushing toward you is great for clearing the mind! Studies of entrepreneurship indicate the same thing: It is a crisis that tends to motivate the entrepreneur. Losing his job or a lapse into frustration and boredom—that is the kind of thing that causes him to try something new.[16] The same seems to be true of social entrepreneurship. When you can be sure that help will always come from Washington, why try anything new? Only when that help disappears, and there is a crisis, do the creative juices start to flow.

The same has been true in the neighborhoods. There is no doubt that in many instances the withdrawal of federal support caused great concern to many poor neighborhoods, particularly during the recent recession. But it has also stimulated creativity and entrepreneurship. The vision of a rapidly retreating federal presence encouraged neighborhood leaders to concentrate on innovative local solutions to their problems and to look once again at the strengths of their communities, rather than parade their deficiencies before federal officials. It was not long before some began to admit there was a positive side to the Stockman ax. While many black church leaders, for instance, bitterly criticized the Administration for abrogating what they saw as the government's proper responsibilities, *Black Enterprise* magazine noted in 1981: that "In fact, some people regard Ronald Reagan's policy of forcing the poor 'to make bricks without straw' as a blessing in disguise. 'It may enable us,' says Reverend [William] Payne [of Baltimore Baptist Church], 'to rely on our own strength, which lies latent, like a sleeping giant.' "[17]

So the Reagan Administration has not *created* community institutions, as the Johnson Administration tried to do. It has not planted the seeds—many were in the neighborhoods already. It has not even applied fertilizer, in the sense that money is a fertilizer. It would be more accurate to say that it has applied a selective weedkiller. By taking financial sustenance away from professional organizations that have overshadowed the true community organizations, it has given them room to grow.

Many types of organization in recent years have significantly expanded their social and economic role in poor communities, at least in part because of the vacuum created by the strong message sent out from Washington by the Reagan Administration. The black church, in particular, has become a central force in a welfare and social system based more on a traditional concept of community than on the fragile liberal notion of national community. It was the strongest institution to emerge from slavery, and in the post–Civil War period black churches organized a vast array of mutual aid social services, even including insurance. Since the 1960s the black churches have played less of a social role, as government-sponsored organizations took over many of their secular functions. But today the black churches are once again uplifting the bodies as well as the spirits of the poor.

Many black churches have become heavily involved in the provision of low-income housing. In Washington, D.C., for instance, the United House of Prayer has built more low-income housing than the city and federal governments combined, and congregation members of the Church of the Savior, including the innovative developer James Rouse, formed the Enterprise Foundation to provide low-income housing. Rouse was the pioneering developer of several recent central city renovations, including Baltimore's Inner Harbor, which have used new construction and rehabilitation as a means to draw inner-city neighborhoods into the life of the central city.

Rouse has used the same approach in Washington. The foundation's first full-scale venture, the Jubilee Housing Project, led to the renovation of more than two hundred apartments. Significantly, Jubilee comprises far more than real estate. Each of the six Jubilee buildings has a tenant committee, which both administers the property and acts as a focus for the Jubilee community. Moreover, Jubilee and the church have become the focus for a number of organizations, including a health clinic, a preschool, an emergency food and medical care group, a business start-up program, a learning center for emotionally handicapped children, and a foster care service. The twin pillars of the church and the housing project have thus become the nucleus of a closeknit community. "Jim Rouse taught us that we have to look at problems in a holistic way," says Jerry Flood, who started the venture with Rouse. "You can't succeed by attacking just one problem like housing or maybe jobs. What you have to do is look at a whole neighborhood and then figure out what efforts and programs will make that neighborhood work."[18]

Housing has been the focus of many successful community-based initiatives. When residents have a feeling that they are in control of their living environment, they often use that as a base from which to launch other community ventures. That has been particularly true in another recent success story: resident management of public housing. Still limited to a dozen or so projects, resident management has often produced dramatic results. While those successes may seem particularly surprising, since tenant management has usually been tried only as a last-ditch attempt to save a project racked with problems, they are really just another demonstration of the crisis-enterprise phenomenon.

The first project transferred to tenants, in the mid-1970s, was Boston's Bromley-Heath complex. Since it has been under tenant control, its residents demand that visitors refer to the complex as a "development" and not a project—a mark of their pride. It was once plagued with crime, but a community security force has cut robberies by almost 80 percent. Bromley-Heath residents now operate their own community center, three day care centers, various social services, and a small radio station.

Not long after the transfer in Boston, St. Louis turned over five projects to resident managers, including Cochran Gardens, a high-rise project within sight of the doomed Pruitt-Igoe complex. The moving force behind the handover was a tenant named Bertha Gilkey. Never at a loss for words, Gilkey is one of those people who just know instinctively how to get things done. The crisis she and the other residents faced was that the building had become what she describes as a "jungle," with several floors abandoned for years, rats everywhere, and drug pushers using empty apartments as business offices. Nothing the city tried seemed to have any effect, so Bertha Gilkey persuaded the city to let her and her fellow tenants try their hand. Once they had control of their project, the tenants had both the power and the incentive to fight back, to the point where Cochran Gardens has become a showcase for successful tenant management. By 1985, the Cochran management association had created 350 jobs, primarily for residents, by establishing its own maintenance teams, day care centers, a catering company, a neighborhood shopping mall, and a company to install cable television connections in public housing throughout the city.

121

Not that the task was easy. The residents discovered early in the game that there were plenty of people who wanted to keep things the way they had been, and many others in City Hall who preferred peace and quiet to confrontation. So the new managers had to battle foot-dragging bureaucrats as well as attorneys representing the pushers and other troublemakers they were determined to evict. Obtaining the right to evict was not easy, but the tenant managers insisted on it. Gilkey maintains that in such troubled neighborhoods, the power to control residency is essential, no matter how objectionable that may be to civil libertarians. Unless residents subscribe to common aims and standards, she says, the community will fall apart—and some tenant-managed projects have failed simply because the power to throw out residents who refused to accept the rules laid down by the majority of tenants was denied.

The same determination and success have been evident at the 464-unit Kenilworth Courts project in Washington, D.C., another public housing complex managed by tenants. Again, it was a crisis that led to the handover. The tenants had grown used to the graffiti, the drugs, the prostitution, and the managers who were well paid for doing nothing. But after two years without hot water, they had had enough. They went to City Hall and demanded the right to run the project themselves. In 1982, after training a resident group in management techniques, the city handed over the rapidly deteriorating project to the residents. The management board: three college students, two mothers on welfare, two working mothers, and one housewife with a working husband.

The results, dramatic by any measure, are carefully documented in a detailed study by the international accounting firm of Coopers & Lybrand.[19] By 1985, rental income had risen 77 percent, thanks to improved collection and a cut in the vacancy rate from 18 percent, the average for the city, to less than 6 percent. By 1984, the project was running a surplus; when board members presented the housing authority that year with a check, instead of requesting a subsidy, housing officials had no idea how to process it.

The success of Kenilworth Courts goes far beyond the efficient management of a housing project. Like so many service organizations created by the residents of poor neighborhoods, the management group had a decisive effect on the economic and social condition of the project. Before the tenants became their own managers, some 90 percent of the families were headed by single women and 70 percent of the population was on welfare. The management team decided to tackle chronic dependency by recruiting residents for maintenance and other jobs in the project and by establishing several on-site businesses staffed by Kenilworth residents, including a co-op food store, a clothing shop, a beauty parlor, a catering service, a trash collection firm, a roofing company, and an insurance franchise. Thanks to the employment opportunities the ventures provide, welfare dependency has more than halved and fathers and husbands are returning to their families. Factoring in the reduced welfare costs, improved tax base, higher rental income, and other results of tenant management, as well as increased renovation costs, Coopers & Lybrand calculates the net benefits to the city between 1982 and 1985 at $780,000. After ten years of tenant management, the accountants say, the net benefits will top $4.5 million.

Just as in Cochran Gardens, the Kenilworth tenant management board runs a very tight ship. Every weekday morning, board chairman Gladys Roy, a mother of nine, looks for uncut lawns. An unkempt yard means a fine for the tenant. Young boys hanging around at street corners are given a stern lecture, and suspicious outsiders are told to leave the project. Tenants in financial difficulties are counseled and helped. Persistent troublemakers in the project either learn to play by the rules or they are evicted.

The power of the board has little to do with official titles. It has a lot to do with the respect that board members can command. A walk through Kenilworth with Kimi Gray, who led the tenant campaign for self-management, demonstrates that very clearly. Like Bertha Gilkey, Kimi Gray knows how to get action. Her large physique and booming voice mean she does not have to tell people a second time to do something. Turning a corner, she sees a young boy lounging against a fence. "Jimmie Green! Why aren't you at home this late?" Jimmie wastes no time moving in the direction of home. "Sorry Miss Kimi, I was just on my way." A short time later she spots a car with out-of-state tags driven by a white woman. It cruises up and down, but nobody goes near it. "Looking for drugs," explains Gray. "She won't find anyone to sell her any here. If one of our young men did so, it would be reported to me by one of our block captains, who watch for such things. And then I would skin that young man—personally."

That kind of toughness works. But it gets results only when it comes from someone who also has a stake in the outcome. It can also work in some very unusual circumstances. In 1969, for instance, David and Falaka Fattah opened their West Philadelphia home to fifteen members of a teenage gang who had become sickened by street violence and the deaths of dozens of gang members every year. With donations of food and money from local churches and well-wishers, they offered the boys a simple but firm agreement—if the gang members would henceforth do nothing illegal, the Fattahs would help them stay out of jail. Since then the House of Umoja, as the Fattahs called their new extended family, has "adopted" more than five hundred former gang members. It was credited with cutting gang-related deaths from forty-three in 1973 to just one in 1977, thanks to the success of the Fattahs in persuading gang leaders to agree to a truce. Members of the House have no easy ride. If they wish to stay, they are required to be out of bed by 6 A.M. for a conference to set goals for the day and to start their assigned chores. They must also attend a weekly session to review their behavior. But in return, they can depend on the strong positive support of a tight family.[20] The deal requires confidence and obligations on both sides. And it works.

Those and many similar success stories are not the products of government. They were not started by private philanthropists. Each involved a group of poor people who had just had enough—usually it was enough of someone else's incompetence or lack of concern. Something finally snapped. Like the hero of the movie *Network*, tired of being given the runaround by bureaucracy after bureaucracy, they too threw open their windows and yelled out, "I'm mad as hell, and I'm not going to take it any more!" Each is faced with a crisis, and that leads to enraged enterprise.

From the perspective of reforming the welfare system, the important thing about all those initiatives is that they do have common characteristics. The same ideas and approaches appear again and again. By appreciating those features, it becomes possible to see how we could begin to change the climate of public policy so that instead of frustrating such community enterprises, as many of the War on Poverty programs ended up doing, or just allowing them to appear by default, as the Reagan Administration has done, we can actually encourage such institutions to develop.

The first very obvious feature of the successful community ventures is that they demand obligations on the part of those being assisted, and they encourage individuals to look to their own strengths to fulfill those obligations. Invariably the organization has a firm code of conduct, even a sense of elitism, that members are expected to live up to if they wish to remain part of the group. And the benefits of the group are provided as a "package," corresponding to clearly defined obligations. Unlike the current welfare system, members do not act as individuals in a supermarket, picking and choosing benefits as a right from an inanimate shelf.

That is why the tenant management groups insist on the right to evict. "Unless every resident has to play by the rules of the group," Bertha Gilkey says, "it is not long before nobody does." At the House of Umoja, the rules are tough, and they are rigidly enforced by the ex-gang members themselves. No bad language is tolerated, and the loyalty demanded of the residents is just as binding as that in the inner-city gangs from which they came. These are not easygoing social clubs.

The second characteristic is that the successful community organizations are primarily social and economic in nature, not political. In contrast with the Community Action Program view of empowerment, where the goal was to create institutions through which the poor could get their fair share of government programs, these organizations are more interested in being allowed to control their own environment. Effective control gives organizations the freedom to be entrepreneurial and to mobilize community resources without first having to persuade some outsider. By contrast, the War on Poverty's political model encouraged groups to focus on outside resources by identifying problems requiring government aid or grants from large private foundations. The tenant management organizations, for instance, are quintessentially economic rather than political bodies. Because they are responsible for the finances of their projects, they are inclined to examine ways of keeping costs down and raising income, leading them to enforce good behavior and to look at ways of employing residents. They behave very differently from "activist" tenant groups, which confine their activities to urging landlords or housing associations to take action.

The third common feature is that they take what might best be called a "frontier" approach to problem solving. Just as on the frontier in the great movement west, the leaders of successful community organizations use unusual methods to deal with unusual situations. Generally they ignore orthodox or accepted professional ways of dealing with issues, relying instead on streetwise tactics. The Fattahs had no formal training in psychology or criminology, so they were not disinclined to try a quite unusual—but very shrewd—approach to dealing with gang warfare. Kimi Gray did not solve the problem of graffiti in the laundry room at Kenilworth Courts by hiring a guard or psychoanalyzing the culprits. She gave the mothers of the suspected vandals the responsibility of keeping the room in perfect shape and told them they would be fined if it became shabby: The graffiti problem stopped immediately. Those community leaders are brilliant entrepreneurs. It is hard not to believe that if they had been born in different circumstances they would be very successful, and probably very rich! It is difficult for most of us to understand why the Kimi Grays and Sister Fattahs choose to remain in poor neighborhoods, when their obvious personal skills would allow them to move quickly up the economic ladder. The reason, it seems, is that they feel a part of the community as much as everyone else: They will rise as everyone else rises.

But just as on the frontier, community organizations can ignore the rules only as long as they are beyond the reach of officialdom. When groups seek government assistance, or even if they are merely discovered, they can come face to face with the dead hand of a bureaucracy, which insists on everything being done according to the book. And not far behind the bureaucrat is the service professional, insisting that "standards must be kept up"—by employing their services, of course.

The Kenilworth managers, for instance, have had to overcome years of foot dragging and outright hostility from District of Columbia officials. The management board has been forced to obtain extra insurance, has suffered crippling delays in recovering rent money from the housing authority to cover essential bills, and has faced enormous union opposition to hiring its own residents.

The House of Umoja discovered that it had to take on a professional social worker in order to comply with the licensing requirements for a group home. Its highly successful security firm, which
kept the streets of the neighborhood so safe that a local mall
reopened for business, had to cease operations under pressure
from private security companies, which pointed out that city ordinances indicated that reformed teenage gang members were too
young to be "guards." The mall subsequently closed.

How to Strengthen America's Communities

Creating a climate to strengthen community institutions in
poor neighborhoods is in no way the complete answer to poverty
and social problems in America, but it is the necessary condition if
other approaches are to work. Fostering strong community organizations encourages the poor to look for strengths in their neighborhoods and themselves. By itself, that can provide the solution to
many social problems, as strong and effective community institutions can replace government approaches that currently do not
work. But by emphasizing the positive, an atmosphere conducive
to self-help community institutions also encourages the poor to
look for ladders out of poverty rather than languish in the safety
net.

How do we revitalize community institutions from the outside,
given the fact that government programs have invariably weakened local institutions? How is it possible to "create" institutions
that must be uniquely local if they are to be effective? The experience we now have of the War on Poverty programs in action,
together with the patterns of successful organizations that have
emerged, suggests a number of strategies.

1. Significantly reduce the scope of federal action.

First and foremost, it must be made crystal clear that the days
when federal officials persuade people they are lame and then give
them a free crutch are over. While government programs at
various points in the federal system are necessary for basic support
and sustenance, creative community responses to social problems
need community leaders who recognize that there is no alternative
to building on the capacities of their neighborhoods. In that re-

spect, the Reagan budget cuts—even though they have been far less draconian than commonly believed—have been extremely important in forcing a sense of crisis, which has led to innovation. Program reductions have also helped to weaken the power of the expensive army of social service professionals who have taken the place of genuine local leaders.

Moreover, neither the morality and common social bonds needed to bind a community together nor the authority to enforce a positive code of behavior can come from government. Government officials cannot make teenage girls believe it is wrong to become pregnant and go on welfare; they cannot make going to college instead of pushing drugs the fashionable thing to do in a public housing project. That requires determined moral leadership from people respected in the community. It cannot be created with government programs. Such leadership has been especially lacking in the black community. With the exception of some political and church leaders such as Jesse Jackson, who is prepared to admit and denounce black-on-black crime and to go into high schools to attack drug use, the official leadership of the black community seems willing to condone almost anything as a product of racism. Fortunately, that kind of sterile leadership is now being challenged by a new generation of blacks, who recognize that while the civil rights era was essential to the breaking down of racial barriers, the way forward is to build on the inherent capacities of the community, not to claim that supposed inherent deficiencies will make blacks forever dependent on special help from ''guilty'' whites.

In addition, it should be recognized that economic development is not a proper function of the federal government. Economic development decisions and funding should come instead from the ''community of interest'' involved. When development affects a city, it is the residents, businesses, and taxpayers of that community who should assess the costs or benefits involved and should raise the money. If there are costs or benefits that flow wider, to the state or region, then it is legitimate for that higher level to become involved in the design and funding of projects. Only rarely would such a project have effects so widespread as to justify the involvement of the federal government.

Countless neighborhoods have been destroyed because ''free'' money from Washington made it economic for developers to go ahead with projects that could never have been justified by weighing the costs and benefits to those affected. When federal money is readily available for new construction, which all too often breaks up communities, there is little incentive to look at ways of rehabilitating existing structures in a way that binds communities together and gives them a shot in the arm. It is rather ironic that so many of the neighborhoods now considered up-and-coming are those that "missed out" on federal dollars during urban renewal and similar programs to pay for bulldozers. Ironic, but not surprising.

2. *Make greater use of vouchers and other forms of direct assistance to turn clients into consumers.*

Limiting the scope of federal activities does not mean that the federal government has no role, only that there should be a decisive switch in emphasis. As discussed earlier, an important change would be to direct government assistance for services as far as possible to individuals and families, to enable *them* to make the choice as to what services should be delivered and by whom. That would provide an enormous stimulus to many community-based organizations.

Housing vouchers, for example, would mean giving poor families a certificate equal to the average cost of adequate housing in the area and allowing them to "shop around" for a unit. The family could add to the certificate to obtain better housing, if they so wished. Such vouchers give much wider choice to families in deciding where they will live, in contrast with the policy of segregating the poor into costly public housing projects or privately operated housing developments sponsored by the government. The evidence from early experiments with the housing voucher and from the limited federal program launched by the Reagan Administration also shows that there would be significant budget savings to the taxpayer.[21]

Vouchers for other services would have an equally significant impact on the power of individuals and communities. Instead of hijacking funds en route to the poor and turning them into services according to their own assessment of deficiencies and needs, professionals would have to compete for the client dollar among themselves and with indigenous organizations. There can be little doubt that many of those professionals would face a lean time. As the urban scholar John McKnight puts it, the current system spends an enormous amount of money on each poor family and yet fails to empower those families to make economic decisions: "They are given a pittance in purchasing power and all the service providers they can eat." Thank heavens, he says, that we did not surround returning GIs after World War II "with a ring of service professionals. We gave them an economic key to educational systems and an economic key to home ownership. We valued our GIs too much to treat them like poor people and substitute service professionals for income."[22]

> 3. Create a "frontier" climate for enterprise creation in poor neighborhoods by cutting taxes and red tape, fostering indigenous capital formation, and experimenting with enterprise zones.

The success of so many organizations in depressed neighborhoods, usually against all the odds, shows clearly that both opportunities and entrepreneurs exist in even the most depressed communities. Moreover, just a cursory glance at successful institutions in poor communities should convince even the most skeptical that entrepreneurship has little to do with the wealth of a community, but much with the attitude of its residents. In Asia and South America, enterprises flourish in the midst of what Americans would consider abject poverty. In this country, the remarkable turnaround of many communities hinges on the entrepreneurial abilities of individuals or organizations within them. None of the board of the Kenilworth housing project went to the Harvard Business School, yet they have an almost uncanny ability to see opportunities for business creation. Entrepreneurship generally runs deeper in poor communities than most people would expect. Once someone has taken the lead, others with ideas soon follow.

One step that government can take to encourage someone to take the lead is to reduce the barriers that discourage risk-taking. At a conference on youth crime prevention a few years ago, one former teenage gang leader explained that he and other members of one gang had decided to go straight and approached the city of Philadelphia with an idea to rid the streets of abandoned cars. "Nobody knew better how to strip the cars down than the brothers we were dealing with," the youth said. "The brothers could take and strip the cars down, take the parts, put them together in some old cars and maybe sell some of the cars they didn't need." The city was quite interested but wanted to know how the young people would pay for the legally required insurance. The frustrated youths went back to the streets. "They always have some kind of blockages. No matter how creative or innovative a thing is, there is some kind of blockage they have, some kind of legal, bureaucratic thing."[23]

The secret behind the high level of innovation on the American frontier and in the early immigrant communities was that there were few barriers confronting anyone with the nerve to try an idea. The problem today is that enormous and costly legal barriers confront the low-income entrepreneur. Occupational licensing, bonding requirements, local building codes, zoning ordinances, and many other requirements make legal business extremely unattractive and illegal business strongly appealing. What is needed is a much looser approach to government regulations in poor communities, re-creating the openness to creativity that characterized the frontier. Let public housing residents establish legitimate businesses, or day care centers, in what are now strictly residential buildings with the minimum of bureaucratic hassle. At the moment we discourage honest, law-abiding people who would make good use of empty units, while drug dealers and pimps operate freely by simply ignoring the law. Let us at last accept the reality that paper credentials are much less important in dealing with juvenile crime or high school dropouts than is the credential of respect within the community.

Many policymakers agree that removing barriers to businesses in poor neighborhoods makes sense but then argue that few can start because of a chronic shortage of capital in those areas. That idea of a "shortage" is encouraged by official representatives of the poor, who would have everyone believe that the only way a poor person can start an enterprise in America is with a special loan from Washington or by classing himself as "disadvantaged" and receiving special contracts from government. How amazing, then, that so many poor Americans somehow got started in the basements of Brooklyn or in the fields of Iowa without Uncle Sam's helping hand! The fact is that enterprises used to get off the ground in very poor neighborhoods because the meager resources that did exist were saved and pooled. Credit unions and cooperatives led to flourishing businesses.

To the extent that there are genuine shortages of capital, government can help—but not by favoring particular entrepreneurs and giving them money or subsidized contracts so that they can overcome the high start-up costs imposed by government itself. Bureaucrats are perhaps the worst people to help entrepreneurs, because by nature they are not risk-takers themselves. The best way for government to help entrepreneurs is by reducing the need for capital and fostering indigenous capital formation in poor neighborhoods. Streamlining regulations to reduce the complexity—hence the cost—of forming enterprises in poor neighborhoods would help a great deal. So would reducing certain taxes. While it is true that very few small enterprises make enough money in their early years for relief on corporate income taxes to make much difference, property taxes, inventory taxes, and other taxes unrelated to profit can make the difference between deciding to start on a shoestring and giving up. Such tax relief on business formation within depressed areas rarely imposes a cost on government. Governments do not collect taxes on derelict buildings or businesses that do not exist. In tax collection as in other walks of economic life, 50 percent of something is better than 100 percent of nothing.

As noted earlier, government can also help business formation in poor neighborhoods by using neighborhood organizations as basic service providers. As the experience with tenant management and other services indicates, that makes good business sense for the city at the same time as it provides a boost to neighborhood enterprises. Local governments are already making greater use of neighborhood contractors. The National Association of Neighborhoods reports that existing contracts include food distribution, park and building maintenance, and weatherization services.[24] In addition to generating income and capital for community institutions, such services tend to be more attuned to resident requirements, thanks to the close ties such groups have with the neighborhood.

In keeping with the federal government's proper role as a sponsor of experimentation, other potential methods of indigenous capital formation should also be explored. Near the top of the list should be a full evaluation of the "enterprise allowance" idea, already being pioneered in Europe. It involves an agreement by the appropriate level of government to continue making unemployment or welfare payments for a specified period, usually six months, to an individual who tries to start a business, provided the person is willing and able to contribute a certain amount of capital to the venture, either from his own resources or from others willing to support him.[25] Essentially the idea is almost an entrepreneurial version of workfare, in that the recipient is creating an enterprise, rather than undergoing employment training, in return for benefits. An American version of the apparently successful allowance idea is being advocated by the Council for a Black Economic Agenda, a new group of black leaders who emphasize economic development rather than political concessions as the best road to improvement for black America.

Many of these business development ideas could be folded into a limited and experimental federal "enterprise zone" program. Such zones are small designated areas of depressed neighborhoods where taxes and nonhealth regulations are cut significantly to spur enterprise formation among low-income residents, and where economic development ideas can be tested.[26] A federal program, coordinated with state and local governments, would provide a laboratory to explore the potential of various self-help proposals. Failed ideas could be abandoned, and the successful ones incorporated into the law at the proper levels of government.

The enterprise zone idea has already won wide support. Most of the country's principal minority and urban organizations have endorsed the proposal. But federal legislation still has not been enacted, despite passage in the Senate, backing from the Reagan Administration, and bipartisan sponsorship in the House of Representatives. Nevertheless, the notion of reducing barriers to enterprise in poor neighborhoods has made progress at the state level. To date, just over half the states in the union have enacted some version of enterprise zones, and the results have been heartening to development officials.

4. Institute a program of "land reform" in poor neighborhoods, whereby low-income people are given control or ownership over land and buildings.

It is often said that in America there is capitalism for the rich and socialism for the poor. Rich Americans can own property, control resources, and make choices. The poor are provided with "free" or subsidized housing and services over which they have practically no control, other than very indirectly through advisory bodies and the political process. Yet we see from the experience of the pioneers, the immigrant communities, the tenant managers, and many other examples that control or ownership of resources encourages poor Americans—just like rich Americans—to build for the future.

The experiment with tenant management shows just what can be achieved when direct control over their environment is passed into the hands of public housing residents. It is now time to move that form of management from its "experimental" status to a standard form of public housing management, where that is desired by tenants. Plenty of hard-learned knowledge is now available regarding what works and what does not, so a basic model can be applied to any project. And both public and private resources are already becoming available for training new managers. The main opposition seems to be coming from the professional public housing managers, who feel threatened by the tenant management movement. Their obstructionism has to be overriden by legislation giving tenants the right to manage. That one step could reproduce the successes of Cochran Gardens and Kenilworth in decaying projects all over America, transforming deserts of hopelessness into positive and strong communities.

But it is time to go farther. In Great Britain, the government introduced a program in 1979 under which public housing tenants received the right to *purchase* their homes at a discount of up to 60 percent of the market value, depending on how long they had lived in public housing. The program made sound financial sense from the government's point of view, since it was obtaining back at least some of its original capital cost while relieving the taxpayer of the operating subsidy on each unit sold. The lure of ownership was also too much for many tenants to resist. By the end of 1986 more than one million units had been sold.

There is a great deal of interest in a similar program in this country, particularly among the existing tenant management organizations. They see it as the ultimate form of control and the way to allow residents to capitalize on the improvements they have achieved with their efforts to upgrade the projects. "Why should the residents of Kenilworth do all the hard work to make this place successful," Kimi Gray asks "and then somebody else gets to keep all the savings?"

Critics of the idea argue that unlike Britain, where residency in public housing is common even among well-paid blue-collar workers, the income of typical public housing tenants in America is so low that ownership can only be a dream, never a possibility. Yet calculations by the Congressional Research Service, taking into account the savings in operating costs achieved by tenant managers and discounts equivalent to those offered in Britain, indicate that as many as one in four of the nation's tenants could afford the carrying costs of ownership.[27]

Such a transfer of government-owned housing, as a means of strengthening communities through resident ownership, need not stop at public housing projects. Many cities, including New York, have had success with various versions of "homesteading," where the city will sell city-owned housing (usually abandoned by private owners) to families for a token sum. The new owner must agree to live in the unit and invest money to rehabilitate the property up to a certain standard, or else do the work himself as part of a "sweat equity" arrangement. In that way the owner has a commitment to the property and is not inclined to walk away at the first problem, as has often been the case with federal programs that enabled low-income people to become homeowners with little or no down payment—hence little or no stake in the building. In some cases, including many of the housing initiatives in the South Bronx mentioned earlier, cooperatives have formed to purchase and renovate entire tenement buildings, often with residents dividing up the renovation tasks and receiving architectural and other technical help from local colleges or foundations.

The process of ownership transfer, especially cooperative ownership, needs to be expanded if inner-city communities are to be strengthened. Community-owned housing becomes the nerve center for business formation and the local services that make a community tick. So city governments should examine ways of accelerating transfers. One would be to forgive tax arrears and to purchase rapidly deteriorating buildings *before* the owner disappears, making the building available for purchase at a discount by the tenants or a neighborhood housing organization.

Other forms of real estate transfers should also be considered as ways of enhancing neighborhood control. One promising idea, introduced in Kentucky as part of the state's enterprise zone legislation, is for a long lease on derelict buildings and vacant land owned by the city in a neighborhood to be given, free of charge, to a neighborhood organization or a special corporation comprising residents of the area. A variant would be to transfer ownership instead. In that way the community obtains effective control over a capital asset in the neighborhood and can benefit from any improvement that takes place. Thus if local associations manage to reduce the crime rate in the area, so that land can be subleased at a good price to commercial enterprises, the community obtains income for its efforts. On the other hand, the community may decide to use part of the "land bank" as low-cost, or free, premises for local service or businesses. The city might help to develop the land and buildings, but only in a manner agreeable to the community leaseholders or owners. Whatever final arrangement emerged, it would be the product of decisions made by the community, not by some development board with token local representation.

No amount of government money can revive such places as the South Bronx if no community organizations are there to form a springboard for recovery. Yet those successful community organizations have tended to flourish in spite of government help rather than because of it. It is time for the whole thrust of policy to change. Community, like family, must become a base upon which an antipoverty strategy is built. Government must not suffocate community initiatives with kindness. It must recognize that the organizations that launch them need the freedom to experiment and first to make mistakes if they are ultimately to succeed. It must create the conditions conducive to strong community organizations—and then keep out of the way.

CHAPTER

5

Welfare and the Family

THE TERM "social welfare spending" actually includes many different programs, from Social Security to veterans' benefits and several other transfer payments that do not go primarily to the poor. But most Americans take the term "welfare" to mean the so-called means-tested programs, that is, programs for which only those with low incomes are eligible. There are more than seventy such programs, often with sharply differing rules and procedures, operated out of various agencies at each level of government. They must be looked at together to determine what we are doing for the poor and what we should be doing for the poor.

An even narrower notion of "welfare" refers to such programs as Aid to Families with Dependent Children (AFDC), Supplemental Security Income (SSI), and state general assistance programs, together with their "satellite" income supplementation programs, including food stamps, housing assistance, and energy benefits. Eligibility for those programs is determined not just by low income but also by several additional qualifications.

Public approval of those programs differs widely. Since SSI goes to the aged, blind, and disabled poor, and general assistance rolls are relatively small and benefits limited, there tends to be broad acceptance of such aid. AFDC is a different story, chiefly because of the costs, the number of recipients (about 10.5 million), and the social issues involved. To the average American, somebody "on welfare" often brings to mind a single-female-headed family with children. Many negative stereotypes tend to be associated with such beneficiaries of public assistance, including the "welfare queen" (a rarity), teenage pregnancy (not so rare), and degrading long-term dependency (also not so rare). Thus, while the War on Poverty tends to bring to mind images of poor Appalachian whites, migrant workers, and jobless inner-city youth, "welfare reform" is generally shorthand for reforming AFDC and its satellite programs. That is the sense in which we shall use the term in this chapter. It is important to stress again that "welfare reform," in that sense, must be but one component of overall social policy reform, or else it will be doomed to failure. The AFDC population does not live in a vacuum.

AFDC was created by the Social Security Act in 1935 and was initially known accurately as Aid to Dependent Children. Additional benefits for the guardians of such children were added only in 1950. It is interesting that the program was not conceived as a principal welfare program for the poor. Indeed, it was almost an afterthought tacked on to the Social Security legislation. Those who stopped to think carefully of its purpose, one historian notes, "considered it . . . largely a bill to help worthy widows and children whose fathers had died. It was thought that as the years went by and social insurance matured, the need for public assistance would just wither away; there would be a residual class, but it would be small."[1]

Needless to say, that is not what happened. Today, there are about 10.5 million AFDC recipients, some two-thirds of them children. The program costs federal, state, and local governments more than $16 billion a year. Only Medicaid is more expensive. The $13 billion food stamp program is close behind in third place. Medicaid costs, of course, tend to be run up by the elderly poor, and not so much by the young and comparatively healthy AFDC population. Food stamps are almost universally available and not limited to those strictly "on welfare." But since being an AFDC recipient makes one almost automatically eligible for Medicaid and food stamps, and AFDC benefit loss frequently means Medicaid loss, AFDC is in many ways the key to the welfare system for the single parent. That makes cutting the caseload a difficult political exercise. Further, because AFDC recipients are eligible not just for those benefits but usually also housing assistance, energy assistance, and various social services as well, the program is actually far more expensive to taxpayers than the AFDC total indicates.

The typical AFDC parent today is not the "worthy widow"

envisaged in the original legislation but a divorced, deserted, or never-married woman. Regardless of extenuating circumstances behind any particular out-of-wedlock birth or the justification for any particular divorce, the fact remains that illegitimacy and divorce have an element of personal choice and responsibility that widowhood does not. Moreover, nearly 90 percent of AFDC children have able-bodied but absent fathers.

Regardless of how difficult it is for individuals to pay for making irresponsible or unfortunate choices, that does not absolve those individuals of dealing with the consequences as best they can, before society is asked to step in to support them and their children. It is not that society should not help those who cannot fulfill their responsibilities, but it should certainly not promote the idea that taxpayers are responsible in the first instance for the ill effects of the mistakes of individuals. Nor should children be held hostage to the good nature of more responsible Americans.

Social assistance has always been based on social norms and expectations. One of the assumptions underlying AFDC was the idea that a mother has an important role to play in the upbringing and socialization of her children. It was the humane intention of the program in 1935 to enable a mother to take care of her children—in other words, to encourage what was left of a family to stay together. It was, in today's parlance, a "pro-family" measure. But now the program finances a subculture whose citizens argue, as several young women argued on Bill Moyer's soul-searching 1986 CBS report on *The Vanishing Family*, that they want children but not marriage, because "you don't want the commitments" and "male figures are not substantially important in the family."[2] It is difficult to avoid a disquieting sense that the welfare system is taking money out of the taxpayers' pockets to pay for perhaps the most bitter fruit of the "Me" generation.

Families, Values, and the Public Interest

One result of the emphasis on traditional values in the 1980s has been a long-overdue reevaluation of the economic role of the family in society and of how policies affect the family. At last policymakers are waking up to a simple fact of life: Poverty in the United States today is inextricably intertwined with family structure and the economic viability of families. Broken families lead to poverty. Nearly half of America's poor live in female-headed families with no husband present, even though such families in the general population are only 16 percent of the total. A second adult in the family makes a significant economic contribution to the family, either through earnings outside the home or by providing child care and housekeeping so that the other adult can work: Two-parent families have a 7 percent poverty rate, as against 35 percent for those headed by women.

The connection between family and poverty—not racism—is the explanation for the high poverty rate of American blacks. While blacks make up just 12 percent of the population, they constitute 28 percent of the poor, and the poverty rate among blacks is a staggering 34 percent. But then, nearly three-quarters of all poor black families are headed by females. Among black married-couple families the poverty rate is 14 percent; among those headed by women it is 52 percent. So the fact that more than half of all black infants born today arrive to unwed mothers is not just a disturbing moral trend—it is a calamity for those babies and for the black community. No one is more likely to become a long-term welfare recipient than a black high school dropout who begins having children as a teenager. And her children are very likely to suffer the effects of long-term poverty.

Of course, the relationship between family dissolution (or nonformation) and welfare is a hotly debated issue. Those go-ahead liberals who feel that the "traditional" family is passé and that female-headed families are an expression of individualism should feel acute discomfort over the fact that one-parent families tend to be heavily dependent on welfare. They have to shrug off a crushing weight of evidence and reject common sense: If a young, unskilled woman has to look after an illegitimate child, that woman is going to go nowhere in the economy. The purpose of the Great Society welfare programs was to reduce poverty and dependency—to get people "off the dole," as President Johnson put it. To the extent that those programs give young fathers the easy assurance that their children would be cared for by Uncle Welfare, they have contributed directly to increased poverty. Throughout the 1960s and 1970s, contrary to the stated goals of the War on Poverty, the mechanics and nature of the programs did just that. Indeed, it became quite normal for officials to say that the poor should "demand" the "entitlements" that were theirs, and liberals began to argue that the function of social workers was to go out and actually recruit eligible people for programs.[3]

Whether or not government programs have actually helped to cause family breakup and nonformation, they clearly have helped to finance it and to make it socially acceptable. Broken families moreover are an open invitation to poverty. Pressing for policies and public attitudes aimed at strengthening the family does not mean you are a Jerry Falwell convert. It means you want to deal with one cause of poverty in a way that can have an immediate effect. As a society concerned about reducing poverty, America has a strong public interest in government policies that help families; encourage strong, self-sufficient families; and recognize the responsibilities of parents to their children. When the family is in bad shape, what follows is poor education, poor skills, and poor performance. The federal government may try to douse the flames, but the fire has already caught hold.

As Secretary of Education William Bennett points out, of course, this does not mean "society is relieved of responsibility to do what it can when the family cannot do or is not doing its job. . . . But society cannot replace the family."[4] From the standpoint of averting poverty, the ideal family is a healthy, two-parent family. Granted, that is not always possible, and granted, a sound one-parent family is usually better for a child than a bad two-parent one. And there is no denying that single parents can bring up children as well as or better than two parents in many cases. But, as any single parent knows, it is much more difficult, simply because of the time and attention both children and work require. In the case of unwed teens or young women bearing children, how can such "families" nurture and educate and instill values in children when too frequently the parent is confused, aimless, and immature? Some people retort that unmarried teens are but a small minority of AFDC recipients and so not the main problem. The bulk of welfare spending, however, is on women who first went on welfare in their teens, regardless of the age profile of the current caseload. That is the group most likely to develop long-term dependency and the group whose children are most likely to suffer the effects of long-term poverty. It is a far more significant social problem than the typical divorced middle-class woman who might go on welfare only until she gets herself organized and on her feet.

141

The welfare system is not a neutral factor in the ethos that leads to single-headed families. The attitudes of those who administer it are part of a network of institutions, part of a climate of values, beliefs, and cultural expectations. The messages the environment sends to individuals can encourage or discourage certain behaviors. Americans clearly believe in family values, but many of our human service institutions, in a misguided attempt to be "value-free," instead send the message that values don't matter. The welfare system is not simply a means of transferring economic goods to needy families; its policies and regulations should also reflect and reinforce the society's values. If we expect men and women to work, to be self-sufficient, and to care for their children in a responsible way, our welfare system should reflect that message even as it humanely assists those who are unable to do so.

Is Workfare the Answer?

Tying work requirements to public assistance for the able-bodied has always seemed the obvious solution to the work disincentives and demoralizing effects of welfare, since work is the apparent means to independence and the basis of man's dignity. The Elizabethans built work requirements into their Poor Law. Conservatives have always been attracted to the idea. In the past few years, the concept of workfare has come to enjoy broad bipartisan support, thanks to widespread public concern about the effect on the recipient and the recipient's children, and about long-term dependency. If the long-term dependency problem were solved, AFDC and related costs could be reduced by more than half within a few years.

Supporters of workfare generally believe that work itself benefits people by inculcating the work ethic and that able-bodied people are not entitled to an income at taxpayers' expense if they don't "earn" their way: No one should get something for nothing. Contemporary workfare reforms either make recipients work off benefits in public service or train and place them in private-sector jobs. But no policy on earth can eliminate the inherent problem in trying to promote both the work ethic and good home care of children by a parent when the family eligible for welfare is a one-parent family, as it is in 95 percent of the cases. The inescapable conclusion is that if we want to turn those single parents into breadwinners, they will not only be unable to care for their own children but they must earn enough to pay for child care. Otherwise society will end up picking up the child care tab. If we also want mothers to care for their preschool children, we cannot force them to work. Moreover, making such mothers work would not be any less expensive to society than letting them stay home.

The changing role of women in our society leads to ambivalence about what is expected of mothers, whether on welfare or not. States tend to offer welfare mothers with preschool children the option of not working. Since the majority of welfare recipients have preschool children, the workfare programs may send a positive and important signal, but they probably will not have much impact on overall caseloads and welfare spending—at least in the short term. Conservatives in particular must realize that though workfare may be good policy, it does not necessarily cut budgets.

There were various attempts in the 1960s and 1970s to encourage welfare mothers to work. The AFDC legislation which began the Work Incentive program (WIN) in 1967 was intended to put more welfare recipients to work, at least on a part-time basis, by not penalizing them on a dollar-for-dollar basis for earnings. The program and income disregards put into place did not work as intended. The income improved the income levels of some AFDC mothers but were a total failure in promoting self-sufficiency or encouraging more AFDC mothers to seek jobs. Some states experimented with a standard workfare requirement: no work, no benefits. On the whole, they failed as well, or at least had little impact on budgets or caseloads besides a general housecleaning effect. Meanwhile, there has been strong resistance from the social welfare establishment against requiring mothers to work off grants. Not only were mothers with small children often exempted from the work requirement, but numerous other exceptions were made. Few if any penalties were ever exacted on those who simply did not want to work. Obviously, if a work requirement does not actually require someone to work, it is not likely to have much effect.

More recently, the 1981 federal budget act made some serious changes in the AFDC program, laying the foundations for subsequent work-related reforms in many states. The budget specifically allowed states to establish workfare programs, called Community Work Experience Programs (CWEP), to help make participating welfare recipients more employable. In addition, states were permitted to set up WIN demonstration projects for three years (called "WIN demos") in lieu of the ongoing WIN program. The CWEPs and the WIN demos now constitute the bulk of ongoing workfare and work-related welfare reform experiments in the country. Almost forty states are experimenting with such programs, though fewer than ten actually have statewide programs. New York and California, which between them have more than a quarter of the entire AFDC caseload, are among those having statewide programs.

The political dynamics behind the recent groundswell of support for workfare and other work-related programs is significant for the chances of fundamental welfare reform in America. Workfare has long been proposed by conservative welfare reformers—and just as long has been anathema to liberals, particularly the "welfare-rights" proponents. But the social climate has clearly changed. There seems to be increasing acceptance in the welfare establishment of the value of work in promoting independence, and over 90 percent of the American public now supports work and job training components in welfare.[5] Undoubtedly the change of heart is not simply a new-found emphasis on values like the work ethic but also a changing perception of the proper role of women in the labor force. Today, more than half of all married American women are in the work force, and almost half of those work fulltime. Moreover, more than half of all mothers with children under six now work, as do well over two-thirds of mothers with their youngest child between six and thirteen. For many of those women, paid labor is a matter not of personal self-fulfillment but of economic necessity.[6] That perception sheds light on one reason for the popularity of workfare as an equity issue: Why on earth should taxpaying working women, who only reluctantly leave their children to work, be taxed so that another group of women are able to stay home with theirs?

Moreover, fewer and fewer welfare recipients themselves seem to view work requirements as either unfair or punitive. Indeed, as conservatives have always maintained, work itself provides a source of pride. The Manpower Demonstration Research Corporation (MDRC), for instance, has conducted studies of welfare employment initiatives in eleven states over a five-year period. The studies have proved an invaluable contribution to the understanding and development of better work strategies. MDRC found "quite similar" results at work sites from Maryland and West

Virginia to San Diego and California: Even in jobs with "relatively little skills development" there were "high levels of job satisfaction, and an acknowledgement that a requirement to work for one's welfare check is a fair principle."[7]

But there are some difficult practical issues with which workfare enthusiasts have to deal. A beneficiary's desire to work is not always consistent with his or her skills or child care responsibilities, particularly in the case of long-term recipients. If workfare is to mean an opportunity for the welfare recipient to end dependency, rather than simply fulfill an obligation to work in return for assistance, there will soon be calls for job placement, job training, and child care services. That obviously raises rather than lowers at least the short-term cost of welfare. Indeed, not much hard data exist about the cost-effectiveness of workfare from a pure current budget standpoint or about its impact on caseload reduction. So conservatives are talking through their hats when they claim that workfare makes people independent and cuts costs immediately. Such data as do exist—and MDRC provides some of the most reliable, given the difficulties of quantifying some of the factors—provide both opponents and supporters of workfare with ammunition. The glass is both half-full and half-empty. One typical MDRC result, for example, showed that 61 percent of the experimental group in San Diego obtained private sector jobs over an eighteen-month period, as against 55.4 percent of the control group, clearly an improvement and good for the individuals involved—but hardly slashing the budget.

So, although the case for workers is usually made on cost-saving and dependency-reducing grounds, there is no clear evidence that any savings will in fact be forthcoming in the short run. Depending on the design and goals of the program, it can be either more or less expensive than welfare without work requirements. Nevertheless, it is important for society to send a clear message, and workfare sends it: Good welfare policy must involve reciprocal obligations. As for dependency, it can be reduced by linking benefits to work and promoting the work ethic, but work requirements in welfare programs—or the lack of them—are only a small part of the total picture. Work requirements will not provide a panacea for dependency.

Moreover, even though policymakers should strive to make existing families, including single-parent households, as self-sufficient as possible, that is not necessarily a sound long-term policy.

Why? Because work requirements within the welfare system do not improve work incentives or opportunities for absent fathers; their effect is to transform mothers into primary earners. Children have two biological parents, and two-parent families are economically and socially more efficient and, all else being equal, better for children. Thus, long-term welfare reform has to focus on strengthening the two-parent family. In families where the parents live apart the policy should be for both parents to assume responsibility for children. We should certainly encourage the work ethic, but it is by no means the only value we should be promoting. Workfare is only a small first step in reform.

What's After Workfare?

If workfare is only the first step, what would a "post-workfare state" look like? It is when one tries to imagine the end result that the current coalition for workfare seems destined to fall apart. Some versions would mean far bigger government and more spending than even the liberal welfare state has thus far demanded. Others see workfare as the way to force the able-bodied poor to get off welfare and reduce the need for programs.

There is general recognition today that wiping out poverty takes more than transferring income. Most liberals acknowledge that to combat the so-called culture of poverty—the illegitimate children, the social irresponsibility, the lack of a work ethic—we need not more of the same but a different approach to welfare. Yet, as a sign of the desperate times that have befallen those liberals disillusioned with the record of the Great Society, some of the "cures" sound worse than the disease.

For instance, in a fascinating two-part article in *The Atlantic* entitled "The Origins of the Underclass,"[8] Nicholas Lemann describes the underclass problem in ways that could have been written by a conservative. Yet he concludes that neither workfare nor self-help, neither liberal job creation nor conservative enterprise zones, can possibly "heal the ghetto without taking on cultural issues."[9] Those "cultural issues" are so intractable, according to Lemann, that the only way to heal individuals in the ghetto is by getting them out. The inner city itself is too sick to cure. When youths join the Army or Marines, Lemann says, they "do seem to respond to the imposition of a different, and more disciplined, culture."

146

Lemann writes off the possibility of any inner-city rebirth and sinks into wistful liberal nostalgia: His "best solution" turns out to be a rehash of the old liberal agenda of the 1930s—a new federal Works Progress Administration that would provide ghetto youth with public sector jobs outside the ghetto at subminimum wages. Now, one might ask, why would young people who would rather hang out and hustle than take minimum-wage jobs flock to a WPA to purge themselves of their bad neighborhood habits? Lemann picks up the stick: "Ideally, the program would be combined with a universal national-service requirement for young people that would bring many middle-class kids into the neo-WPA too."[10]

So big government and coercive public service are put forward as some novel answer to the problems of long-term poverty in the ghetto, even though out-of-wedlock births, in Lemann's view, are "by far the greatest contributor to the . . . misery of ghetto life."

In a similar vein, Mickey Kaus in the *New Republic* claims that the only way to break the culture of poverty is to set up a "work ethic state." Like Lemann, Kaus does not think much of the potential for self-help and rejuvenation from within. His solution is to replace all welfare programs assisting the able-bodied poor over eighteen (except Medicaid) with a government guarantee of a job to anyone who wants it, also at a subminimum wage. That, he says, would take care of the antifamily incentives of welfare, because the same requirement would apply to everyone, married or single, with or without children.[11] There would be no welfare, except for those who work.

Since not everyone could support a family at a subminimum wage, Kaus argues that the government should supplement the wages or expand the Earned Income Tax Credit (raising costs, of course). Those who did not work would be "thrown into the world of austere public in-kind guarantees—homeless shelters, soup kitchens and the like" (raising the demand for those services). Mothers would become eligible for government-provided day care (which alone would cause public expenditures to skyrocket). And for mothers who didn't want to work? Well, the laws "already provide for removal of a child from an unfit home" (and where would we put them?). In all the years that conservatives promoted what liberals called "punitive workfare," they never came up with a scheme as crushing and punitive as this!

It is characteristic that liberals disenchanted with the Great

Society approach and newly concerned about values and the work ethic begin to flounder when it comes to developing alternative solutions. Liberals have accused conservatives of wanting to turn back the clock, but what else can one call the liberal nostalgia for the New Deal? Promoting the work ethic at the expense of individual freedom is an inevitable consequence of seeing the federal government as the sole source of authority and power in effecting social change, which is precisely why the liberal welfare state became bogged down in the first place. That kind of authoritarian control, of course, costs money. "Who cares?" Kaus says. "The point isn't to save money. The point is to enforce the work ethic" and to give liberals "a chance to achieve, through the back door, the ancient Democratic dream of a guaranteed job."[12] Michael Harrington could not have put it better. Dreams of a beneficent all-powerful welfare state die hard.

The problem with such visions, of course, is that they simply repeat the pattern of what we already have. Social structure is more than a series of transactions between individuals and a central government. Family, community, and such mediating structures as the church have a far greater impact on the social well-being of individuals than government can ever hope to have. When the social contract is defined as one between the individual and the state, the potential value of intermediate social structures is automatically ignored. Parents are not responsible for children: The state will provide. Indeed, the very definition of the problem as the "poverty of children," so much in vogue today, masks the fact that there is no child poverty without family poverty, and we must look to the causes of family poverty to help children, not set up an impoverished federal government *in loco parentis*.

Rebuilding the Family

There is an alternative vision, however, in which government plays a different role—a supporting role to family and community. Support for the family as the primary unit of society is essential if we are serious about fighting poverty. All the evidence shows that cohesive families with strong family ties and loyalties are the best guarantee against poverty. Much has been written about the success of recent Asian immigrants. In spite of discrimination and language barriers, a strong work ethic and unified family effort bring success. But that work ethic must be a foundation of the community itself, or else must be pushed on the community by its own leadership. It cannot be created artificially by government programs or as a requirement for government aid.

Census Bureau data on household wealth and asset ownership in the United States indicate clearly and strongly that home ownership and an intact husband–wife family is the best route to permanent economic security. No income redistribution scheme can change that fact. The work ethic is but one of the key values we need to reaffirm in welfare. Parental responsibility is another.

There are limits, of course, to what government policy can accomplish with respect to reversing trends in divorce rates and illegitimate births. Government officials are not good at persuading people to embrace cultural norms and moral standards. So policymakers have to recognize that government can do only so much and cannot have the same impact as other, more immediate institutions such as church and community. On the other hand, the welfare system obviously should not encourage family and community dissolution, nor should the law turn a blind eye to parents who ignore their responsibilities. Efforts to step up the collection of child support payments from absent fathers are an appropriate and long overdue step toward encouraging parental responsibility. In the case of unwed mothers, especially teenage mothers, enforcing paternal responsibility is more problematic. Yet we have an obligation, for the child's sake, to attempt to enforce it. There is no reason why the new wave of workfare reforms should not include job clubs, mandatory job search, and fathering courses for unemployed fathers of illegitimate children. Whether or not they "worked" initially, society would be sending a firm message to tell those parents what is expected. Government should not allow children to be held hostage so that parents can have their chosen lifestyles financed at public expense. Nor should parental responsibility be passed on to the state. A teenage mother should be expected to live with her parents and not establish a separate household paid for by the rest of us. Both sets of grandparents of illegitimate children born to minors should be held legally responsible for supporting their grandchildren.

But ultimately, in attempting to arrest "cultural drift" there is no substitute for grassroots self-help. Self-help as a solution to the culture of poverty has sometimes been derided by the big-government liberals as ineffective and an abdication of government's responsibility. But small is not necessarily ineffective, particularly in human relations and social development. Many small steps can lead to far more progress than a giant stride onto a banana skin. Self-help as a strategy is not a substitute for government responsibility for the general welfare but a recognition of the limitations of government. There is no more powerful force for social change than the concerted and organized efforts of genuinely engaged people, and it is the strength of our society that government can allow and foster such spontaneous activity.

The National Center for Neighborhood Enterprise (NCNE), for example, which approaches the problems of the ghetto not as a spectator but as an active participant, does not see the problems of inner-city families as hopeless. It works within communities not to "cure" deficiencies but to build on the strengths it identifies. Its family-to-family initiative and other such efforts by it and other groups are likely to be more effective in turning around the lives of families than any neo-WPA. One approach, created five years ago by a black physician in Los Angeles, involves having a committed lay or professional team "adopt" a family in trouble and work with it on a continuing basis as an extended family would. That involves helping kids with homework, taking them to sporting events, and counseling and assisting the mother in continuing her education or finding work. Another approach involves reciprocal self-help among welfare mothers themselves—a "sisterhood" that provides a network for moral and concrete support for fostering positive values in the home. Such efforts complement the welfare system, because they attack problems that have defied solution by traditional social service providers.

In the final analysis, people cannot be helped unless they are encouraged to make the decision to help themselves, and that kind of motivation can develop only from within the community. In an era when it has become popular to talk about the weaknesses of the black family, it is characteristic that Robert Woodson, President of the NCNE, says that the key to success in breaking the bleak cycle of poverty is the black family. The "vanishing" black family will reappear if we encourage more ideas like Woodson's family-to-family network of assistance, which can provide poor and disorganized black families with middle-class role models, counsel, and continuing moral support and assistance. Such were the functions of the traditional extended family networks of blacks that provided the black community with strength and resilience in the pre–civil rights era. The NCNE is also documenting examples of families that flourish even under miserable social conditions, so that their success can provide a guide to teach others how it's done.

Government can do only so much in rebuilding the family as a bastion against poverty. It cannot make Americans change their philosophy. Nor can it turn miserable, crumbling marriages into strong and happy marriages. But government can do a great deal to help those who try to live up to their family responsibilities by removing legislated barriers that make life difficult for them. It can attach different requirements to the provision of welfare—making it clear that society is not going to stand for behavior that imposes enormous burdens on those Americans who take their family responsibilities seriously.

1. Reform the tax code to strengthen low-income families.

For years the federal tax system has been biased against low-income families, adding considerably to the disincentives holding back the poor. Until 1985, for example, inflation-induced bracket creep meant that taxes rose automatically unless adjustments were legislated. Moreover, single persons and married couples with no dependents paid roughly the same proportion of their income in tax in 1984 as in 1960, but average tax rates rose steeply for households with dependents: The average tax burden on a couple with two dependents rose 43 percent in that period, while it soared 223 percent for a couple with four dependents.[13]

Indexation of the tax rates since 1985 has at least halted that drift, but it does not make up for ground already lost. The real value of the personal exemption, for example, is now about half what it was in 1955. Since that year it has fallen from 14 percent of median family income to just 4 percent.[14] Fortunately the tax reforms of 1986 will go a long way toward improving the situation for families and the poor by reducing tax rates and increasing the standard deduction, personal exemptions, and the Earned Income Tax Credit amounts.

Ideally, the tax code should be neutral with respect to a wife's decision to work or not work outside the home. But in practice, perfect neutrality among the various categories of taxpayer is hard to achieve. The "marriage penalty," for example, increases the tax burden of two earners in marriage compared to what it would be if they were single. Many other aspects of the current tax code also are unintentionally "antifamily." For example, two-parent families with only one earning spouse are not eligible for the child care credit; that is a bias against "traditional" families in favor of one-parent households and two-earner households. A family of four earning $15,000, with a wife working outside the home, currently is eligible for a credit potentially worth nearly $1,300. But a family earning only $10,000 with the wife at home is not eligible.

There is a closer relationship between tax policy and welfare policy than many people realize. All increases in all taxes, but especially the flat Social Security tax, put a heavy burden on the working poor and increase the disincentives to work. That is particularly true for large families, because welfare benefits increase with the number of children, while wages do not. A similar problem, known as the "poverty wall," confronts many women trying to support a family. Leaving welfare for a low-paying job generally means losing Medicaid, having to pay for child care and transportation, and paying taxes. The way the system works, in many cases, makes it irrational for many women to go off welfare.

We need to move toward a tax code that does not tax poor people and does not put tax disincentives in the way of those who want to leave the welfare rolls. It is absurd for us to have a system that tries to squeeze taxes out of the working poor, and then spends those same taxes on those who will not work.

2. Eliminate or streamline regulations that impede poor families that try to stand on their own feet.

Various regulations have an impact similar to the tax code. In the name of protecting the poor, and at the behest of unions, social workers, and many others who claim to be protecting the poor, government at all levels has created regulatory barriers to jobs and self-help efforts for many of the poor, particularly poor women. Rules setting standards such as occupational licensing restrictions and building codes exist ostensibly to benefit the poor. But in reality those regulations make it impossible for parents to work at home and thus combine family duties and paid work.

Regulations promulgated in the 1940s, for instance, banned the production of certain women's apparel in the home. Those were intended to protect workers from sweatshop conditions and wages. But increasingly their effect was mainly to make it difficult for some women to combine their household duties with earning a living at home. Continued enforcement of the ban on "homework" by the Labor Department destroyed jobs and opportunities for women, particularly in rural areas, where a need for transportation, day care, and social services posed obstacles to employment away from home. It was not until 1986 that the Reagan Administration took action to end the ban on homework.

Most barriers confronting women trying to help their families are erected by state and local governments, and Washington makes the situation worse through guidelines attached to federal funds for local programs. Although affordable day care is increasingly important, for instance, those who wish to provide day care in their homes encounter occupational licensing and zoning ordinances emanating from state and local government. Most states limit the number of children who can be cared for in a home. If the limit of children is exceeded, the facility may have to meet the stringent and prohibitively costly building codes designed for schools, including separate toilet facilities for boys and girls and accessibility for wheelchairs.[15]

Such extensive regulation hurts working women in two ways. It makes child care more expensive for women who work outside the home (but not necessarily better or safer, as several recent court cases involving child molestation demonstrate), and it limits the opportunities for women who prefer to work at home. In a time when there is increasing pressure for child care services in the workplace to accommodate changing social realities, it is astounding that the possibilities of paid work at home have not been more fully explored or promoted by the women's movement. Certainly as we attempt to get mothers off AFDC, the possibilities for them to undertake either day care or other entrepreneurial activities from the home ought to be encouraged, and regulations that impede their road to independence ought to be waived.

3. *Base welfare programs on the assumption that parents are responsible for their own actions and those of their children. Mothers and fathers of a minor, whether married or not, should be required to provide for their child, with welfare only supplementing their efforts. In addition, parents should be held responsible for the consequences of the sexual behavior of their minor children.*

The purpose of welfare should not be to validate and shore up such social pathologies as illegitimacy and paternal irresponsibility; it should be to express the compassion and expectations of the community at large. It is all too easy for adults who wish to evade their own responsibilities to rely on the compassion of others by pleading that the children involved are innocent and deserve help. To be sure, society should be compassionate and willing to help innocent children. But responsible parents are far better than welfare.

Requiring a sense of family responsibility does not mean we should force incompatible people to live together. It does mean, however, that the parents of a child—in particular the father—have obligations that extend at least until the maturity of the child. Various studies have shown that divorce, as a general rule, impoverishes women and children, while the men may actually move to a higher standard of living than before. Granted, there are instances of financially exploited males, and every newspaper story about the miserable lot of women in such cases invariably generates letters from aggrieved males, but the weight of the evidence is clear. In general, the fathers in broken families simply are not doing their share. Regardless of their feelings toward ex-wives, they have an obligation to their children that they should not expect us as taxpayers to shoulder just to allow them to nurse their grievances.

About half the women potentially eligible for child support have no payments awarded to them, and about half of those to whom payments are awarded never receive the full amount due them. Many women receive nothing at all. That creates a tremendous personal burden for the custodial parent as well as a burden on society. Indeed, about 90 percent of AFDC children have able-bodied but absent fathers, and only about 10 percent receive any child support from those fathers.

When fathers shirk their responsibilities, children suffer and society pays. That holds true not only for divorced and separated fathers but also for the irresponsible young males who think fathering children—the physical act, not taking care of them—is a mark of virility. There is no reason why any of us should have to pay the cost of an illegitimate child so that a young man can boast about the number of children he has sired. The law should come down decisively and heavily on absent fathers.

The complicated and extended legal process for child support claims must be reformed. Although in 1985 Congress allowed states to garnish the wages of delinquent fathers, that hardly goes far enough, since it imposes no requirement on the father to obtain a job. Moreover, many states do little to secure payments from fathers. States should face reductions in their federal AFDC support if they fail to take tough action. There should also be reciprocal laws in each state to allow for the automatic deduction of a certain percentage per child of an absent parent's income and the payment of child support to a custodial spouse. The federal Internal Revenue Service should back up states by providing tax information and facilitating withholding. The absent parent should be required to work full time or enroll in a workfare program to offset state support for the child. Refusal to do so should lead to a prison term.

Such obligations should apply to all fathers, whether or not they were ever married to the mother, and whether or not they are currently employed or minors. This could have important social consequences. Perhaps surprisingly, one of the best arguments for tough action was advanced in the 1986 report of a policy committee of the U.S. House of Representatives Democratic Caucus. In giving tentative approval to a Wisconsin experiment along the lines of the reform suggested above, the report observed: "Young men who know that a portion of their wages will be withheld for 18 years if they father a child without marrying the mother may be compelled to consider more carefully the consequences of their actions. Similarly, the threat of wage withholding if a family breaks up may induce the breadwinner in the family to make more of an effort to deal with family problems and to hold the family together."[16]

The actions of children should also be made explicitly the responsibility of the parents. While government should not preach morality, it should make clear that society will not pick up the tab for the disastrous economic consequences of out-of-wedlock births by teenagers. The parents of those teenagers should be required to take a greater responsibility for the socially costly behavior of their children. Rather than have welfare pay for a teenage mother to leave her parents' household, the parents of both the teenage mother and the father of her child should be required to make a contribution to the support of the child. Wisconsin has already taken the step of making both paternal and maternal sets of grandparents of illegitimate children born to minors legally responsible for supporting their grandchildren. The rest of the nation should follow suit. In the same spirit, a teenage mother should be expected to live with her own parent or parents as a condition of welfare, and not establish a separate household at public expense.

4. Extend the AFDC-UP program, which assists needy two-parent families hit by unemployment, to all states.

AFDC-UP provides assistance to two-parent families meeting income eligibility requirements if the principal earner has a specified work history but is currently unemployed. Only about half the states currently offer the program. Since family stability should be a primary policy goal, it would be a wise exercise in prevention for all the states to provide that assistance to help intact families on hard times, rather than restrict their assistance only to families that have already collapsed. Admittedly, given the limited framework of the current AFDC-UP program, it is unlikely that such a change would have any effect on family stability in the short term, but it is important for AFDC to conform to society's values.

5. Add a work component to every welfare program. States should design work programs according to their own evaluations of their fiscal and economic condition and needs.

A blanket national workfare program would be a mistake. It could end up costing the federal taxpayer far more than it saves, and like other national programs, it would not be sensitive to local conditions. On the other hand, states should be encouraged to experiment with innovative work requirements.

A work component is important to sound welfare policy. Whether or not it produces savings in the short term, it sends a strong message about obligations and expectations and should be a requirement for welfare benefits. The only exception should be teenagers—but only to the degree that they need to continue their education without interruption. In addition to the self-respect and independence work brings an adult, a working parent is also teaching his or her children the work ethic by example. But since the majority of welfare recipients are only in the midst of a temporary crisis and manage to leave the rolls on their own, states would be wise to attach costly day care or education and training programs to work requirements only after recipients have been on welfare for an extensive period. Again, teenagers should be exempted.

6. Adopt a national consumption standard to set benefit levels for state programs, such as that described in Chapter 2. States should be allowed flex-

*ibility in setting income standards and determining program design to
achieve nationally mandated goals.*

It was argued earlier that the best way to combine the goal of a
national minimum welfare standard while encouraging experimentation and sensitivity to local factors would be for the federal
government to require states to meet a federal standard while
allowing them wide flexibility to meet that standard in their own
way. In addition, states should be free to increase benefit levels
beyond any national minimum, provided they raise the funds to
finance the program.

The purpose of means-tested federal welfare programs is to
raise the level of consumption of the poor to an acceptable level.
There is no good reason for widely differing income standards for
eligibility for housing assistance, energy assistance, food stamps,
school lunches, cash aid, and various other programs. If states set
their own poverty income thresholds based on what the federal
government determines are appropriate consumption standards,
then assistance could be targeted to the neediest—those whose
income falls below the level necessary to reach the consumption
standard. But it should be remembered that according to various
poll data, most Americans do not expect welfare to keep able-
bodied recipients out of poverty, just to help them until they can
stand on their own two feet. Second, a significant number of
Americans do not feel that government welfare necessarily ought
to bring the recipient all the way up to the consumption standard;
they feel that other institutions ought to make a significant contribution.

7. Make AFDC explicitly a temporary program.

Limiting AFDC support during a beneficiary's lifetime to a
total of perhaps four years would not affect the vast majority of
welfare recipients, since most remain on the program for less than
that. But it would create a different incentive structure for teenage
mothers, who are the most likely to develop long-term dependency.
Essentially it would say "Get your act together, because you are
not going to become a permanent beneficiary of this program." In
a poll conducted in 1985 for the Heritage Foundation, 94 percent
of the American public agreed with the idea of welfare as a temporary program.

Every effort should be made to enable the mother to become
independent. Education and job-training for teenage mothers, for

157

instance, should be provided and mandatory for the mother. But if the mother is unable to achieve independence at the end of four years, public assistance should be limited to job placement services and in-kind benefits such as food assistance. Otherwise the mother should be required to turn to state-funded programs or the private assistance network.

Though a cutoff may seem harsh, it makes good sense for two reasons. First, the four-year limit would make it clear that AFDC is not a permanent income-support program. Permanent government support should be for those who are disabled, not for able-bodied parents. Second, if government cannot do the job of helping an individual achieve self-sufficiency in four years, it probably can never do that job at all, and it is time for society to try other approaches. The more personalized approach of the private sector is often the only thing that can help such individuals avoid the tragedy of self-perpetuating poverty.

8. Combine the AFDC and food stamp programs.

AFDC and food stamps are both designed to provide assistance to the poor for basic necessities. In the case of current AFDC recipients, it would be simpler and administratively easier if the two programs were folded into each other under the same eligibility criteria and given entirely in the form of cash. The food stamp element of other welfare programs could also be merged into those programs, while working food stamp recipients could receive the equivalent benefits through an expanded Earned Income Tax Credit.

Thus the largest federal welfare program (save Medicaid) could be eliminated as a separate entity without jeopardy to the consumption standard of the eligible population. Initially the combined program could be administered by the Department of Health and Human Services, although the ultimate goal should be to devolve the programs to the states and limit federal support as far as possible to the poorer states. It would also make more sense for nutrition programs designed to improve the health of at-risk populations to be administered as public health programs by the appropriate health agency.

Although administrative savings and greater simplicity would be achieved by cashing out the food stamp program and combining it with other programs, it might seem strange for us to argue for the scrapping of a voucher program, when we point out the advantages of vouchers in many other cases. But it should be remembered that cash is the form of support to the poor which gives them the greatest flexibility and degree of choice (whereas direct services is the most restrictive and inflexible method). Vouchers are a halfway house. They are most appropriate when the beneficiary is able to act like a consumer in the market, but there is reason to believe that if provided with cash he would not use it for the broad purpose intended. A cash grant to pay for a child's education, for instance, might well end up paying for a better apartment.

But food is treated by almost everybody as the most basic necessity, ranked above all other items on the scale of priorities. It is very rare for somebody with enough money to buy food to spend it on other items and go hungry. Those who do so are not usually helped by a voucher. Vouchers should therefore be reserved for the services where the poor's consumer power needs to be directed in some way, to achieve the goals of the particular program. In the case of food, cash is almost always quite sufficient.

The ability of government to solve social problems is very limited. It can always throw money at a problem, but that only solves the part of the problem resulting from a lack of money. It is not simply the lack of money that creates the social pathologies of the underclass, but more subtle cultural influences. Such problems can be solved only within the most basic institutions of a society: family and community. Of course, Americans always tend to want quick solutions to problems—indeed, sometimes Americans appear to prefer rapid action that probably will not work to a patient, slow course of action that is likely to succeed. But those who feel that strengthening social institutions and encouraging self-help is too slow a solution should come up with a speedier solution that actually shows promise of working. They are not very good at doing that. The high hopes of the Great Society were typical of the quick-action philosophy. The dashed hopes of that great social crusade are what has made us look more deeply into the root causes of poverty in America.

CHAPTER

6

Better Education for the Poor

OF THE STUDENTS who enter Boston's schools as ninth-graders, 43 percent do not finish high school. That is not an unusually high rate for one of America's large urban school systems. In many school systems, even those who are officially in school are conspicuous by their absence. In troubled inner-city schools, the attendance rate on a "good day" is about 50 percent.[1]

Even when a school system manages to coax a student through high school, often the high school graduate effectively cannot even read. According to one disgusted union leader, high school graduates in his city "can't even read their own names on their diplomas."[2] A 1983 report of the National Commission on Excellence in Education indicated that such stories were not atypical. Some 13 percent of American seventeen-year-olds, the study found, are functionally illiterate.[3] A recent analysis of Census Bureau data by the U.S. Department of Education found a similar rate among the general population. One-third of those nonreaders are immigrants, but two-thirds are a home-grown problem.[4] If so many Americans cannot fill in a job application and address an envelope, or even figure out correct change, is it any wonder that they cannot find or hold down even an entry-level job or function as responsible, informed citizens? How can we expect them to provide for themselves and their children, and to escape the cycle of poverty?

It should come as no surprise to anyone that there is a direct connection between a poor education and poverty. About half the nation's adult poor have less than a high school education. The poverty rate for high school graduates is 9.5 percent, but for those with less education than that, the rate shoots up to 21 percent. And who is the most likely candidate for long-term welfare dependency? Again no surprise: the female teenage dropout who bears a child out of wedlock.

Poor education breeds poverty. It is like a ball and chain holding a person back. Needless to say, there are plenty of stories of Americans who rose from rags to riches with no education to speak of. As the black millionaire J. D. Gaskins once reminded an audience, it is better to be able to say "I is rich" than "I am poor." But such anecdotes mask the grim reality that ignorance goes hand in hand with poverty in a modern industrialized society. Immigrants to America have always seemed to realize that. If there were no schools nearby, the community would create its own. A recent crop of refugees to America, the Vietnamese, recognize the importance of education more than most. Go to a school in northern Virginia or in California, where many of the Vietnamese settled, and look down the lists of those who stand first in the class in mathematics or even English. The chances are you will find a Vietnamese name.

Good schooling, of course, helps children to escape adult poverty by giving them valuable skills. But it can and should help in another very important way. Schools once saw it as their duty to teach the values and standards of the community, and indeed to impose them on the child. Teachers saw those values not as a straitjacket but as a foundation, giving the child a firm set of tried and tested principles on which to base his life. Unfortunately, public education for the poor in America no longer upholds that tradition. But then it is bound to be hard for public schools to uphold high standards of education when so many teachers vigorously oppose competency testing or pay tied to merit. Moreover, obsessed with the idea that schooling should have nothing to do with inculating values, there are some in the public education establishment who tell us that far from schools castigating teenage pregnancy—usually a life sentence of poverty if the mother is already poor—schools should provide clinics to dispense contraceptives and day care centers for single mothers. Although that view is in the minority, it is the logical outcome of an attitude that is all too common. After all, the argument goes, they are going to have sex anyway, so at least let us make it as safe as we can for them, and as easy as possible to stay in school if they do become pregnant. It is no longer the purpose of a school, these days, to tell a child that something is wrong and will not be tolerated. But as every parent knows, you get the behavior you accept.

The inadequacy of the public schools exacerbates the underlying problems of poor communities, denying the poor the educational rung on the ladder out of their dismal condition. Middle-class children, of course, are not trapped in the public system. They come from families that can more easily move to districts where the schools are better or transfer to private education. But the poor are denied that opportunity: The poor cannot afford private schools, and the public school industry protects its monopoly with vigor—it even has the nerve to tell its critics that the poor must be kept in the system in order to uphold the great traditions of American education. Meanwhile its barely literate victims go out into the world, where business and "training" programs try to provide them with the rudimentary education and positive attitudes to life that they should have acquired years before.

We shall never come to grips with poverty in America until we deal with the disaster area of public education. Together with a stable, two-parent family and a positive community environment, a good basic education is a key to escaping poverty. But over a period of many years, the public school system has lost its moorings. Too many of the professionals who run it have looked more to their own interests than to those of the parents and children they are supposed to serve. Instead of setting a standard schools seek to emulate, many public schools and public school teachers reject any attempt to compare their performance and block every effort by parents to vote with their feet. Rather than provide the children of the poor with the means to escape poverty, they add to the suffocating pressure to fail.

The Great Society: A Failing Grade

The architects and supporters of the Great Society well understood that knowledge is the key to progress and power, and that the uneducated are disfranchised in the most basic sense. Indeed, a prominent theme of the War on Poverty was the idea of "full educational opportunity." Government education and job training programs were to "equalize" opportunities. Federal action was said to be needed because it was patently clear at the time that some states and localities were either unwilling or unable to put the necessary resources into educating the children of the poor. Public education in those areas, in the words of the eminent sociologist Kenneth B. Clark, seemed to have "rejected its role of facilitating social mobility" and to have "become in fact an instrument of social and economic class distinctions in American society."[5] The school system, it was said, perpetuated the segregation of poor Americans from the national community. And as long as the poor continued to be segregated, they would remain an underclass. Equal educational possibilities were to be that first rung on the ladder out of poverty.

It was not just that bad education meant the poor lacked essential skills. Architects of the War on Poverty argued also that deficiencies in education reinforced the other dampening social pressures that made poverty almost inevitable for some Americans, encouraging the poor to resign themselves to their condition. The Great Society education programs were thus designed to remove the depressing features of the "culture of poverty" and thereby liberate the poor. In the case of education, improved schooling and training programs were intended to "free" the poor from the lack of skills and low horizons that kept them in poverty. As Lyndon Johnson put it, "Poverty has many roots but the tap root is ignorance. . . . Just as ignorance breeds poverty, poverty all too often breeds ignorance in the next generation."[6]

The Great Society advocates emphasized the material deficiencies of the education system among contributors to the culture of poverty. They also recognized that a lack of resources was but one factor in the complex problem of poverty in America. Yet when it came down to the design of specific programs, the direct connection between educational performance and the support given by family, community, and often local institutions was misunderstood. The simple fact that people from similar material circumstances respond quite differently to the same educational opportunities and problems should have given policymakers a clue that the progress of an individual is only slightly related to his economic circumstances or to the material condition of school buildings—or even the quality of teachers. Family and community values are probably the single most important determinant of a person's potential to take advantage of educational and employment opportunities in the larger society; they are an individual's essential primary education.

Dozens of federal education and training programs were either launched or expanded to assist the poor. Head Start was intended to prepare children better for school at the preschool level, both mentally and physically. The Elementary and Secondary Education Act of 1965 provided funds for programs for dropouts, the educationally deprived, and bilingual education, among others. Head Start "graduates" could progress to a Follow Through program. At the secondary level, there were the Upward Bound, Special Services for Disadvantaged Students, and Talent Search programs. The Emergency School Aid Act, the Teacher Corps, and a significant expansion of federal funding for vocational education were also enacted. For young adults Congress offered the Job Corps and the Neighborhood Youth Corps. As for the college level, not only was aid given to institutions, but disadvantaged individuals were eligible for grants, loans, and work-study programs. Nor were adults ignored: The Adult Education Act of 1966 and the Manpower Development Training Act, together with programs for migrant workers and others deemed to be disadvantaged, attempted to address the poverty problems of undereducated adults. Nothing was left to chance. There would be nothing less than a cradle-to-grave strategy in the educational War on Poverty.

It was not long, however, before some of the more unpleasant dynamics of federal action began to show up in education, just as in other areas subjected to strong federal action in the 1960s. In particular, those just outside the orbit of eligibility began to press for inclusion, and service providers came to Washington in an effort to secure more clients. Soon the definition of "disadvantaged" came to include the handicapped, minorities regardless of poverty status, and women—even the lower middle class somehow managed to get itself included. Subsidized student loans were available to everyone. Consequently the war effort became diffused and fragmented. It was not even clear exactly what each program should or could accomplish, but the federal money machine kept rolling. The bottom line was that a $1.2 billion federal investment in education and training for the poor in 1965 grew sixfold by the mid-1970s and doubled again by the mid-1980s. In fiscal 1984, the federal government spent $12.6 billion on education and job training specifically aimed at lower-income individuals. There have been plenty of individual success stories and progress at the margin as well as for some particular groups, but a reasonable bystander would be hard-pressed to detect any significant general improvement in the quality of education received by the poor.

The dismally low education and training standards now reached routinely by the residents of urban slums or poverty-stricken rural areas make the bold rhetoric of the 1960s sound very hollow indeed. Even if one rejects the thesis that the programs actually exacerbated the deepening crisis in the ghetto, it is clear that they have been totally ineffective in coping with it. To those who would argue that insufficient funding has been the reason, one might pose the obvious question: Considering the 1,000 percent increase in spending over the last two decades, how much is enough?

Why Schools Are in Trouble

American schools did not begin their downhill slide the day Lyndon Johnson entered the White House. Deep-seated problems were evident well before that. The War on Poverty programs tried to correct those problems, but in many respects they made them worse. The reason was that federal initiatives attacked the symptoms of the failing educational system, not the causes.

Public education in the United States has always been, by law as well as by tradition, primarily a local responsibility. Until the mid-nineteenth century, when free and universal schooling was established in America, parental fees were normally levied to provide for "common school" education. That direct method of financing meant strong elements of both parental responsibility for and parental control over education. The movement to establish governmental responsibility for the funding of schools was not a rejection of the ideal of parental control. It was an attempt to make education both universal and professional. Still, until well into the twentieth century, local funding, thus local control, was the rule: In 1920, local funds made up 83 percent of public school revenues. At that time federal funds accounted for less than 1 percent of school spending. Even by 1940 it had not reached 2 percent.

165

By the 1960s it was quite obvious that there were severe problems with the public school system, especially the schools serving the poor. Violence, poor attendance, low expectations, lack of motivation, vandalism, drugs, and a host of other ills were typical and chronic problems in the inner-city public schools and a feature of many schools elsewhere. A lack of resources also plagued many school systems. But the civil rights issues involved in the attempts to eradicate both legal and *de facto* segregation meant that the Johnson White House, perhaps unavoidably, devoted most of its attention to questions of access and the political environment in which the schools existed. Yet those pressing concerns masked even deeper problems in the schools. Slowly but surely, community and parent control of local schools had been replaced by control through the political process. The federal initiatives launched by Johnson only intensified the trend.

Further, the monopoly status of the public schools—at least as far as the poor were concerned—had become an end in itself. Rather than a vehicle to ensure a quality education to all Americans, the monopoly was serving the interests of the educators themselves. Most educators were and still are well-intentioned, but in a monopoly it is very easy to confuse one's own interests with those of the client. The moribund and top-heavy administrative apparatus of the system protected too many incompetent and lazy teachers. The rules and regulations of the monopoly seemed designed to serve its teachers and bureaucrats, not the students. The guiding philosophy and values of the schools were those of teachers and administrators, not parents. Yet the War on Poverty assumed that the inadequacies of the education system were due, if not to segregation, then to the deficiencies of the poor and their communities, not the system itself. So it spent money to graft new programs onto what was essentially an unsound stock.

At the preschool and elementary/secondary levels, the federal approach was to try improving basic cognitive skills through special programs intended to compensate for the deficiencies in the education received by the poor. The preschool Head Start program, for instance, was part of the broader community action strategy, and it provided medical, nutritional, and other social services, as well as schooling. The emphasis of local Head Start programs could vary widely, however, reflecting both the strategy of drawing parents actively into the program as volunteers and the necessity to be creative with the very limited federal resources available.

Such efforts were supplemented by school-based vocational education and by job training programs for those less academically inclined. The most disadvantaged of all were to be reached by "total immersion" programs, such as the Job Corps, which placed the disadvantaged person into a totally new environment. Federal funds were also made available for higher education programs, financial aid, and education and training programs for adults.

Rather than reduce the bureaucratization and self-interest goals of public school teachers and administrators, however, the federal programs added considerably to the paperwork burden. More important, the programs accelerated the shift toward control by teachers rather than parents. Moreover, the federal involvement added a new fly to the ointment: the same interest-group politics that have undermined the integrity of other social services. The resulting political dynamics have enabled the education establishment to protect and expand programs even when the evidence regarding their effectiveness was far from clear.

Take the case of Title I, the compensatory education program that formed the heart of the 1965 act. Studies have shown consistently that the goals of the program have never been achieved. As early as 1969, reports mandated by Congress were finding complaints about red tape from educators and about the meager improvements in children's progress from parents. A fullscale study launched in 1975, which reported its findings in 1981, found that any beneficial impact of the remedial program on a child normally had disappeared by the time he or she entered junior high school. A recent review of forty-seven studies of compensatory education found a clear pattern of early gains that eroded over time, and a poor relationship between the money spent and the improvements realized.[7] Nevertheless, the education lobby has managed to keep funds flowing to the program, denouncing those who demand standardized tests as elitist and those who question continued funding of the program as antipoor. Needless to say, the same lobby has been in the forefront of the opposition to attempts by the Reagan Administration to introduce vouchers into Title I programs so that parents can begin to decide for themselves which providers of compensatory education are doing a good job and should be funded.

The political dynamics surrounding federal education spending have been most pungently described by the educator Diane Ravitch. Describing what she calls the "new politics of education" after 1965, Ravitch explains:

> In elementary and secondary schools, almost no area of administrative discretion was left uncontested: students demanded new rights and freedoms; teachers' unions asserted a new militancy; political-action groups complained about books in the classrooms and libraries, for reasons of sexism, racism, or immorality; the courts ordered the busing of students in many communities, as well as reassignment of faculty, to achieve racial integration; Congress, the courts, federal agencies, and state legislatures imposed special mandates across a wide range of issues, such as restricting or requiring certain tests, setting standards for promotion and graduation, and establishing new requirements governing the treatment of handicapped students and of students who were either female or members of a racial or linguistic minority. Considering the traditional reluctance of the courts to intervene in the internal affairs of educational institutions, of the federal bureaucracy to violate local control of schools, and of the Congress to bestow federal aid upon education, it is all the more remarkable how rapidly the courts, the federal bureaucracy, and the Congress shed their doubts and hesitation after 1965.[8]

Thanks in large part to the power of the education lobby, per-pupil expenditures have soared since the 1960s. But also thanks to the lobby, an increasing proportion of the money has been spent on administration and support services. During one five-year period in the 1970s, for instance, when the number of teachers and other professional staff increased by 15 percent, the number of supervisors went up 44 percent.[9] Meanwhile, academic standards have taken a nosedive. In a 1986 survey, the Congressional Budget Office concluded that the past two decades have been a period of decline in academic achievement across the whole country. The 1983 report of the National Commission on Excellence in Education put it with characteristic bluntness: The nation's schools are "at risk," and if any outside power had imposed such a system of mediocrity on us, "we might well have viewed it as an act of war."[10]

Of course, the education lobby continues as always to maintain that the root cause of the continuing problem is money. If the existing federal programs are not doing the job, then just make them larger and more comprehensive. Above all, pay teachers more. Yet it is very difficult for anyone to argue plausibly that money is the crucial factor in explaining the dismal standards in today's public schools. Private schools, on average, spend half of what public schools spend on each student. Yet they produce, as a group, consistently better academic results than public schools.[11] Even when they do not require teacher certification and pay their teachers less, private schools consistently outperform public schools.

There is no magic to the success of private schools. Unlike the public schools, they have to compete for the parent dollar, and to be successful at that they must demonstrate that they are providing value for money. Public schools, on the other hand, operate as a politicized government monopoly, offering "consumers" little choice or control and developing the inefficiencies of all noncompetitive bureaucratic enterprises. That view is by no means restricted to conservative educationists. The Brookings Institution has never been accused of being conservative, but two Brookings scholars, John Chubb and Terry Moe, share the conservative view that freedom of choice is essential for good public education. The differences in performance, they argue, derive from the schools' "methods of social control: the public schools are subordinates in a hierarchic system of democratic politics, private schools are largely autonomous actors 'controlled' by the market."[12] Their conclusion: The public schools, by virtue of their effective monopoly, have become the creatures of the interest groups providing educational services. They are no longer sensitive to the needs and demands of the communities they were intended to serve.

> The public schools are captives of democratic politics. They are subordinates in a hierarchic system of control in which myriad interests and actors use the rules, structures, and processes of democracy to impose their preferences on the local school. It is no accident that public schools are lacking in autonomy, that principals have difficulty leading, and that school goals are heterogeneous, unclear, and undemanding. Nor is it an accident that weak principals and tenured, unionized teachers struggle for power and hold one another in relatively low esteem.[13]

The Brookings scholars are part of the emerging consensus on what is at the root of the public school problem. The reason public schools serve the poor so badly is not that they are underfunded or in bad neighborhoods. Nor is it that children from poor communities are somehow incapable of learning. Public schools fail to educate the poor adequately for two basic reasons, quite similar to the reasons why other services to the poor are so inadequate. Low-income "consumers" of educational services have little choice and less power; the monopoly public school providers of those services pursue their own interests while refusing to see themselves as the guardians of the community's fundamental values.

The middle class has the political clout to pressure school administrators to give their children the kind of education they want. Failing that, most have the resources to choose another school, even if it means paying twice for schooling—once in taxes and again in tuition fees. The poor, on the other hand, do not have that choice. Dropping out is about the only way the poor have of registering discontent with the system. When that happens, the schools blame the student, the home environment, a lack of resources, or Ronald Reagan—but never themselves. It is not a coincidence that dropout rates are much higher for inner-city youth, Hispanics, blacks, and the disadvantaged, or that being two or more years behind grade level is one of the best predictors of dropping out.[14] Without meaningful choice, and thus power to influence the educational system in a direct way, all the remedial education and compensatory programs in the world will not provide the poor with "equal educational opportunity" or give them the incentive to try harder. Only when the poor can exercise clout with public school administrators and choose private over public education will they have "equal educational opportunity."

Similarly, public school teachers must accept the fact that they have a responsibility to uphold the positive values of society. They are not neutral observers of other people's values. At one time, school teachers considered it their civic duty to uphold conventional morality. They taught "good" attitudes and demanded "good" behavior. At one time, for instance, smoking cigarettes was forbidden on school grounds. Even though "daring" students could always sneak a smoke in the lavatory, being caught meant trouble—even suspension. Later, schools decided it was not up to them to correct the behavior of students, so they designated "smoking areas," usually on the school grounds, where students could smoke without disturbing anyone else. And the daring students have moved up the drug scale. Admittedly, the attitude to smoking has begun to harden again, but that results from the mounting evidence that smoking poses serious health hazards. It has nothing to do with the moral health of students.

From the perspective of poverty, the changed attitude to pregnancy is even more disturbing. It used to be that when a teenage student became pregnant, school officials were outraged and the girl was disgraced. Invariably she had to leave the school. To continue her education, she would probably have had to attend evening classes with others in a similar situation. Harsh though that might be, it sent a clear message to every student about what would be tolerated and what would not. But these days we are more "caring," and teachers are less inclined to take sides in the moral debate. In some communities, becoming a mother while at school is all too often a status symbol; fathering such a child allows a boy to walk tall. The schools do not interfere. They provide special services so that children can enjoy their enhanced status and remain in school.

What Should We Try to Achieve with Education and Training?

The poverty of public education has denied many of the poor any chance of succeeding in the world of work. Thanks to the failure of the school system, America's business community has to find innovative ways of dealing with the semiliterate, and the vocational education system has become a dumping ground for the slow learner and the potential school dropout. The Committee for Economic Development, a leading business research organization, complains that "many high school graduates are virtually unemployable, even at today's minimum wage." It points out that vocational education rarely teaches adequate basic skills and even graduates with "academic" backgrounds often fall short: Fully two-thirds of U.S. colleges (and, though the Committee does not note this, fully 94 percent of public colleges) now provide remedial reading and writing courses to compensate for the shortcomings of the school system. When high school graduates or dropouts go directly into the job market, it is employers rather than colleges who must pick up the slack. While about 60 percent of school dropouts are functionally illiterate, some 44 percent of seventeen-year-olds still in school are only "marginally literate."[15]

The deficiencies in basic education pose serious problems for American business. After twice revising an already simplified training manual, for instance, Delta Foremost Chemical Corporation of Memphis, Tennessee, had to hire a teacher "to work on employees' basic skills for two hours a week." The Bank of New England has had to offer entry-level workers courses in basic math.[16] But perhaps most disturbing of all, some companies are now simply giving up on the education system and turning to technology to enable them to make allowances for poor education. In some fast-food chains, for instance, to ring up sales and make change the employees need only press buttons displaying pictures of the products. Twenty years ago schoolchildren were told that they would have to learn the complexities of technology to work in the modern world. But they are not even learning the basics. The short-term good news is that technology seems able to adapt to people with even minimal skills. That gives some young Americans the idea that really they do not need good schooling to make it in the world. The bad news, of course, is that such ideas are wishful thinking. If the only way you can make change is to punch a button with a hamburger on it, then you are condemned to jobs that supply buttons with pictures. Unfortunately not many jobs do that, and an increasing volume of young people can function only in those jobs.

The long-term picture for the poor is even bleaker than that. Their employability is going to depend on more than just the technical ability of American industry to adapt to their low skills. It will be affected too by America's ability to stay competitive in industries that can get by while accommodating young people with little education. Employment in fast food may be safe; Americans have to eat. But what about basic jobs in manufacturing? Obviously international competition in such industries is an ever growing threat to young, poorly educated Americans. The Committee for Economic Development notes that Japan boasts close to a 100 percent rate of high school completion and literacy. When the Japanese graduate from high school, the committee says "they have completed the equivalent of the second year at a good American college."[17] The same could be said for many European school systems. It is no wonder the National Commission on Excellence in Education termed the situation in our schools "unilateral educational disarmament."

Vocational education and job training programs are not the answer to those fundamental problems with routine skills. They can only build on a solid educational base; they cannot make up for failings in the general education system. Today's rapidly changing job market means that employers wishing to provide specialized training generally look for workers with the ability to learn and adapt. So school-leavers need to show competency in the basic skills, such as reading and writing. Training programs can show good results only when those core skills are present, but remedial education is fast becoming a central component of those programs.

Nor does vocational education adequately prepare youth for jobs after high school. Long a part of the American high school system, enjoying federal support years before the Great Society, vocational education is supposed to supplement a core education of very basic skills with practical workplace subjects such as carpentry or automobile maintenance. Conceptually that makes sense. It was designed to provide a high school track for the student who is more inclined to leave school for the factory rather than go on to college. But in reality, vocational education has become in many instances a dumping ground for low achievers, where the basic skills are neglected. That was tacitly recognized in 1984 amendments to the federal legislation dealing with vocational education. The amendments attempt to restore the original emphasis on a core of basic education, but given the entrenched "culture" of vocational education in high schools, it is doubtful that the good intentions will lead to tangible results. Without that core, vocational education cannot hope to make the ghetto youth employable, even if it gives him some practical skills. Today's rapidly changing technologies and job opportunities mean that employers generally look for workers with competency in basic skills, like reading and writing, together with sound work habits. A narrow vocational training at the high school level might conceivably enhance employability in specific situations, but from the employer's perspective, vocational education "cannot substitute for education in the core competencies."[18]

The federal government provides approximately 10 percent of vocational education funding. But instead of helping, that modest support may have made things worse. Like other federal money, it comes with strings attached. The strings here require the program to be open to various special groups, straining the resources available. As the National Institute of Education concluded in a 1981 report, the federal Vocational Education Act "attempts to accomplish too much with too few resources.''[19] With vocational education already fighting an image problem as a dumping ground, federal requirements to expand vocational opportunities to the handicapped and disadvantaged, including those with limited English proficiency, reinforces that image and limits the funds available for modernization of vocational programs, many of which hobble along with obsolete equipment. The providers of vocational services are seriously disturbed by the trend. "We're concerned," a spokesman for the American Vocational Association says, "that the federal government not send a signal that vocational education is a compensatory program."[20] Too late—it already has! And any effort now to end the earmarking of funds for the handicapped, the poor, and the disadvantaged would meet with stiff political resistance.

The federal involvement in job training is equally flawed and bears the same uncomfortable relationship to the educational system as does vocational education. The fact is that much of what passes for "job training" is nothing more than remedial education. The majority of out-of-school youths do find jobs and are able to change jobs without suffering long spells of unemployment. The serious youth employment problems are found primarily among the disaffected, those hanging out on the street corners of the nation's cities. The National Research Council confirms the impression one has driving around any large city: The youth employment problem is "highly concentrated among minority-group, inner-city, low-income, and high school dropout youths" and "young unwed mothers"[21]—in other words, the underclass that is so ill-served by public education.

Any effort to overcome the basic educational deficiencies of those young Americans by grafting remedial education onto government employment and training programs is doomed to failure. That does nothing to deal with the underlying problem—which is with the school system—and it undermines the integrity of training, turning many programs into little more than holding tanks for misfits. It is no wonder that the National Research Council draws attention to "the stigma which has plagued [employment and training programs] and their participants."[22] According to the council, isolating disadvantaged youth breeds failure. They need to be integrated as far as possible into the mainstream, and training must be viewed in its relationship to a reformed school system.

The only way to develop this proper relationship is for the educational system to do a satisfactory job in providing the basics. Training can build on that. Securing that firm base requires a fundamental reform of public education for the poor.

The confused relationship between current education and job training programs becomes quite evident when one examines the goals, problems, and successes of the Job Corps, which has been referred to as "the flagship of the fleet of federal [youth employment] programs."[23] The Job Corps originally started as a War on Poverty program, with the passage of the Economic Opportunity Act in 1964. It was designed to give high school dropouts a second chance by supplying them with practical skills to prepare them for meaningful jobs. The program was transferred to the Department of Labor when many youth employment training functions were streamlined and restructured under the Comprehensive Employment and Training Act (CETA) in 1973. With the demise of CETA in 1982, the Job Corps was placed under the new Job Training Partnership Act (JTPA).

The Job Corps costs approximately $600 million annually, which finances about 40,500 training slots at a cost exceeding $15,000 each. It delivers remedial education (including work habit and attitude modification) and job skills training at 107 residential centers around the country. Thirty are operated directly by the federal government and the others by private contractors or by state and local agencies. The centers provide various services and allowances, including room, board, and medical and dental care.

Even strong supporters of employment training tend to admit that the results of most programs are mixed. By contrast, they generally tend to view the Job Corps as being fairly effective in cost-benefit terms, despite a shaky start.[24] Its critics, of course, are more skeptical. Yet the criticism from many conservatives that the $15,000-a-year cost per trainee means "you could send someone to Harvard for what it costs to put them through Job Corps" is just a little too smug. As one Job Corps advocate put it to the authors: "I would be happy to train a Harvard student at a fraction of what Job Corps spends, if Harvard would take our people and train them for less than we spend."

The program's comparative success seems to be the result of a trial-and-error process in which many mistakes were made. There is no doubt that much of what the program attempted to do in its early years was idealistic and perhaps bound to fail, and it is easy to point to weaknesses even today. But there is equally no doubt that the Job Corps has achieved some heartening success. They should not be dismissed lightly without pondering the alternatives.

Visiting a successful center brings the ethos of the Job Corps into sharp focus. The Woodstock, Maryland, Job Corps Center operates in an idyllic rural setting on the campus of a former Jesuit seminary. The center's more than five hundred trainees live in austere dormitories and spend their working day under strict rules in a disciplined atmosphere. Beds are made, graffiti is nonexistent, and the youngsters are kept busy. Academic classes—in math, English, social studies, and other core subjects—are small and quiet. Most students appear to be working diligently. The contrast with the chaos and threatening atmosphere of the inner-city high school is obvious to a teacher who has taught in such schools, as one of the authors has. Yet those are the same kids who were the "losers" in those hopeless schools—the wise guys who played cards in the back of the room, the girls who got pregnant, the "cool dudes" who got their kicks from harassing the teacher.

Training classes, ranging from welding and bricklaying to landscaping and food services, mean hard work in the noonday heat. The trainees are dressed in the "uniforms" of their trades, and they are respectful and polite. A few instances of under-the-surface tensions, such as a potential fight in the dining hall, are quickly controlled. The trainees understand the rule: One fight, and you are out. There are no second chances, no excuses. They also know the Job Corps is probably their last chance to make something of themselves. The effort involved in this self-discipline is visible, and the results are admirable.

John Peoples, director of the Woodstock Center and a two-decade veteran of the Job Corps, believes in the efficacy of the "tough love" approach to instilling self-respect, responsibility, and good work ethics into young people who could easily have been written off as failures. Like the successful community organizations in the inner cities, Peoples knows that you have to demand standards and values if you are going to get results. Accepting excuses helps nobody, least of all the young person on the brink of the poverty trap. Job Corps directors like Peoples show what can be done, even with those who are supposedly maimed by disadvantages and deficiencies. What a shame, then, that kids have to come to him. If the public schools did their job, the few young Americans who reach Peoples would not need to be rehabilitated, nor would the many who don't have to flounder in the underclass.

The Job Corps can never be much more than an heroic rear guard action, an attempt to compensate for the failings of the public schools. To the extent that it succeeds it simply demonstrates that supposedly hopeless young people can be saved and makes the bankruptcy of the public school system serving the poor all the more obvious. If the Job Corps can be effective in its tough approach to discipline and hard work, why wouldn't the same approach work in local public schools, especially if it started with grade one or even earlier? Obviously it makes sense to concentrate our efforts on preventing failure before it happens. It is a cop-out to say it cannot be done because of the "negative environment" in the public schools. That assessment in and of itself contributes to defeat. By ascribing too much influence to some nebulous "environment," which somehow prevents teachers and administrators from doing anything about teenage pregnancy or schoolroom violence, the public schools have been able to write themselves off as a positive force for change of that environment. And by dumping "hopeless cases" into the lap of business and the government, the schools help to perpetuate a dual educational system in America: a mainstream system for those who can readily make it, and a remedial system that tries to make up for the deficiencies of the schools, stigmatizes young people, and undermines the noble commitment to equal educational opportunity.

How to Save Public Education

At long last there are signs of positive changes in the public school system. Just as in other areas of social policy, it is the states that are taking the initiative. According to two leading education scholars, Denis Doyle and Terry Hartle, "states and local governments launched a dizzying number of efforts to improve the schools," beginning in the early 1980s.[25] Some states have instituted merit pay systems, others have required teachers to submit to competency tests, others still have instituted standardized testing for all schools. The State of Texas recently even instituted a requirement that high school athletes must attain certain grades before they will be allowed to take part in school games—a remarkable development in a school system that practically workships high school football.

In part, those efforts were aided politically by highly critical national reports and the focus on educational excellence by the Reagan Administration, which put the teacher unions on the defensive. However, many of the reforms predate the national attention given to the problems of schools and are much more the result of the growing sensitivity of state government to issues, and their new willingness and ability to take decisive action. The Reagan Administration certainly boosted those actions, but mainly they originated in state capitals.

The current wave of educational reform at the state level owes much to a change in thinking in recent years about the relationship between schools and children from disadvantaged backgrounds. In particular, the notion that the primary reason for the failure of disadvantaged children in the schools is their deprived background has taken some particularly hard knocks. More and more cases in which low-income parents take action themselves, leading to sometimes dramatic results, have come to light in recent years.

The residents of Washington's Kenilworth public housing project, for instance, have done more than just improve the physical condition of their complex by taking over its management. Even before tenant management, the residents were coming to grips with the poor educational level of children in their neighborhood. In 1975 the 464-unit project had a typically dismal record of educational failure. Most of its young people had trouble finishing high school, and only two had ever gone on to college. But then things changed. Parents and young people began to take control of their own educational lives. They established a campaign to send kids to college and named it "College Here We Come." The two residents who had graduated from college, who by then had good jobs, were brought back to the project to show the kids just what they could aim for if they were prepared to work. A vacant unit has been turned into a set of study rooms for students willing to abide by tough rules laid down by a council comprising mainly children in the program. Absolutely no drugs are allowed, specified grade point averages have to be maintained in school, and older students are required to coach younger students in the evenings.

Membership in College Here We Come has now become a status symbol within the project, precisely because of its rigid self-discipline and frankly elitist rules. Students in the program are big shots in the project—they can hack it. Just as in the Woodstock Job Corps Center, any breach of the rules and the student is thrown out in disgrace. Being poor or disadvantaged according to some government handbook cuts no ice with College Here We Come. The results? Superior expectations have led to superior performance. Between 1975 and 1985, high school performance increased dramatically and the project sent 582 students on to college.

The successes of highly disciplined and community-supported initiatives like College Here We Come strongly suggest that making undue allowances for a poor background is a discriminatory way of educating the poor. Moreover, they also show up the stark failure of the public schools—schools that act on the assumption that private programs like College Here We Come must be an aberration, while they dump "failures" into training programs that have to remedy the structural deficiencies not of the children but of the schools themselves. When children from poor neighborhoods are told by well-meaning people that they cannot be expected to succeed like other children because of the deficiencies of their environment, then they fail. When they are told that their intellectual abilities are no different from anyone else's, that they are expected to succeed and will be encouraged to do so, and that behavior that leads to failure will not be excused, then they do succeed. That is why an organization like College Here We Come produces results that dumbfound the experts. It is why an inner-city teacher like Chicago's Marva Collins can take illiterate basketball players and teach them to love Shakespeare. It is why low-income blacks and Hispanics work at second and third jobs to pay for tuition at the hundreds of independent minority schools that have sprung up around the country.

It is also the reason for much of the success of Head Start, one of the few products of the Community Action Program that still commands wide-based support. Head Start provides federal funds to assist local efforts to upgrade schooling for the very young, supplementing pure education with health care and other services. Head Start runs parallel to the public school system. Not that the program has escaped criticism: A study in 1969 raised serious questions as to whether the modest academic gains by children were temporary or permanent. Others have accused the program of being little more than a glorified day care system. Nevertheless, the program seems to show progress that generally eludes the public school system, and it does so at lower cost than other "compensatory" programs.

The reason appears to be that Head Start is by its very nature a neighborhood program. Head Start classes are not taught by highly paid teachers who can boast plenty of paper credentials. Parents routinely volunteer as teacher aides and are closely involved in setting policy. Generally no unions intervene between supervisor and staff. And Head Start centers are typically housed in spare accommodations in a church or housing project, rarely in school buildings. Above all, Head Start is a *community* program, run by and for the community. One analyst of the program explains that

> . . . in neighborhoods around the country, residents can readily point to the nearest Head Start center. To them, Head Start is not just another federal program, but a place around the corner where young kids go to get their teeth fixed and learn the alphabet. . . .
>
> Head Start bears a likeness to the neighborhood public schools of a generation ago. It also resembles them in other ways: Like the old neighborhood school, Head Start is sustained by many informal relations that give it roots, and make it a palpable expression of shared community values. . . . [L]ike the old neighborhood school, Head Start is a "permeable institution," one that raises few bureaucratic or professional barriers against parents and neighbors who wish to be part of it.[26]

The common feature of all these approaches is communities of parents that make educational decisions. In some cases they simply provide the encouragement to their children to shake off the suffocating stigma of "disadvantaged." In others they opt out of the public school system altogether. But in every case they are involved directly, and they make key choices. The involvement of communities in education—even poor, supposedly deficient communities—is critical to any strategy to provide good education to poor Americans. The question is how to stimulate that parental and community involvement on a much larger scale, so that it can help to correct or to compensate for the deficiencies of the public school system.

There is no absolute guarantee that closer involvement will come automatically from the innovations now taking place at the state level. Just as many federal reforms were shanghaied on the way to implementation, some of the state reforms, after the education establishment has finished with them, may end up as a coercive, trickle-down approach to improving education for the poor. Admittedly, that is less likely to be the case at the state level, because state government is closer to the people and less under the thumb of the professional lobbies, but it certainly can happen. The best news for the poor from the state initiatives is that they are concentrating on upgrading standards.

For those who believe poor people cannot be expected to reach the standards of other mortals, this is actually bad news. They maintain that raising academic standards will simply increase the number of school dropouts and failures, meaning that overstretched remedial and training programs will be further burdened. Yet there are several reasons why that does not have to happen. First, the very idea that expecting high standards must lead to more dropouts rests on the condescending assumption that failures in inner-city schools are caused by lack of ability resulting from a disadvantaged background. But all the evidence points to one simple fact, which ought to be engraved in stone above every entrance to every inner-city public school: When poor children have clear goals to reach, and when teachers apply enough inspiration and students enough perspiration, it is remarkable what can be done.

Second, if low or nonexistent standards are the only things keeping some students in school, then we are perpetrating a fraud on the students and society. The reason for keeping children in school is not to provide them with day care but to assure academic progress. If a child is determined not to learn or accept the standards applied to all, then he should not be in the classroom undermining the school's efforts to provide a reasonable education to other children.

Third, equity in a democracy must mean equality of opportunity, not equality of outcome. The perversion of the idea of equity as equal outcome is a dangerous denial of individual responsibility. All it can guarantee is equality at the lowest possible level. Encouraged to make it look as though everybody is succeeding, schools allow students to pass even if they make only minimal effort. That is why high school diplomas mean nothing.

Giving true equality of opportunity to the poor will require the education establishment to haul itself out of its rut by enabling the parents of poor children to exercise an influence over service providers that they do not now possess. Just as in other areas of social services and community development, it is remarkable how people in depressed neighborhoods respond when effective power over their circumstances is given to them. When that happens, one-time passive clients of the service industry become aggressive pursuers of their own interests. The only way to give them that leverage in the case of education is to give them the chance to exercise real consumer choice between education services, thereby introducing some competition among education providers. Thanks in large part to the civil rights campaigns of the 1960s and to Johnson's determination to break down racial barriers, access is no longer the central bone of contention. Quality is. And as in any other field of social endeavor, quality is best guaranteed by competition. Only when parents can threaten to take their child somewhere else, at some cost to the school, can they expect to get the attention of teachers and administrators.

Public education exists today because nineteenth-century reformers believed that the previous system of private community schools was insufficient for those children who needed it most, those whom we define today as "at risk." Today the situation is the exact opposite: It is now the public schools that serve the poor least well, providing them with inferior education and hence unequal opportunity. Yet the federal government is doing little to correct the imbalance. As Daniel Patrick Moynihan points out, the federal government merely "feigns neutrality" in the struggle between public and private education. "As program has been piled on program, and regulation on regulation, the federal government has systematically organized its activities in ways that contribute to the decay of nonpublic education."[27]

The solution is the same now as it was in the last century: alternative providers. Giving poor people the right and the power to choose their children's schools would not constitute a death blow to the notion of public education in America. Public education implied a system of quality education for all the public and a school system that bound communities together by teaching the prevailing values of the country. But the buildings with teachers inside that are called public schools today do not, in most poor urban communities, belong to those communities in any real sense. Making those schools more sensitive to the views of parents, and ultimately enabling poor parents to send their children to independent schools, is the best way of achieving the elusive promise of the Great Society.

Reform of that kind requires grassroots effort and an end to the public school monopoly imposed on the poor. With education deregulated in that way and more sensitive to consumer pressure, there is every reason to believe that poor people will flex their muscles and demand better quality, just as they have when allowed to exercise greater control over other services. The shift in power will lead to innovation and improvement in the nation's school system. The federal government can help the process by encouraging experimentation at the state and local levels. Policies at all levels of government should also seek to promote parental choice and competition among providers by empowering the consumers of educational services. There are several ways in which that can be done.

   1. Maximize parental choice, and hence competition, within the current
      public school system.

Simply extending the right to choose within the existing education framework has been shown to result in more parental involvement and improved student performance, even in "hopeless" districts. Such choice and competition can be fostered in various ways. One is to allow open enrollment within a district, so that parents can choose a school for their children instead of being assigned to one. That puts public pressure on bad schools and encourages them to shape up. This approach is also sometimes associated with the "magnet school" idea, where schools are allowed to become more specialized by concentrating on certain subjects beyond the core curriculum to attract students who would not normally be assigned to attend them. That type of approach has its limits, of course, since "good schools," unless expanded, will have waiting lists, while "poor schools" will not necessarily lose either enrollment or funding.

But it is a good start, and numerous school districts have already implemented such approaches, often with impressive results. One example is the East Harlem Community School District

4, which ranked last in New York City in reading scores in 1974. Reacting to that dismal status, the district instituted the "magnet school" concept. Teachers in each school are allowed to develop their own educational programs, emphasizing a special interest (for example, performing arts, math and science), or a specific philosophical approach to education (open education or traditional instruction). Parents and students are provided with information on the available alternatives to give them what school officials call "a voice and a choice." Healthy competition among schools is encouraged, and any school with insufficient enrollment must close. In-district school zoning, which assigns children to specific schools based on geographical area, is now a thing of the past.

The program began with federal money, which had been made available for such "magnet" projects in minority neighborhoods to promote voluntary integration. From just three schools and ninety students in 1974, the magnet system has been expanded to about fifty schools serving about half of the school district's more than 12,000 students. Each "alternative concept" elementary and junior high school has between two hundred and three hundred children, which is considered the maximum workable size. Some 1,500 students—many white and middle-class—enroll from outside the district.

The result has been solid progress. At many of the district's schools, reading performance is now ahead of the city average. And from its last-place ranking (thirty-second place) among New York's school districts in reading scores, the district now ranks nineteenth. Attendance has improved throughout the district, and suspensions are down. The encouraging results, in short, show just what can be done when schools and educators gain some autonomy and poor families receive the power to choose.[28]

Another approach is to allow interdistrict enrollment. That widens parental choice considerably. The strategy has been adopted in both large and small school districts, often providing interesting local twists to the concept. In Colorado, for example, a plan was proposed in 1985 to enable state money to "follow" dropout students into any public or private school, giving poor parents in effect the financial power to try a new school when the local institution failed their child. The education establishment, of course, objected to the inclusion of the private schools as an option, and the final version of the plan allows only public school options. Nonetheless, the fact that state money can be transferred from one school to another establishes the principle of consumer choice and provider competition within a state system.

Open enrollment and choice among public schools is now the rule in Minnesota. But Vermont, in its inimitable and individualistic New England style, goes even farther. In that state, many local school districts do not even have a public high school; they are allowed to designate a local private school as the town high school and can pay students' tuition with public monies. It is also possible to obtain voucher support to attend another approved and nonsectarian school. The Vermont voucher system has been in existence since the nineteenth century. In Iowa, parents are provided with some limited opportunities to have an unsatisfactory school district pay their children's tuition in another district.

In general, opposition to such plans comes from those whose entrenched power is threatened. But states have been responding to widespread parental pressure for such reforms. Governments at all levels have to recognize that the possibilities for improving the quality of education through expanding and promoting such reforms have barely been explored. There is room for much more experimentation. And such efforts are most important, of course, in very poor areas, where they can do much to reverse the sense of powerlessness that is the worst barrier erected against the poor.

> 2. *Bring basic values back into the classroom. Schools must resume their critically important role of inculcating basic values and transmitting culture, so that all students, regardless of background, can gain access to mainstream American society through schooling.*

Although American notions of justice and ethics are based on the Judeo-Christian tradition, moral education should not be confused with religious education. Irrespective of their religious beliefs—or lack of them—Americans built the country and their neighborhoods on some very fundamental notions: honest dealing, hard work, mutual respect, and a sense of responsibility to family. It is ironic that many of our children must now learn from recent Oriental immigrants how those values and success in life go hand in hand.

Of course the most obvious dispute over those basic values does concern the purely religious aspect of American life, although that is just the tip of the iceberg. The overzealous crusade to eliminate any vestige of religion from public schools over the last few decades has gone overboard in interpreting the idea of separation of church and state. Not only was school prayer eliminated, but the important role of religion in history—a fact—is totally ignored or minimized in many textbooks for fear of offending someone, leading to historical distortion. It is ironic that Congress starts its day with a public prayer, while schoolchildren may not.

The attack on and disappearance of such long-standing traditions in public education was part of a general questioning of mainstream values by schools, an attitude that continues today. Rather than attempt to teach children what was right and wrong, teachers began to talk about cultural and moral relativism. Values were not demanded and explained, they were presented for the children's consideration; they were "clarified." Children were taught all about "situational ethics" associated with lying or stealing. Today they are taught to contemplate the "choice" of suicide. That's fine for college courses in philosophy, perhaps, but not for elementary- and secondary-level schoolchildren who do not have the base of knowledge necessary for such sophisticated analyses. Teachers no longer feel it their duty to pass judgments on the behavior of students or to tell them what is right and wrong. And that has led predictably to the moral confusion and declining behavioral standards schoolchildren suffer from today.

One of the authors saw all that from the inside in various types of schools, especially during two years as a substitute teacher in an inner-city school system. One lesson she was expected to teach asked students whether stealing was not justifiable in certain circumstances, giving the example of a man with a dying mother who needed but could not afford medicine. The man in the story stole the medicine from his local pharmacy in order to save his mother. Was he right or wrong? The teacher's guide explained that the problem was supposed to help children think about whether a human life took precedence over property rights. In the discussion that followed, everyone quickly agreed, as might be expected, that the man "did the right thing." But unlike the guide, the students were quick to explore the potential implications. One student argued that cheating in school was justified if the teacher was "prejudiced" against a student, because it evened out his chances. Another came to the conclusion that she had the "right to litter" because her parents paid the taxes that helped pay for public cleanup efforts. It soon became clear in discussions with young people about values that not many were mature enough to know the difference between a real moral dilemma and a rationalization for improper behavior.

When the author's purse was stolen from a desk drawer in one classroom, the principal told her it was useless to reprimand the class and the perpetrator probably could not be found; anyway, she should never leave things "lying around" in a school like that. Nobody ever said, "It's wrong to steal." Even in the well-to-do suburbs of Washington, D.C., students stealing from each other's lockers is not an infrequent occurrence, and perpetrators are rarely caught. Instead of a stern lecture about the evils of such behavior and an attempt to influence peers to ostracize thieves, students at the beginning of the year are warned that "this happens" and that they should get good locks and never forget to lock their lockers.

The notion that things "just happen" and that schools should just accommodate to them is a dereliction of duty on the part of the schools. Teaching the values of a society and demanding standards of civilized behavior are not like returning to an intellectual stone age; it is a matter of giving immature young people a foundation. They can always question it in later life, when they have the experience and maturity to do so. Saying that it is wrong to become pregnant as a teenager is not an invasion of privacy. It is a commonsense message that needs to be shouted at young girls by teachers as well as by everyone else.

We have to rethink what the function of schools and teachers are in children's lives. Teachers are certainly right that families should be the first place where values are inculcated. But when families fail to do so, and the schools say "not my job," young people have no standard to guide them. For those with few material resources, that is a quicker road to permanent poverty than living in the most squalid public housing project.

3. Enact tuition tax credits for the parents of children enrolled in nonpublic elementary and secondary schools.

Many parents, of course, exercised choice for some time before the wave of public school reforms by sending their children to private schools. For the less affluent, such private schools are frequently religious or independent schools with moderate tuition.

But those parents end up paying dearly for the exercise of choice: They pay the taxes that support the public schools they do not use, and then they have to pay tuition, too.

States and the federal government could foster a healthy educational pluralism and provide the less well-to-do with greater educational choice by allowing some portion of tuition payments to be credited against their tax liability. After the years of "value-free" teaching in the public schools, it is not surprising that today we see a revival of interest in religious and traditional education. It has happened, moreover, in spite of government impediments to freedom of choice in education.

Two arguments tend to be advanced against tuition tax credits. First, it is alleged that credits will undermine the principle of public education, and second, such tax credits are said to violate the constitutional separation of church and state. Both arguments are specious. The "principle of public education" refers to a social obligation to ensure that appropriate education is available to all—a desirable outcome. It was never meant to be a justification of the "principle of government monopoly." The children of the poor were not intended to be held hostage to the interests of public school teachers. And the state–religion argument is based on a remarkable interpretation of the Constitution clearly never intended by its framers. Indeed, in 1787 the Congress specifically stated that "religion, morality and knowledge being necessary for good government and the happiness of mankind, schools and the means of education shall forever be encouraged."[29] If the tax deductibility of charitable contributions to religious institutions passes constitutional muster, it is hard to see why the tax deductibility of tuition paid to church-related schools should present constitutional concerns. It is a misguided secularism that interprets the principle of separation of church and state to mean an antireligious state.

Tax deductions and credits can always be limited to the poor. The objective of giving greater choice to the poor does not mean we have to give tax relief to the rich. On the other hand, tax deductions and credits are of only limited use in helping the poor, because most poor people have little income tax liability. They would certainly be helpful to those hard-working Americans who have to struggle to make ends meet. But for the very poor, we need a much more powerful method of expanding choice—vouchers.

4. Establish a system of state and federal educational vouchers for the poor to broaden the "voice and choice" of the disadvantaged and to foster community-based education.

The most potent way to give choice to poor parents would be to fund public schools indirectly, via the parents, through the use of vouchers. That would mean parents of school-age children would be provided with certificates with a monetary value equal to the average cost of educating children with their particular advantages or handicaps in the area (learning-disabled children, for instance, might receive a larger voucher). The voucher would include money from different levels of government according to their contribution to a particular educational program. Ideally, the parents would then be able to use the voucher at any public or private school of their choice that met reasonable state criteria. The school, in turn, would "cash" the voucher at the level of government that issued it.

Such a "pure" education voucher seems a little too radical to most people. But even very mild versions of the idea have been bitterly attacked by the public schools teachers' unions, which recognize the threat it poses to their monopoly. The usual arguments are brought out. Vouchers will mean a subsidy to religion. Vouchers will destroy public education. Vouchers are just a free handout to the middle class. But of course, there is no more truth to those charges than to similar claims about tax credits.

As we mentioned before, several states have already instituted modified voucher systems, taking the sting out of many of the objections. Although it would reduce the range of choices available to parents, vouchers can be restricted to public schools within a state (but parents would be able to cross district lines), or they could be limited to secular schools (so independent neighborhood schools could qualify). And they can be restricted only to parents below a certain income level. Any of those less-than-ideal versions would still mean an enormous increase in the power of poor parents to demand quality education for their children.

A voucher program would give an enormous boost to the kind of community-based initiatives typified by College Here We Come or the independent inner-city schools. And it would almost certainly mean more programs like Head Start in poor neighborhoods—not because Congress took action, but because parents took action. A voucher program would truly liberate the poor from poor-quality education, and they know it. Polls show that the greatest degree of support for vouchers comes not from the wealthy or the middle class but from blacks and inner-city parents whose children are most victimized by the public school monopoly.[30]

5. *Reform teacher training and certification procedures at the state level to attract talented teachers who are knowledgeable in their subject matter and dedicated to teaching.*

The teacher unions always maintain that good teachers will be found simply by offering higher salaries. Yet there is a considerable body of evidence that high pay is not one of the crucial factors determining career choices or the quality of education. In any case, on average, teachers are not as poorly paid as their rhetoric would imply, and private school teachers, who produce better educational results, are usually not paid as well as public school teachers. Emily Feistritzer, director of the private National Center for Educational Information, explained recently that

> . . . as it stands now, with teachers on 9–10 month contracts considering themselves full-time, year-round employees, their $25,000 a year salary is about the median for males with four or more years of college who are working full-time, year-round. It's in the top quarter of college-educated women working full-time for 12 months.[31]

One factor frequently ignored in the quality-of-teacher debate is the effect of state regulation and certification requirements on the supply of able teachers. Those requirements, just like the credentialing requirements of many social service professions, seem designed more to protect teachers from competition than to ensure quality. There is very little evidence that state certification requirements or simplistic courses at most colleges of education do much to guarantee that teachers are of high quality. There is plenty of evidence, however, to suggest that they keep good people out of the public school classroom. One Ivy League honors graduate with an out-of-state teaching certificate was unable to gain certification in Virginia to teach history, for example, just because she lacked three college credits in physical education, for which her university gives no academic credit. So she decided to teach at a private school instead, at lower pay, rather than take a college course in physical education to correct the "deficiency." Many talented potential teachers are probably more discouraged by that kind of bureaucratization and anti-intellectualism than by supposed deficiencies in pay levels.

There are two basic components to good teachers. One: They actually know what they are talking about. Two: They impart it to the child. Neither component is guaranteed by the nation's education schools, which at the undergraduate level take in students who score well below the national average on standard achievement tests and often turn out teachers who know little more than their own students. Nor is either ensured by certification requirements, which rarely test either knowledge or competence. What a teacher really knows is best measured by rigorous testing at the state level, much like the bar examination for lawyers. A teacher should also be required to go through at least a year-long internship under a "master teacher" to acquire schoolroom skills, rather than the few weeks or months of "student teaching" under the current system. States are moving slowly in that direction, but they need to move faster. It appears that the public would support such tough action to get certified but incompetent teachers out of the schools and replace them with people who know their subject. Whether a teacher can actually teach what she or he knows is best assessed by the customer—ultimately the parent. Giving parents real choice means giving them the chance to say, "I don't want that person teaching my child. He doesn't do a good job." There could be no better test of teaching skill.

Americans know that a good education means a giant leap forward out of the clutches of poverty. That is why America saw a comprehensive and universal system of education as a vital part of the national interest. But that system is now failing the very people who depend on it the most. It is clearly unwilling to tackle its chronic deficiencies, preferring instead to pass on the results of its failure to others to deal with as best they can. During the 1960s the Great Society made some improvements at the margin, and today the states are making some further improvements, but the only way to solve the underlying deficiencies is to recognize that they stem from the simple fact that a monopoly does not have to satisfy its customers. As long as poor Americans cannot exercise effective choice the school system will fail them. As long as it fails them, it will condemn them to poverty.

CHAPTER

7

Making America Healthy

EARLY IN 1981, former Secretary of Health, Education, and Welfare Joseph Califano received a brusque telephone call from Lee Iacocca, the Chrysler chairman. "Meet me in New York," the automaker said. "I want you on this board." Califano agreed to the meeting and was soon persuaded to join the company. His role was to be far from cosmetic. Iacocca was deeply worried about the cost of Chrysler's health care benefits—Blue Cross and Blue Shield were the company's second largest suppliers—and he feared that the health bill alone could "sink this ship."

Iaccoca's concerns were by no means unique in the private sector. In 1983 his rivals at Ford spent $742 million, equivalent to $300 added to the price tag of every car the company produced and the fastest-growing cost item. For the Fortune 500 companies and the largest 250 nonindustrial firms, the average rate of increase of health insurance between 1981 and 1983 was a stunning 20 percent, and their health care costs in 1983 amounted to 24 percent of average after-tax profits.[1]

Califano's agreement to join the board was clinched when Iacocca asked him to chair a board committee to tackle the health cost crisis, a committee comprising Iacocca, Califano, and United Automobile Workers chief Douglas Fraser, who was also a board member. Iacocca explained his rationale for the committee's membership with characteristic bluntness: "The three of us did more to create this mess than any other three people in America. You with those Great Society programs. Fraser with his crazy demands for health care benefits in union contracts. And me—I agreed to damn near every one of them."[2]

Iacocca's anxiety about the cost of health care is just one element of what is shaping up as a time bomb in America's social welfare system. In the 1960s Johnson tried to deal with what many saw as a gaping hole in the country's health care services. Despite the enormous wealth of America, many of the poor lacked the most basic, routine health care, which was available to everyone in Europe and elsewhere, and the elderly and even middle-class Americans lived in dread of costly serious illness. But the system Johnson put in place, Califano and others now concede, also contained many deep and serious flaws. The Great Society's hybrid public–private system has led to the worst of both worlds instead of drawing from the best of each: Federal support has by no means assured access to all, while perverse incentives are causing costs to rise at an alarming rate.

Pressure to do something decisive about health care costs and availability is growing. Americans are rapidly coming to the conclusion that, one way or another, everybody must be able to count on obtaining adequate health care services, whatever their situation. Whether conservatives like it or not, the shifting consensus in America now believes that adequate health care is an item, like food, education, and decent shelter, that this society must guarantee to its citizens. Although we do have an extensive system, there are gaps that need to be filled. And the country is going to do that in one of two ways. If conservatives continue to keep their heads in the sand, the old-style diehard liberals, led by Senator Edward Kennedy, will continue to exploit the gaps in the system, persuading Americans that they are indicative of a structural problem. Then one day the liberals will have the votes and popular support to enact a massive extension of the welfare state in the form of a federally financed national health system. That would be an economic disaster, but it will happen if no alternative is put forward that meets the need with an effective combination of public and private resources.

The alternative is for conservatives to stop trying to deny the inevitable and instead seize the initiative. If they do so, they may discover some surprising allies. The experience of the last few years, for instance, has convinced many onetime Great Society enthusiasts that the health care market place is a remarkably powerful institution, capable of rapid innovation and adjustment. Even Califano, who as Lyndon Johnson's Special Assistant for

Domestic Affairs actually helped design the Great Society's health care strategy, is now convinced that at least on the question of how to deal with the runaway cost of health care, "our best hope to change the health care system rests on an awakened, competitive world of business purchasers demanding and bargaining for high-quality care from a variety of providers at much lower cost." The former Johnson aide maintains that the remarkable degree of innovation in the private sector is nothing short of a "health care revolution." The states have also shown a remarkable ability to use the competitive market place to provide better health care to the poor. The insurance and health care delivery industries have become far more sensitive to consumer demands in recent years.

The potential coalition is there to create a comprehensive health care system in America that addresses the needs of all income classes and all ages. But unlike the systems of Europe, which provide a shabby service at heavy public cost, or the proposals of the American liberals, who think only in terms of price controls and new federal spending, it can be a system that uses the innovative power of the competitive market place to ensure quality, and the financial power of federal and state treasuries to ensure access for those in need.

The Johnson Revolution

In the early 1960s there was a growing appreciation that decisive action was urgently needed to deal with very basic deficiencies in the availability of health care for millions of Americans. Americans could obtain the best health care in the world—but only if they could afford it. And that was the catch. The market worked extremely well in delivering high-quality care when money was there to pay for it. If the patient did not have the money or adequate insurance, he had either to rely on the willingness of a physican or hospital to treat him for nothing (which was by no means uncommon), or to go for care to one of the nation's many charity hospitals or community clinics. If none of those were available to him for any reason, or if he was too proud or insufficiently concerned to seek out free care, he simply went without treatment.

Three groups were particularly ill-served by this system. The most obvious, of course, was the poor. Not only did the poor have to fear the effect serious acute health problems would have on family finances, but the lack of routine preventive care made those problems more likely. Widespread deficiencies in dental care, prenatal and postnatal care, and similar routine services often turned preventable problems into major and costly medical disasters for many poor families. As Michael Harrington's influential account of poverty pointed out, there was a marked difference in the health of rich and poor Americans, occasioned by the latter's lack of access. The poor, Harrington bitterly remarked, "are physically victimized in America."[3]

The second group was the elderly. Many retired Americans, of course, set aside more than enough in cash or insurance to deal with the health problems they could expect to face in their retirement. Others could rely on younger family members to care for them if they became infirm. But if an older person had been unable to earmark enough of his earnings to deal with all normal eventualities, or if he was beset by an unexpectedly severe illness, he could easily find himself reduced to penury by health bills, joining the poor in total reliance on charity. Aging and the dread of destitution through ill health went hand in hand in the America of the early 1960s. Surveys show that fear of ill health is still the number one concern of the elderly.

The third group comprised millions of working Americans with insufficient insurance coverage. That was a very different problem, because in most instances it was not a matter of insufficient money to pay for health insurance protection. Rather, they decided not to pay the cost, and gambled on their continued good health. Given other pressing wants and needs, in other words, millions of Americans chose of their own free will to purchase little or no health insurance. So when anything more than routine, reasonably predictable health problems occurred, even fairly prosperous families could find themselves ruined by medical bills. The problem was compounded by the complexity and nature of health care economics. Many Americans could not make informed choices about the protection they might need. When it came to the crunch, during an illness, they were rarely in a position to bargain as consumers or make careful purchases: "Buying" an emergency heart operation is not like shopping around for a new car.

Pressure was growing for action to tackle those deficiencies well before Johnson entered the White House, but heavy lobbying by the medical industry bolstered congressional opposition to a potentially very expensive expansion of the welfare system. So during the Kennedy Administration and the early part of Johnson's tenure, little progress was made toward significant change. After the landslide election victory for the Democrats in 1964, however, resistance to ambitious new programs began to crumble, and sweeping health care legislation was enacted.

The health care bill passed in 1965, in the words of the Ways and Means Chairman, Wilbur Mills, was a "three-layer cake." With various amendments, it still forms the core of today's federal health programs. Two of the layers deal with the elderly (Medicare), and one with the poor (Medicaid). Medicare seeks to deal with the concerns of the elderly in two ways. The first layer, known as Part A, pays for hospital care for almost all Americans over sixty-five—although there is a deductible and a copayment, and Medicare only covers up to ninety days for any one spell of inpatient care for an illness. Part A also covers sixty additional "lifetime reserve days" which a patient can use at any time. That part of Medicare is financed through the Social Security payroll tax. The second layer, Part B, is voluntary and covers 80 percent of physicians' services in and out of hospital, together with additional service costs, including ambulance trips. Part B requires the elderly person to enroll and to pay a premium ($17.90 a month in 1987), which covers approximately 25 percent of the more than $20 billion annual cost of that segment of Medicare, with general revenues picking up the remainder of the tab.

The third layer of the cake is Medicaid. Unlike Medicare, which is basically a federal health insurance program for the elderly, Medicaid is a grant program, under which the federal government joins with state governments to finance health care for the poor. The federal government pays just over half of the more than $50 billion annual cost of the program, which includes coverage for inpatient and outpatient hospital care, skilled nursing home costs, and physician services; but because the federal contribution depends on per capita income, and states have the option of providing additional services beyond the basic mandatory service, the program varies widely between states. Eligibility requirements also differ considerably, depending on state welfare policies. At a minimum, all states must cover all who receive assistance from the two principal welfare programs, Aid to Families with Dependent Children (AFDC) and Supplemental Security Income (SSI). About 22 million Americans annually are served by the program, although many more qualify for benefits. Since there is no limit on the assistance that can be provided to an individual, Medicaid effectively serves as catastrophic medical assistance for the poor— and as the last resort for Americans whose savings have been exhausted by health bills.

Like so many of Johnson's other Great Society statutes, however, the stunning congressional victory on Medicaid and Medicare required significant political compromises and seat-of-the-pants cost calculations that continue to haunt the programs. Johnson was determined to see the legislation passed. If deals had to be made to get the bill through, and if these deals might cause problems later, well, so be it. Johnson would take care of that later. The President agreed to many costly demands of the medical industry, Califano says, "because his focus was almost entirely on access, rarely on cost." So in his eagerness to push the legislation through and to avoid the possibility that doctors and hospitals might refuse to participate in the new programs, Johnson essentially allowed the health care industry to snatch victory from the jaws of defeat. One deal, in particular, boomeranged badly. In response to criticism that the bill might introduce crippling price controls into medicine, hospitals were allowed to charge Medicare the "reasonable cost" of treating the elderly, and physicians were permitted to charge "reasonable" and "customary" fees for their services. In practice, the effect of that concession was to allow doctors and hospitals to write checks to themselves drawn on Uncle Sam's account.

That is not to say the beneficial effects of Medicare and Medicaid were not dramatic and significant—it just took time for the flaws to become obvious. The Medicare legislation took effect on July 1, 1966. Within one year, about one in five of the elderly received hospital services under the program, and approximately 70 percent of those enrolled in part B—93 percent of the elderly— had received services. Hospital admissions of the elderly were increasing by between 2 and 5 percent annually toward the end of the decade, and there was an increase in real medical services to the elderly of 36 percent between 1966 and 1973. The increase in available services did vary from place to place, but there were improvements for all income groups, especially among low-income elderly Americans.[4]

Considerable progress was also made in dealing with the health care problems of the poor. In the early 1960s the poor visited physicians far less often than the nonpoor, despite the fact that generally they suffered more illnesses. By the 1970s the poor were visiting physicians more frequently than other income groups. Minorities made significant gains in access, as did the rural poor. Pregnant women also began to seek medical assistance, leading to better prenatal care. By 1970, 71 percent of low-income women received attention, as against 58 percent in 1963. Moreover, the length of hospital stays and the average number of physician visits showed substantial increases by the early 1970s.[5]

But the underlying economic dynamics of Medicare and Medicaid, built into the system by Johnson's compromises, quickly began to dominate the programs. At the time of passage, there was wide disagreement about the potential price tag of the legislation. The Administration felt that by pushing through companion legislation to boost the supply of services to meet the demand, costs would be kept under control. "By 1967 and 1968," Califano admits, "we realized how misguided this assumption was. The rise of health care costs was accelerating dramatically."[6] Indeed, the cost of the federal programs exceeded the expectations of all but the most pessimistic of their critics. In its first year, Medicare made care available to 19 million elderly Americans at a cost of $4.7 billion, or less than 3 percent of the federal budget. By 1984, the federal government was spending $65 billion, or 7 percent of the budget. Total Medicaid expenses have risen even faster, with combined government outlays jumping from $2.5 billion in 1967 to $9 billion in 1973 and to more than $32 billion ten years later—a rate of increase of almost 25 percent a year. The share of national medical expenditures paid for by all levels of government has risen dramatically. In 1967 alone, government payments jumped from 29.5 to 37.0 percent of national health expenditures. By 1984 the proportion had reached 42 percent. Total expenditures on health, both public and private, have risen from 6 percent of gross national product in 1965 to more than 10 percent in the 1980s.

Such massive increases in public spending might have been acceptable—even though they surpassed all reasonable estimates—had they been due simply to an increased volume in medical services used by the poor. If that had been so, then the Great Society advocates could have said that costs were higher than projected simply because the legislation did a better job of opening hospital doors to the poor and elderly than anyone had expected. Unfortunately, the medical industry's new check-writing privileges proved to be the driving force behind the rapid rise in health care costs. Between 1965 and 1972, for instance, price changes accounted for 45 percent of the increase in the country's spending on health care; 46 percent was due to greater utilization and 9 percent was due to population growth. In the 1970s price rises accounted for more than 68 percent of the additional spending.[7] In 1967 alone, physicians' fees rose 7 percent, and the average price of a hospital room skyrocketed by 20 percent, as against the consumer price index that year of 3 percent. After increasing at between 3 and 7 percent a year throughout the 1950s and early 1960s, hospital charges have risen at an average annual rate of about 12 percent ever since 1966. Price rises in the health care sector typically have been about double the general rate of inflation.

Price rises in the health care industry, of course, occur for many reasons. It would be unfair to assume that doctors and hospitals simply pocket every extra dollar they feel they can charge their patients. Improvements in technology, for instance, may mean that prices go up in conjunction with a rise in quality services. Nevertheless, recent studies indicate that pure inflation has been the main cause of increased health outlays since the 1960s.[8]

The problem of rising costs has proved to be the Achilles' heel of the Great Society health care programs. By agreeing to pay doctors and hospitals essentially whatever the health industry itself decided was a reasonable set of charges, Medicare—and to a lesser extent Medicaid—invited medical cost inflation. Still, it would be wrong to blame the runaway price tag of federally funded medicine solely on the design of the federal programs. Had the private sector financing of health care provided a check on the cost of medicine, the cost of federal programs might have been kept within bounds. But until very recently, the private sector system of health care finance encouraged an upward spiral of prices. What the Great Society programs did was pour gasoline on the flames.

The root cause of the problem is the nature of health insurance. Because health care expenses for an individual can be heavy and unexpected, Americans have increasingly resorted to insurance to cover at least part of their health costs. In recent years the proportion of health costs covered in that way has increased significantly. In 1966, for instance, 49 percent of such payments were made directly by patients. Spurred by the growth of federal programs and private insurance, that figure had fallen to just 27 percent by 1983. That trend has had significant implications for costs.

Health insurance, however, is not like most other forms of insurance. Most insurance, such as homeowner or automobile protection, bases premium rates on various risk categories. But unlike automobile insurance, for example, where the individual's annual premiums are linked to the size of previous claims he has submitted, health insurance is based generally on group risk, where the premium cost is related to total claims made by the group, not by the individuals within it. There are very good reasons for such an approach, of course. When you or I think about buying a car, we can make a choice between a high-performance sports car and a utilitarian station wagon, knowing that there will be a big difference in the cost of insurance. If we can't afford the insurance cost of our dream car, thanks, perhaps, to our poor driving record, we can do without it. But we do not make a choice about becoming ill, and so a poor health record could shackle us with financially crippling insurance premiums if companies based their charges only on our own record. We might not be able to obtain insurance at *any* price if we were judged too high a risk. Group rate insurance, in contrast, means that those judged likely to remain healthy subsidize the insurance of those with less certain health, and everyone can thereby obtain the necessary care.

But there is a flip side to this, known as "moral hazard." Moral hazard refers to the fact that if insurance protects a person against potentially costly decisions, he tends to make more of them, in turn pushing up the cost of insurance. To understand why that occurs with group rate insurance, imagine what might happen if all automobile drivers were treated as a group for insurance purposes, and the individual premium was set at the average insurance cost of the whole group, without regard to each person's driving record or level of claims. The result is not hard to envision:

There would be no insurance incentive for reckless drivers to be more careful; that would lead to more accidents and higher premiums for all—although the reckless drivers, by virtue of the averaging of premiums, would pay only a small fraction of the additional costs their actions imposed on the group.

A similar principle applies to medical insurance. Group health insurance gives hospitals and doctors the incentive to charge as much as they think they can get away with. Since insurance is paying, and premiums are averaged out over a large group, any individual patient has little reason to question costly procedures recommended by his doctor, and every reason to walk into a costly emergency room to get treatment for a minor ailment, rather than ask a drugstore pharmacist. Since the patient is not paying directly, it is hard to lure him with lower prices. The result? The doctor and his hospital are always inclined to propose costly procedures and to purchase the latest technological wonder— leading, Califano says, to a "medical arms race," where hospitals seeks to lure patients with "the latest, the best, the gold-plated version of every medical weapon."[9]

Medicare and Medicaid add to the private sector cost pressure, because to an extent they also operate like group insurance. The Part B premium of Medicare is not related to the risk or case history of the elderly person. In the cases of Medicaid and Part A of Medicare, the beneficiaries do not pay *any* premiums. So there is no incentive operating through premiums to discourage unnecessary services and charges. Both parts of Medicare, however, do require beneficiaries to pay a proportion of the cost, and this does place some restraint on demand. A patient must under Part A pay a deductible of $520 for each hospital visit and $130 per day for a stay in hospital exceeding sixty days. The Medicare beneficiary must also pay 20 percent of physician fees under Part B. About 70 percent of the elderly, however, possess private "Medigap" insurance which must, under law, cover the cost of these Medicare copayments, and the premiums are priced at group rates. Thus the incentives within Medicare are significantly blunted in practice.

Hence in both private and public sector medicine in the United States, we have a system in which the private providers of health care have the incentive to mark up prices as high as they can, within federal or other guidelines; the users have no reason to shop around for price; and the tab is picked up by a third party, virtually without any questions asked.

Such craziness is made worse by the way we treat group insurance for tax purposes. If an individual provides himself with his own insurance or pays for routine medical expenses out of his own pocket, he must generally pay the cost with after-tax dollars (medical expenses can be deducted, but only if they exceed a signification percentage of the taxpayer's income *and* he itemizes his deductions). But if he is covered under a group plan, provided by his employer, for instance, the premiums are tax-deductible by the business without limit. It is hardly surprising, therefore, that in union–management contract bargaining, tax-deductible health benefits have often been more attractive to both sides than the same dollar amount as an addition to the taxable paycheck. Moreover, it is in the interest of union negotiators to press for the inclusion in the "insurance" of even the most routine, minor, and predictable health costs in company plans, to make those costs tax-free. Yet workers are still inclined to take a chance on very serious illness, seeing even tax-deductible premiums for unlikely situations as little better than money down the drain.

That has led to the paradox of American health care: Many workers have "first-dollar" coverage (meaning that insurance covers every penny of the cost) for the most routine and minor dental and medical costs, and yet those same workers do not have full coverage for unusual "catastrophic" health expenses. So tax-supported health "insurance" actually performs the opposite role that insurance should play: It covers predictable, small, and everyday costs, yet it rarely covers the real disasters.

Despite the huge cost of both federal and private health care programs, significant gaps remain in the system. Awareness of those deficiencies is generating the pressure toward some form of comprehensive national health care system in America. Take the elderly. Medicare certainly removes the financial worry of serious short-term illness. But the elderly are still not shielded from the devasting financial impact of chronic illness or infirmity. When the limit on Medicare coverage is exceeded, they must rely on their own resources unless they have purchased private insurance— which most, in fact, do. Only when those avenues are exhausted, and the elderly person descends into poverty, will the public sector again enter the picture in the form of Medicaid. Obviously that can be a traumatic experience. When an elderly American is struck down with debilitating chronic illness, such as Alzheimer's disease, or is incapacitated by a stroke or just simple frailty, what might first appear to be substantial life savings can be quickly eaten away by hospital bills and nursing home care. As America ages, and new life-prolonging technologies are developed, the problem of paying for the care of the elderly will intensify. Just in the last decade, expenditures on nursing home care have quadrupled, and the burden is such that nearly half of that price tag, nearly $14 billion a year, has to be picked up by Medicaid. Clearly a rich and civilized country like the United States has to find a better way to provide long-term care for its senior citizens than to require them first to reduce themselves to penury.

But first, we must recognize clearly what the problem is in the case of the elderly. What has been happening during the last twenty years or so is that middle-aged Americans have come to assume—wrongly—that the government, in the form of Medicare, will be there, as the first as well as the last resort, to take care of their health needs during retirement. That has discouraged workers from undertaking sound retirement health care planning. Consequently, many now retired or reaching retirement discover that they do not have the means to cover the enormous gaps in Medicare. Hence there is a clamor for federal action to finance care with dignity.

Expanding Medicare, however, invites a Pandora's box of political and economic problems, as the Reagan Administration has discovered. In his 1986 State of the Union address, Reagan instructed Health and Human Services Secretary Otis Bowen to study ways of dealing with the general issue of catastrophic health costs. Later that year Bowen released his study, which included, among other recommendations, a proposal to offer Medicare protection for the elderly against catastrophic hospital costs. His plan was to increase the Part B premium by $4.92 per month to finance Medicare coverage of all of a patient's hospital charges after a deductible of $2,000 a year.

The political reaction to the Bowen plan was predictable, although apparently not to the White House officials who had permitted Bowen to release his proposal before a decision had been made as to whether Reagan would endorse it. Liberals in Congress saw the opening and rushed through it. Simultaneously they applauded Bowen's "boldness" in accepting the idea of federal responsibility for dealing with the issue and attacked the Administration for not going far enough. They argued correctly that catastrophic hospital costs are not the greatest concern of the elderly, but that Bowen had not proposed any immediate solution to the most pressing problem—nursing home costs.

The Reagan White House quickly found itself on a slippery political slope. Despite Reagan's philosophical opposition to an expansion of the federal government, his top health official had conceded the argument, and the only remaining issue was the degree to which Medicare coverage should be widened. Under intense congressional pressure to deal with the problem he had identified, and beset by the Iran arms scandal, Reagan finally caved in and supported the Bowen plan, reversing more than twenty years of deep-seated opposition to Medicare. Yet the decision simply drew Reagan deeper into a political bidding war over the elderly. Having conceded the principle of Medicare expansion, the Administration found itself being condemned for not going far enough and thereby being "anti-elderly."

Compounding the philosophical defeat for Reagan, it is difficult to see how reimbursing catastrophic hospital care costs through Medicare can do anything other than push the system heavily into the red. Advocates of Medicare expansion claim that the system will remain in balance because premiums will cover costs. That is naive in the extreme. On the one hand, with an unlimited commitment by Medicare to pay for hospital care and with new and more expensive treatments continuously on the horizon, there is every reason to believe that Medicare outlays will skyrocket. On the other, it is difficult to imagine congressmen voting year after year to raise premiums. It is more likely that politicians will try to curry favor with the elderly by holding down premiums below outlays, as they have done in the case of Part B, and simply shift the funding problem to the next generation.

The financial condition of Medicare is likely to deteriorate further because of quite rational decisions of working Americans. Increased federal support for retirement health care means simply that we take more money from one generation and give it to another. Today's young workers will find even more is taken out of their paycheck to bail out the current problem, and they are assured that they will be taken care of when they reach retirement.

What is the average worker likely to do? Told that money he might otherwise save is to be taken by Uncle Sam to care for him in his retirement, he has even less incentive than before to make adequate provision for his retirement health needs, and a greater incentive to rely on the government. That will make even more Americans dependent on the government for their retirement health costs.

A financially sound and permanent solution to the health care needs of the elderly must start with a recognition that for the vast majority of people who have good incomes during their working lives, the issue is how to get them to put aside a sufficient amount of money in savings and insurance to take care of their last years. There should be no question of America allowing one generation to coast along without making adequate provision, knowing that the federal treasury will always step in to take care of them by taking money out of the pockets of the following generation—which in turn expects the treasury to raid the paychecks of the next generation of workers. That is like hanging on to a tiger's tail: It's fine until you have to let go. What we have to do is explore ways of encouraging—or even requiring—Americans to take steps to build up savings and insurance reserves to take care of routine care and reasonable health risks when they become aged. In those cases where a person does not earn enough to put sufficient aside, or where an elderly person faces medical costs that he or she could not have been expected to insure against, then it is humane and legitimate for government to step in as the last resort—the final insurance underwriter. But when people begin to think of government *instead* of proper foresight, we have a problem.

The Medicaid system also suffers from many flaws besides its cost. It is often said that one of the worst is that because eligibility for Medicaid is linked to eligibility for other welfare payments, and because most low-paid jobs provide few, if any, health benefits, Medicaid leads to a perverse incentive: It encourages the low-skilled poor to opt for welfare dependency instead of taking a job and losing much of their health care coverage. So the able-bodied poor, struggling to make ends meet in a marginal job, are encouraged to drop out of the work force, pushing up the cost of many other welfare programs besides Medicaid itself.

This "Medicaid trap," as one might call it, may be a factor in the growth of the welfare class in America. It should not be overstated, however, because the evidence does not indicate strongly that people work or fail to accept jobs because they lose Medicaid benefits.

Another wide gap in the health care system is underinsurance, and sometimes even a complete lack of insurance, among working Americans. Other than the tax treatment of employer-provided group insurance, there is no encouragement or requirement for working Americans or their employers to obtain adequate health insurance. And so, as explained earlier, there is a tendency for workers to play health care Russian roulette every day. But why is that a problem, many might ask; surely people have the right to take chances? They certainly do, *if* they and society are prepared to accept the consequences.

In theory, of course, society could say to those who wish to gamble: "Okay, blow the money that the rest of us use to purchase adequate protection for ourselves and our families. But don't come to us for help if the odds come out against you." Yet in practice most Americans are not prepared to enforce the consequences of that choice. When the self-employed businessman who puts money into more stock rather than more insurance, or the autoworker who has dental insurance but no catastrophic protection, suddenly faces a medical disaster, we do not turn away. We may force him to use up any financial reserves he has, but then we step in with Medicaid to help him. But an American who does without some frills to buy adequate protection should not then be expected to dig deeper into his pocket to save his next-door neighbor who chose instead to have those frills and gamble, relying on the taxpayer to bail him out if disaster struck. Just as we need a method to make sure that workers obtain adequate protection for their retirement, so that they will not then fall into poverty, we also need a method to make sure that workers who choose to forgo the expense of current health care protection cannot then hold our collective conscience hostage. The only way to do that is to *require* those with adequate means to buy sufficient protection.

That is no easy trick. A considerable number of Americans go without any insurance at all at some point during their lives. Various estimates conducted by the U.S. government and private organizations put the number of Americans without health insurance at any one time, and lacking immediate eligibility for public programs, at as many as 35 million. The 1977 National Medical Care Expenditure Survey still provides the best indication of the extent of inadequate insurance. It put the figure at 25 million. The exhaustive survey found that almost one-third of young adults are uninsured for at least part of the year, and 16 percent for the entire year.[10] Employees of smaller firms are also far less likely to be insured than those who work for large enterprises. A survey of its members by the National Federation of Independent Business, for instance, found that only about 65 percent of small firms provided health insurance in 1985, up from 57 percent in 1978.[11] And despite Medicaid, 27 percent of those below the official poverty line lack any protection.

But that is just part of the gloomy picture. On top of those with no insurance at all are millions more Americans whose insurance is insufficient to protect them financially from heavy medical bills. That probably brings the total number with inadequate coverage to well over 50 million. Depending on one's definition of catastrophic medical costs, as many as one-quarter of the privately insured population actually lacks sufficient coverage, with the proportion rising to two-thirds among those outside group plans (chiefly the self-employed and those working for small firms).[12] The underinsurance problem is particularly acute among those nearing retirement, but the phenomenon is spread throughout the population. About 60 percent of the underinsured are full-time employees or their dependents, and half would be considered middle or high-income earners.[13] Thus the problem of insufficient insurance cannot be eased simply by spending more on Medicaid, even if the eligibility requirements could be reformed to target the poor more effectively. Inadequate insurance is a condition spread throughout the population, not just among some of the poor. What is needed to cure most of the problem, therefore, is not a massive extension of federal programs, but a policy change requiring Americans to protect themselves. Like the federal commitment to provide disaster aid to regions of the country hit by unusual, uninsurable disasters, government can always be there in reserve, should an uninsurable personal catastrophe strike.

The Second Health Care Revolution

At the time of the Great Society, it would have been reasonable to ask: "Well, it is all very well telling most people they must provide for their own protection, but how can they be informed consumers in such a complex market?'' Certainly health care is not like having your car fixed. The bills can be much higher, the services more complex, and you cannot afford to make many mistakes. Indeed, few of us can act like rational consumers when it comes to health care. Moreover, if we are knocked down at the intersection, we are hardly in a position to scan the price lists of competing hospitals before we give the ambulance driver our preference. In that sense health care certainly is a ''special case'' market without the usual hard bargaining between buyer and seller. That feature of health care has always been a key point in the argument for government taking a key role in the provision of health care in America.

But that argument carries much less force today. The health care market has undergone some fundamental changes in recent years, mainly because spiraling costs due to the old dynamics have forced new dynamics onto the system. In particular, what we are now seeing is the rise of what might be called the ''third party consumer.'' Business organizations and the states, in the private and public sectors respectively, are beginning to step into the picture in a big way. They have come to realize, belatedly, that as the organizations who are paying most of the bills, they have a strong self-interest in making sure that the worker or the poor person makes informed and economical choices. So those third parties are taking on the role of informed consumer on behalf of ordinary Americans, driving the kind of bargains that are necessary to make a market work. Consequently, it appears that we are indeed in a position to put together a new kind of public–private partnership in health care, leading to a comprehensive national system based on the private market, with government making sure both that individuals do not shirk their responsibility, and that there is always a last resort available.

This growing activism among larger businesses and states has altered the underlying dynamics of health care in America. By introducing new and powerful players who have the incentive to organize effective but also efficient care, this change has improved the situation facing health care policymakers. During the 1970s the prevailing view during each Administration was that the only practical way of constraining the rapid growth in health care costs was somehow to control the supply of health care services, so that unnecessary costs could be avoided, while restricting the freedom of doctors and hospitals to charge what the industry felt was reasonable. In addition, price controls were instituted in an attempt to limit health industry price rises. Yet those strategies, like most controls, proved to have few benefits and many unfortunate side effects. The main reason, Duke University's Clark Havighurst notes, is that such approaches were

> . . . based on a misconception of the cost problem and an overestimate of government's political ability to contest spending decisions in the private sector. These strategies were acceptable politically only because they addressed symptoms of the problem rather than its fundamental causes and did not seriously threaten the customary autonomy of established interests. . . . Because they did not seek to alter the monolithic character of the industry or to change payment ground rules, the early government controls were essentially conservative, constituting only a small shift in the locus of decisionmaking authority in the system.[14]

Costs in both public and private health care programs skyrocketed during the 1970s, with the inflation-producing incentives of the system compounding the underlying rapid inflation of the period. As Ronald Reagan was coasting to victory in 1980, frustration over health costs was reaching new heights. Double-digit annual rises in health costs were ravaging industry; government outlays on Medicare and Medicaid were going through the roof; and Congress seemed incapable of dealing with the problem. The result was a decisive change in strategy in both the public and the private sectors. The Reagan Administration chose the strategy of indirect attack via the Medicare reimbursement system, while American business finally recognized that it alone had to challenge the health care industry.

The decisive step by the government was a 1983 amendment to the Medicare law, which required the Department of Health and Human Services (the successor to HEW) to draw up plans for a new system of payments to hospitals and nursing homes. Medicare would set in advance a schedule of payments it would make for particular diagnoses. If the hospital could treat the illness for far less than the "prospective" fee, it would pocket the difference. If its actual costs exceeded the fee? Too bad, it had to swallow the excess and find ways to economize in the future. In all, Medicare has established 468 "diagnostic related groups" (DRGs), each with a fixed payment to hospitals. So instead of the old system, where the government said "Tell us what all the procedures cost and we will reimburse you unless it sounds outrageous," Medicare moved in a different direction, along the lines of "Look, as the organization paying the bills, this is what we are prepared to pay for you to treat this diagnosis. And if you can't do it for that we'll use somebody else who can."

Medicare accounts for about 30 percent of hospital revenues, so the prospective payment system soon caught the attention of hospitals and doctors by causing cost-consciousness and competition to enter the picture. Nearly twenty years after Johnson unwisely agreed that Medicare would pay hospitals on a cost-plus basis, DRGs allowed the government to escape from that costly trap. The system has also broken the unholy alliance between doctor and hospital, whereby the hospital had every incentive to agree to every expensive procedure recommended by the physician. Now hospitals routinely monitor procedures authorized by doctors, challenging unusual costs and even withdrawing privileges from persistently high-cost physicians.

Of course, there are many drawbacks to the DRG approach. Every year there is a congressional battle over the specific rates to be applied, leading to uncertainty and dislocation for the industry and an opportunity for lawmakers to try to micro-manage health care. There has been a tendency for hospitals to avoid admitting patients for procedures that cost less. There have also been accusations that some hospitals prematurely discharge patients who are atypically costly to treat.

The cost-saving effects of DRGs are likely to be reinforced by another change authorized by Congress in 1982, which encourages "alternative delivery systems" (ADS) for Medicare services. Under the new approach, which went into effect in 1985, Medicare allows beneficiaries to sign up with prepaid medical plans, and it will pay 95 percent of the average per capita cost of the fee-for-service system toward the subscription. The ADS system establishes the principle that the federal government will encourage the elderly to keep themselves healthy instead of picking up the tab only when they need treatment. Needless to say, the federal government should not really be in the "wellness" business at all, but it has committed itself to taking care of the current generation of elderly Americans, and it cannot break that commitment, unwise though it was. So it is sensible for the government to meet its legal and moral obligation in the least costly way. That means giving incentives for prevention and economies.

The new approach has been a considerable shot in the arm for innovative methods of delivering health care, such as Health Maintenance Organizations (HMOs). These plans obtain their income from regular subscriptions by their members and consequently have the incentive to keep those members healthy on a long-term basis. Subscription plans encourage doctors and hospitals to take prompt action, even when that involves expensive procedures, to reduce later problems. Under the traditional fee-for-service system, the income of doctors and hospitals depends on how ill you are. So by giving Medicare beneficiaries what amounts to a voucher, the elderly have the incentive to search for the best value for money—which the current system does not—and health professionals the incentive to stay ahead of the competition. The new system has begun to loosen the stranglehold of fee-for-service medicine without requiring the federal government to micro-manage the health care industry.

The Reagan Administration has extended the revolution in the public sector to the Medicaid system, thanks to a highly effective stick and carrot strategy. It has squeezed the states financially, with budget cutbacks, but simultaneously it has eased the restrictions that made it difficult for states to find ways of economizing. As the National Conference of State Legislatures puts it, "the federal government loosened their Medicaid shackles" in 1981, and since then "states have taken the lead in developing innovative hospital cost containment programs."[15] That year Congress gave states the flexibility to adopt new purchasing arrangements, such as prospective payments; altered the regulations to allow states to enroll Medicaid beneficiaries in "capitated" payment plans, such as HMOs, where the health care provider receives a fixed fee for each person under his general care; and granted waivers from "freedom of choice" requirements (under which beneficiaries can select the care provider), so that states could develop management and purchasing arrangements to bring down costs.

The changes have had a dramatic effect, stimulating a degree of competition and innovation never before known in state health programs. The 1981 reforms effectively made the state both a consumer and a financier of health services, on behalf of the poor, and so gave the states the power as well as the responsibility to ensure economical care for the poor. Thus the states became "third party consumers," with the incentive to shop wisely for the poor. States responded quickly to their new power, as they have done in other cases where the federal government has given them both the obligation and the flexibility to manage social programs.

In 1982 more than two-thirds of the states applied for waivers and subsequently restructured their programs. Many have switched to subscription health care programs. Wisconsin and Florida, for instance, introduced a copy of the Medicare capitation initiative by enrolling the poor in HMOs, which agree to charge 95 percent of the average fee-for-service cost. California requires hospitals to "bid" for patients. Many states have also adopted "case management" strategies, under which each beneficiary is assigned to a primary physician, who must approve all additional services outside his practice. The case manager earns a greater profit by minimizing hospital admissions and specialty referrals. Others require second opinions before they will agree to pay for costly nonemergency operations. And others still, such as Kentucky, now require doctors and hospitals to obtain the agreement of the Medicaid program before admitting a beneficiary for all but emergency treatment. Admissions for elective surgery dropped 30 percent during the first six months of the Kentucky program.

The aggressive action by the federal government and the states to control their health care costs has added to the pressure felt by Lee Iacocca and other managers in the private sector. Traditionally, the medical industry has operated by means of cross-subsidies. Below-cost care for the poor would be subsidized by transferring overhead and other costs to the bills sent to government, insurance companies, and rich hypochondriacs. Now DRGs and other controls imposed by the public sector have made it difficult for doctors and hospitals to fund services for other patients with proceeds from government programs or to recover the full cost of treating difficult cases. Hospitals have responded by passing on more and more costs to patients covered by private insurance.

That "cost shifting" has exacerbated the rises in health benefit costs for industry, generated originally by the perverse incentives implicit in tax-free group insurance. By the 1980s the cost of company health plans had reached crisis proportions. In 1981 health coverage became the second most common employee benefit, available to 97 percent of industrial workers. According to surveys by the U.S. Chamber of Commerce, the average annual cost of health insurance per employee rose from $165 in 1965 to $775 in 1979. By 1984 it had jumped to $1,423. Employer-paid health benefits accounted for 2.7 percent of payroll in 1965, but that had climbed to 6.6 percent by 1984.[16] Moreover, many large companies are sitting on another health time-bomb: health benefits for their retirees. A 1986 survey by the *Wall Street Journal* found that almost 80 percent of firms provide health benefits for retirees.[17] The Labor Department estimates that total company health care obligations to future retirees could top $125 billion. Joseph Califano puts the figure far higher—closer to $2 trillion for the Fortune 500 companies alone, exceeding their total assets.[18]

Faced with those staggering present and future costs, companies have drastically changed their role in the provision of health care. Instead of simply paying premiums to an insurance company and allowing the process to take its course, firms have begun to act like states, taking on the role of "third party consumer." They have changed the incentives facing their employees—for instance, by encouraging the use of alternative health delivery systems, such as HMOs—and have instituted in-house "wellness" programs to cut the need for health care. In addition, many large firms are now "self-funding" their health plans, paying at least some hospital and doctor bills directly, and substituting their own decisions regarding how care should be provided and priced for the decisions of an outside insurance company. A 1985 survey of companies by the Health Research Institute found that two-thirds of the nation's firms have banded together in coalitions to flex their muscles as purchasers of medical services, striking more favorable deals with local hospitals and doctors.[19] The St.Louis Area Business Health Coalition, for instance, comprises thirty-seven businesses covering 160,000 workers. The coalition has developed a data base to identify cost-effective hospitals and has instituted its own prospective pricing system. Its hefty purchasing power has forced many area hospitals to reduce their charges.[20]

Unions are generally quite willing to help management cut the cost of health care, provided quality is not unduly reduced; workers have no interest in seeing hospitals rake in money that might otherwise go into their pockets. General Motors, for instance, holds teleconferences among the company's ninety U.S. facilities, during which management and union leaders explain strategies to the workers on the line. GM cut its health care outlays by $200 million in 1985, the first decline in the company's history, chiefly through greater use of HMOs. Chrysler has also moved swiftly, cooperating with workers to reduce costs. The company developed an incentive program called One Check Leads to Another. When a Chrysler employee or retiree spots an overcharge, Chrysler shares the savings with him. Chrysler has also turned to HMOs for health services.

The twin attack by private and public buyers has forced the American health care industry to wake up and start competing. Traditional fee-for-service doctors and hospitals are on the ropes. The new kids on the block are the low-cost "walk-in" clinic for outpatient care and the Health Maintenance Organization. By the summer of 1985, nearly 19 million Americans were enrolled in close to four hundred HMOs, a 38 percent rise in enrollments since the end of 1983.

Competition has also begun to change the insurance industry. Blue Cross and Blue Shield are now offering a variety of subscription health plans, including HMOs. Many hospitals are confronting the HMO threat by introducing their own insurance plans and other innovations. Others have chosen to switch rather than fight: 1985 even saw five New York City teaching hospitals joining the for-profit Maxicare HMO chain, one of the largest in the country.[21]

The HMOs and similar innovations, however, are not above criticism. Cost-cutting steps have always opened them up to the charge of "assembly line medicine." More damaging, however, is the charge that a good deal of their savings comes simply from attracting comparatively low-risk people as members; there is a tendency, for instance, for younger people to enroll. The effect can be that even if the subscription cost is below the average health care costs for a company or for Medicare, an HMO skimming off the cream of low-risk beneficiaries could actually raise total costs. Honeywell found that to be precisely the case. In a study of its Minneapolis workers, the company discovered a significant age difference between those enrolled in its HMOs and those under the regular plan. Company executives calculated that the difference cost them $5 million over the three years of the study. Honeywell responded by lowering the contribution it would make to the HMOs and by requiring employees to pay a fee to join.[22] It is not yet clear whether this is a general problem. Companies seem to feel that HMOs normally lead to substantial overall savings. But even if it does turn out to be the case, companies will no doubt respond, as Honeywell has done, with steps to link their contributions to HMOs with the risk-experience of particular categories of workers. Medicare and Medicaid could do the same.

Increasingly, then, private companies have taken over the function of consumer in the health care market, correcting a basic deficiency in the private health care market. At one time it was assumed that insurance companies would be the health industry's watchdogs, but they actually had little incentive to challenge costs, especially when there was little resistance from premium payers. Higher costs meant higher premiums, which meant higher revenues for insurers. Some experts had concluded from that apparent breakdown in the market that health was simply not subject to the same economic rules as other industries, and so it was assumed that extensive governmental action would always be necessary. But the sudden plunge into the market by corporate America has changed all that thinking. There is now a new player in the game, willing to acquire the knowledge to scrutinize the purveyors of health care, and with the financial resources to make them listen. That makes a comprehensive private national health system possible.

Creating an American Health System

Americans are clearly coming to the conclusion that adequate health care ranks alongside food, clothing, and shelter as a basic necessity. Conservatives can spend all the time they want trying to argue that health care is not a right, but the fact is that unless the existing gaps are closed, and Americans conclude that they and their families are free of financial catastrophe because of illness, some form of national system is going to be enacted. And if conservatives do not seize the initiative and press for a system based on sound economic principles, the country is likely to stumble into massive federally funded extensions of Medicare and Medicaid. That might seem very attractive to many Americans. Even those of us with good private insurance often get very tired of the seemingly endless paperwork associated with claims and disputes. Besides, however comprehensive we think our coverage is, there is usually something that is not included. Moreover, there is always the nagging fear that some disaster will overwhelm our insurance and leave us destitute. If we are reaching retirement, there is the additional concern about long-term care: What if we simply live for a very long time but need to have constant nursing care? Faced with those concerns, "free" national programs like Britain's National Health Service can look very attractive.

But a national system of that kind would be a disaster. When we look at the problems of Medicare and Medicaid and the comprehensive, taxpayer-financed systems abroad, such as Britain's National Health Service, we begin to see why publicly financed national health systems cannot work.

When government directly funds health care, making it free or at least well below cost to the consumer, certain dynamics begin to appear. When the tab is picked up by the federal taxpayer and the patient does not pay more than a nominal charge, there is little incentive for patient, hospital, or doctor to question price. That leads to rapid increases in costs. If the total budget for government health care is fixed politically, as in the case of Britain, rising demand and fixed spending can have only one result: shortage. Such a system forces rationing of some kind. The tourist to Britain may not see it, as he admires the "free" system, but any resident of Britain, as one of the authors was for the first thirty years of his life, cannot escape it.

Sooner or later a Briton has to sit in a crowded doctor's waiting room knowing that his physician will spend only a few minutes with him, because price controls on the physician's charges mean that he has to see many patients to make what he considers an adequate living. If the Briton needs an emergency operation or long and complex treatment, he does not have any of the financial worries that would trouble many Americans. But large expenditures on acute care mean there have to be savings elsewhere in a system with a fixed budget. So the Briton may have to face a wait of many months of incapacitation for nonemergency heart surgery or literally years for some orthopedic surgery. If he suffers from kidney failure and is over fifty-five, he has virtually no prospect of dialysis. Indeed, if he is old and needs expensive treatment to make his life a little more comfortable, he may be told that there is nothing that can be done. It *can* be done, of course, but taxpayers demand budget controls, and controls force priorities. It is little wonder that more and more Britons are turning to private medicine, in many cases supplied by American health centers set up in Britain in recent years.

In America there is a different problem. Rather than impose tight medical budgets on a "free" system and face shortages, as the British have done, we have a system that delivers more and more services to those who have coverage, while leaving holes for the others to fall through. On the other hand, we also have a system that can provide state-of-the-art services to the poor and that is becoming highly sensitive to the financial concerns of the customer, thanks to the rise of third party consumers.

If America is to have a comprehensive health care system, we should seek to devise one that combines peace of mind with the innovation and economies of a competitive marketplace. We should also recognize that the deficiencies of the current system do not stem from a lack of government dollars. They are due to government dollars unwisely spent, incentives that force the poor to choose welfare if they are to have access to care, and incentives that encourage the middle class to choose "insurance" for routine dental care over real insurance for catastrophes. The answer to those deficiencies is not some giant new system. It is to keep government at all levels as a genuinely last resort and to insist that Americans who can do so provide themselves with protection against heavy medical costs. That will take a number of decisive steps.

1. Require all working Americans to furnish themselves with adequate protection from large health care costs, and modify the tax code and regulations accordingly.

The first step toward comprehensive care without massive new federal programs is to adopt the principle that Americans cannot choose to avoid protecting themselves from financial disaster and then expect somebody else to take care of them if disaster should actually strike. That implies a law requiring Americans to provide themselves and their families with sufficient protection against catastrophic health care costs. The details of "sufficient" would require considerable debate: What counts as catastrophic would differ from situation to situation. But the important step is to establish the principle that self-protection is a social obligation.

Since health insurance is generally provided through the place of work, most Americans would no doubt respond to such a requirement by pressing for the incorporation of catastrophic coverage into their firm's health benefit package. For the majority of large firms, that would involve only a minimal change from the current situation and would be achieved through routine negotiation. Recent experience suggests that most firms would in turn press unions for other modifications to hold down the total cost of the package, such as cost-saving incentives for workers. Firms would also be likely to negotiate tough contracts with health care providers to obtain the best-quality care for the fewest dollars.

The big problem would come with the self-employed and workers in small companies, where underinsurance is common. That could be eased through changes in the tax treatment of health insurance. Under the current tax code, where company plans are tax-deductible but individual premium costs are not, the requirement would lead to strong pressure on small firms to provide health insurance as a standard benefit. Small firms, in response, would point out that the cost—including the cost of managing a plan—would be onerous, forcing payroll cutbacks or even placing them in financial jeopardy.

That problem would be reduced, however, if individual premiums and HMO subscriptions received the same tax-free treatment as company group plans. Since company health benefits do not count as taxable income to employees, individual premiums would have to be made an "above-the-line" deduction for all taxpayers, whether or not they itemize deductions. In that way, workers in small firms might be more inclined to join group plans other than those provided at the place of work. Moreover, movement between jobs—which is more common in the small business sector—would pose fewer difficulties if the health plan were separate from the place of work. Changing the tax treatment of health care in this way would provide more choice for the self-employed and workers in the small business sector.

Ideally, such a change should be part of an overall reform of the tax treatment of health benefits. As noted earlier, the limitless deductibility of benefits has helped to distort the whole notion of insurance and to push up the general cost of health care. So the best step, if political factors did not enter the equation, would be to aim for a reasonable limit on the deductibility of both company and individual plans (with a requirement that all deductible plans must provide catastrophic care). That would discourage first dollar coverage and stimulate more cost containment by firms. But political factors *do* enter the picture. Unions and businesses alike have resisted Reagan Administration efforts to cap the deductibility of health benefits, as has the medical industry, all fearing they have a great deal to lose. Even moves to place the cap at such a high limit that few plans would be seriously affected have gained little support in Congress. Nevertheless, the effort should be renewed. Perhaps a "package deal" linking the cap with more generous tax treatment of individual plans and out-of-pocket medical expenses would have better prospects of passage.

An insurance requirement raises a number of tricky questions, of course. How would it be enforced, for instance? For workers in large firms there should be few problems. The law could require that the firm either provide the required coverage to each worker or verify that he is covered by an alternative plan. But the best approach in general might be to require individual taxpayers to supply proof of insurance with their tax returns. To be sure that families did not drop their coverage during the year, health plans could be required to inform the IRS when a person either joins or leaves the plan. There could be a short grace period during which anyone leaving one plan would have to join another, after which there could be stiff tax or other penalties, similar to the enrollment requirements for Individual Retirement Accounts.

Another issue concerns the high cost of insurance for families with a poor medical history. There is not much point in trying to require someone to buy something they simply cannot afford. The problem has been made more acute as competition has intensified by reducing cross-subsidization and encouraging plans to seek lower-risk enrollees.

There are a number of possible ways to deal with this. In some cases the problem would take care of itself. Large firms, for instance, expect a certain proportion of their workers to fall into high-risk categories and simply cross-subsidize within the company itself, with healthy employees subsidizing care for their less healthy workmates. But if a high-risk individual leaves a plan, or if he does not work for a large company, he may face an enormous premium. The problem requires cross-subsidization in some other form.

The simplest solution would be to pool high risks. For instance, let us say a person had to switch from one plan to another to take up a new job, but he had a history of medical problems. The new health plan could be required to enroll him with similar coverage at a comparable rate to whatever he paid the former plan, without regard to preexisting conditions. The danger is that good-quality plans could become inundated with costly patients. To avoid that, individuals or families could be assigned "risk ratings" according to their health record. Insurance or subscription plans could be required to carry at below-market premiums a certain proportion of families with higher risk ratings, according to their share of business in a state. In that way, each plan would have to treat its enrollees as a group and would be unable to concentrate only on low-cost patients.

States could also be required to set up risk pools for very high-risk patients, like the assigned-risk pools that many states have for automobile insurance. The medical costs of uninsurable individuals would then be paid out of a central fund, financed partly by health care providers in the state and perhaps partly by the state itself. The pool would mean that nobody would be denied treatment because he was too high a risk. The state, the insurance companies, and the health care providers would then have every incentive to find ways of providing care to the high-risk individuals in the most economical way.

> 2. *Encourage states to experiment with a "Medical Assistance Voucher" for families with incomes up to double the poverty standard, sufficient to purchase basic health services and catastrophic coverage, with a sliding scale charge to the family.*

Since the 1981 amendments to the Medicaid law, which allowed states much greater flexibility to manage Medicaid, the states have demonstrated their ability to take on the role of health care consumer and to develop a host of innovative cost-saving methods of providing health care to the poor. Unlike the federal government, the states are able to design approaches that fit local conditions and circumstances, working with public and private institutions within the framework of the existing Medicaid program.

A problem continues, however, because of the "Medicaid trap" caused by the reduction in health benefits suffered when a family leaves welfare. The severity of the problem remains unclear, however, and so solutions need to be tested carefully. One approach would be for states to experiment with a voucher to pay for mandatory medical coverage for those willing to leave welfare for a low-paid job. That would be an extension of Medicaid, but there should be a contribution toward the cost of the voucher by the recipient, according to a sliding scale based on family income. The effect would be to reduce the current disincentive to take a job, since the worker would no longer face a loss of health coverage by leaving welfare. A pilot program should first be launched to test the effect of the voucher on the decision to work. If a company were to provide adequate health coverage to the individual as a fringe benefit, the voucher could be transferred to the company, which could cash it as taxable income up to the cost of the group health premium.

> 3. *Require working Americans to purchase insurance plans to cover cata-
> strophic acute care or long-term health costs during their retirement
> years. In addition, enable corporations to treat limited employer and em-
> ployee contributions to retirement health insurance plans like any other
> pension plan for tax purposes. Eventually the private plans should replace
> Medicare. Further, allow large firms to manage existing Medicare obliga-
> tions for their retirees on a capitation basis.*

The solution to health care for the elderly has little to do with finding new ways for the government to fund their health care needs. It is a matter of developing ways of ensuring that working Americans make reasonable provision for their retirement. The government should always be there in reserve for the extremely unusual situation against which a person could not be expected to insure himself. But there is no justification for a system in which one generation avoids taking the necessary steps to protect itself from health costs during retirement, then expects the government to tax the next generation to pay the medical bills.

To avoid that in the future, the federal government should require working Americans to make contributions to private health plans designed either to accumulate savings for large health expenditures and long-term care during retirement or to purchase insurance now that would pay retirement health and nursing care bills. It would be necessary to make this a requirement, rather than simply encouraging Americans to purchase such insurance, because of the moral hazard problem associated with the belief that government ultimately will pick up the tab for retirement health costs. With Medicaid as the insurer of last resort, and with continuous pressure to expand Medicare, workers currently paying taxes to finance those programs have little incentive to buy insurance so that the next generation of taxpayers will save money by not having to pay for today's workers' retirement health care needs. The only way to break this cycle of intergenerational cost-shifting is to require current workers to make provision for their retirement. The enforcement mechanism would be the same as that for mandatory insurance for a worker's current health costs.

The easiest way for most workers to do this would be for the government to allow them to modify existing savings and pension plans. The law might be changed, for example, to allow individuals to fulfill their obligation by making tax-deductible contributions to a special personal account, much like an Individual Retirement Account, that could be used only to purchase health insurance that would pay out during retirement. Several versions of the accounts have been proposed, under such names as Health Bank IRAs, Individual Medical Accounts, and Health Care Savings Accounts.[23] By paying insurance premiums during their working life, workers could expect low rates, since the insurance company would be able to invest the premiums over many years, and the insurer would be making a commitment well before the individual neared retirement and perhaps a pattern of ill health had begun to emerge. Early insurance is also the answer to long-term nursing care costs, which can turn out to be enormous in some cases. If long-term care insurance is purchased early in a person's working life, the premiums are very low. Moreover, the fledgling and highly competitive long-term care insurance market is continuously developing more attractive new plans.

In addition, the federal government could make it easier for workers to purchase health and long-term care insurance through their company pension plans. The law allows companies to deduct contributions made to an employee's pension and to health plans designed to insure against current health costs. But thanks to a change enacted in 1984, companies cannot deduct contributions to plans to pay for retirement health coverage. That has discouraged company-based plans and should be reversed.

With a new generation of workers enrolled in such plans and with private employers and insurance companies competing to find less expensive new ways to provide comprehensive health care for the elderly, the need for Medicare would steadily diminish. Eventually the program could be turned into an insurer of last resort like the FDIC, which is there to give backstop protection to our bank deposits. Medicaid would provide for those who have insufficient resources or insurance to cover retirement eventualities, as it does now.

Requiring workers to make provision for their retirement years does not, of course, address the problems of today's elderly. But in trying to deal with those needs, we must not set up programs which undercut strategies to encourage the next generation of Americans to be self-sufficient.

The health cost problems of the current elderly fall into two very different categories. The first is large hospital bills for acute care. To the extent that Medicare leaves gaps unpaid, this can cause serious financial problems. But turning Medicare into a program to pay hospital bills without limit is not only an invitation to runaway federal spending, it is also unnecessary. About 70 percent of the elderly possess Medigap insurance, which under law must cover Medicare copayments and pay for up to a year in hospital. Half of the rest are eligible for Medicaid. Many insurers provide additional benefits to those required by law, including unlimited catastrophic protection. For all but a few thousand retirees each year, the combination of Medicare and Medigap insurance is not exceeded. In other words, virtually all retired Americans effectively have protection against catastrophic hospital costs.

Moreover, a small change in the law could reduce the cost of those private Medigap plans and increase the number of Americans choosing to purchase them. The existing law requires those plans to cover all but a few hundred dollars of a short hospital stay but does not, in fact, require them to provide catastrophic coverage. As every automobile owner knows, it is low deductibles which push up the cost of insurance, not generous coverage; that is also true for health insurance. If the law were changed to require Medigap policies to provide catastrophic hospital coverage, while allowing them to raise deductibles to, say $2,000 in out-of-pocket expenses each year, the cost would drop to below $100 per year, according to insurance analysts, making policies affordable for almost all retirees. And unlike an expanded Medicare, the soundness of private insurance protection cannot easily be undermined by politicians.

The second problem of the elderly, nursing home costs for nonacute illness, is much less easy to deal with. Few of the elderly possess insurance to cover those costs, and even reasonably affluent individuals can soon be ruined by an extended stay in a nursing home. Yet federal action to pay for those costs could involve staggering outlays. About two-thirds of the $50 billion Medicaid program goes to the elderly, and nearly half of that is for nursing home care. But Americans spend billions more in personal assets before they are eligible for Medicaid. If they could obtain help before liquidating their assets it would add to current Medicaid costs. Moreover, if a "short-term" federal program were to pay the nursing home costs of middle-class Americans until private insurance could be organized for the next generation, there can be little doubt that there would be enormous political pressure to make it permanent.

To avoid undermining the incentive for future generations to act more responsibly, it may thus be necessary simply to muddle through, recognizing that there will be many cases of hardship. The elderly will have to continue relying on their own assets, rather than expecting the government to take the assets of others, and families will continue, as they should, to shoulder part of the responsibility. Ultimately, Medicaid is there as a last resort. If we are to avoid an enormous new federal commitment, it must remain a last resort.

To reduce the cost burdens on the elderly, there needs to be pressure on medical costs. Actions already taken by the Reagan Administration to stimulate greater competition in Medicare are important steps toward curbing costs by changing the incentives for patients and health care providers. In addition to encouraging retired Americans to enroll in lower-cost health plans, the federal government should make greater use of corporations as managers of Medicare benefits for their retirees. Since many large companies have developed considerable expertise in designing health plans, and since those companies often have health plans for their retirees, permitting them to integrate the retirement plans with Medicare would make sense—and would yield savings to both the companies and Uncle Sam. Chrysler board member Joseph Califano has already proposed this to the Reagan Administration.

"We are prepared to provide all Medicare benefits for eligible retirees," Califano has offered. "The company would put itself at risk, paying anything above 95% [of the average insurance value of Medicare] and keeping anything below 95%."[24] In effect, Chrysler wants to become a group health plan for Medicare, according to the 1985 capitation rules. That means the company would receive a voucher equal to 95 percent of typical annual Medicare costs for its retired workers. Califano reckons that with Chrysler's expertise and with the flexibility to combine Medicare privileges with the company's own benefits, he can come out ahead.

The goal of making health care available to all Americans thus does not require a comprehensive government-financed health service, like that of Britain, nor does it need a massive expansion of Medicare and Medicaid. What we have to do is recognize that the deficiencies of the American health care system break down into two distinct problems. First, we have some impoverished people who simply cannot afford good care and will not be able to do so however we try to make it available to them. That is a legitimate reason for government involvement. But, as we have seen, that does not always mean the government has to pick up the tab: Risk pools and similar methods can allow the cost of serving some of those individuals to be absorbed by the private sector.

The second problem is very different. It arises because Americans who have the means to provide themselves with protection now and in the future simply decide not to do so, trusting to luck and the humane instincts of their neighbors. The answer to that is to refuse to accept antisocial behavior, not to create new tax-financed programs to enable Americans to avoid their responsibilities. Just as we must insist that parents take first responsibility for their children if we are to avoid runaway welfare costs, the only way to have comprehensive health care without bankrupting the country is to insist that all but the poorest Americans bear the responsibility for protecting themselves against crippling health care costs.

CHAPTER

8

Advancing the Agenda

THE GREAT SOCIETY GREW OUT of the self-confidence of the mid-1960s—an optimism not like that of today, based on a belief in the social institutions of America, but grounded in the idea that federal power can solve all problems, right all wrongs, make up for all shortcomings. Kennedy's uplifting vision of Americans serving their country laid the moral and emotional foundation for a massive expansion of confident federal action, but Johnson's powerhouse politics supplied the muscle. There seemed to many at the time to be no limit to what the federal government could and should do. So the states are not willing to play ball? Well, open up their election process and bypass them by running programs out of Washington. Poor communities and families are in bad shape? Create a national community instead and build a welfare state that does what they are incapable of doing themselves. Insurgents in South Vietnam? Give them a taste of American firepower.

The leadership was bold, and the politics were right on target. But the results shattered the myth. Now we must start again, and do it right this time. We must recognize the limitations of federal power in dealing with the complex problem of poverty. They are not limitations in Jimmy Carter's sense of the term; the country has plenty of resources, as it did in the 1960s. They are limitations in the sense that federal power is the wrong weapon in the urban ghetto, just as it was in the Vietnamese jungle. Instead, as we have sought to demonstrate throughout, America must seek victory over poverty by building on the basic institutions of this society. The enormous financial resources of federal and state government should always be there to underwrite our commitment as a society to those who genuinely need help. But it is time to demand that Americans take real responsibility for their actions rather than rely on the welfare state to take care of all problems. It is also time we recognized that the only way to reverse a culture of poverty is to strengthen the cultural institutions and ethos of moral responsibility that have enabled millions of Americans to rise out of poverty. And it is time for us to base a strategy on the thesis that decentralization and pluralism will always outsmart centralization and uniformity—something that Americans understand instinctively in everything except welfare policy.

The federal government cannot literally create the positive social institutions, but fortunately it does not have to. They are already there, even if they are battered or dormant. What it can do is pass some laws, and repeal others, to create a climate conducive to grassroots change and to channel an appropriate level of resources to where they can be used most effectively.

But creating that climate and reforming the government's role are political exercises, not academic ones. As a logician would put it, debating the issues in a scholarly way is a necessary condition for sound policy, but not a sufficient condition. When it comes down to cases, reform requires votes, and votes turn on far more than the facts of the matter. Nobody would ever have accused Lyndon Johnson of forgetting that. Johnson was a master of the political arts. He knew just when to coax, when to threaten, and how to reward. But, as we have seen, his brilliant use of political leverage to push programs rapidly through Congress also had its price. Satisfying constituencies, arrogating power to Washington, and relying on bureaucrats to write the fine print have left us today with a welfare system containing serious flaws. Johnson overcame coalitions of interest groups opposed to change, but he did so by creating other interest groups within the federal bureaucracy, the human services "industry," and among the poor. While those groups were the agents of change during the 1960s, in most cases today they are the obstacles to reform.

The proposals laid out in this book constitute a direct challenge to many of those groups that grew up around the programs launched during the War on Poverty. Federal bureaucrats tend not to be thrilled about the idea of relinquishing power to state or local officials, and social welfare professionals are not exactly known for their inclination to hand over power and money to their own clients. Nevertheless, there are good reasons for believing that we have entered a rare "window of opportunity" for welfare reform, very different in its specifics from the peculiar circumstances of the Johnson presidency, but in some ways even more conducive to fundamental reform. By seizing that opportunity with boldness, America can move beyond welfarism into an era in which the underclass at last faces a ladder of opportunity rather than a trap of dependency.

The window has several panes, not the least of which is the agonizing debate over welfare taking place within the liberal movement. It is hard to pick up a copy of *New Republic* or *Atlantic* these days without finding an article reviewing the poverty problem in terms that would have been unthinkable for liberals just ten years ago. A lot has changed. There can be no doubt that the acceptance among liberal scholars of the need to rethink the welfare system has much to do with its dismal record. The persistence of poverty in America has forced many whose hearts are in the War on Poverty to turn their minds to analyzing why its programs have not secured victory. The willingness of such Johnson lieutenants as Joseph Califano, Bill Moyers, and Daniel Patrick Moynihan to come forward and talk about the shortcomings of the Great Society has made it acceptable for others to discuss the deficiencies of Johnson's legacy. Michael Harrington has not changed, of course. He still speaks eloquently of the structural inequities of American society. But somehow it all sounds hollow now. The rest of the liberals have learned from their mistakes and moved on.

Conservatives have also played a key role in breaking what was once an intellectual impasse. While liberals continue to attack Charles Murray, the man they love to hate, it is very clear that the conservative challenge to the welfare state has hit its mark. When Murray disputed the record of the programs established during the War on Poverty, saying, in effect, "The emperor has no clothes!" he forced liberals to conduct in public a debate that previously had taken place behind closed doors. Now it is liberals who are openly discussing work requirements, incentives and dependency, and the virtues of decentralization to states and nongovernment groups— ideas that until recently were in the exclusive intellectual domain of conservatives.

Liberal scholars have opened the door, and conservatives have an invitation to walk in. Needless to say, the door will be slammed firmly in their faces if they talk of the wholesale abandonment of the welfare system or harp on waste, fraud, and abuse and the shiftlessness of the poor. But if conservatives are prepared to recognize the good intentions and the legitimacy of many of the goals of the War on Poverty, and to focus on mechanisms within and outside government to achieve those goals, the liberals show every sign of readiness to open peace negotiations. The conditions are ripe for that to happen. If it does, a remarkably wide intellectual consensus could be created as a base for welfare reform—an important ingredient that Johnson was not fortunate enough to have.

The winds also seem fair for a wider and deeper political coalition for change than Johnson faced in the 1960s. These days it is sometimes hard to tell Northern and Southern governors apart on the issue of welfare, and Democratic and Republican state houses are trying out similar ideas to combat social problems. As was inconceivable in the 1960s, the states are taking the lead on welfare, experimenting with new ideas, and showing a new determination to get results. State politicians are no longer the resisters of change; they are the agents of change.

The debate within the Democratic Party, moreover, has shifted significantly toward a position that only recently would have been unacceptable for most Democrats. The old New Deal *cum* Great Society school of thought, which tended to view federal power as an unmixed blessing sent to correct the sins and shortcomings of others, seems to have met its Waterloo in the crushing election defeat of Walter Mondale. Nowadays young, influential Democrats at the state as well as the federal level are far more skeptical of federal action and far more willing both to examine private sector mechanisms and to accept that solutions to fundamental social problems may have to come from outside government. The old partisan rhetoric is still there, but underneath it the whole tone and direction of the debate have been altered.

The mood of the country is also conducive to change. Americans may not know what to do about the welfare system, but they are in no doubt that it clearly is not working. Even within the leadership of the black community there seems to be a growing acceptance that you cannot simply blame all of life's miseries on racism, Ronald Reagan, or insufficient federal money. Having castigated black conservatives for years as apologists for repression and the white establishment, the traditional black organizations are at least prepared to talk to men like Glenn Loury, Thomas Sowell, and Robert Woodson, who recognize the importance of the civil rights era but dispute many of the central tenets of today's civil rights movement. On the streets of the black community, increasingly it is charismatic self-help advocates, like the Washington tenant-manager Kimi Gray or Philadelphia's gang-buster Falaka Fattah, who are today's folk heroes.

This is not to say, of course, that a liberal–conservative coalition is actually emerging and will inevitably achieve radical yet sound reform. Yet the conditions are favorable for an initiative no less significant than the Great Society itself. Turning potential into reality will take leadership and a greater degree of mutual trust than currently exists. What can be said is that perhaps the preconditions for such a coalition have rarely been better.

Nevertheless, there are some rather large flies in the ointment. One is the welfare industry created and financed by welfare programs. For that industry, change constitutes a threat, and it is ready to defend itself. Through skillful public relations and no-holds-barred lobbying, the service providers have managed to convince the American people that the interests of providers are synonymous with the interests of the poor. Whenever there is a move in Congress to eliminate or reduce spending on a welfare program, the industry moves swiftly into action. The media are directed to "typical" beneficiaries who will explain that they cannot continue without the program. Obscure academics are trotted out to give authority to industry spokesmen. Sobbing and well-rehearsed welfare mothers are brought to Capitol Hill to testify before equally well-rehearsed lawmakers, beside themselves with outrage at callous conservative attempts to reduce the poor to rags. The television cameras dutifully record it all for the evening news. The image is strong and persuasive. It is a brave politician or official who stands firm in the face of such an onslaught.

Each segment of the welfare industry has its allies in the corresponding government agency. Like the service provider, the preservation or expansion of welfare programs means the bureaucrat can have a long and happy career. Although the bureaucrat, in theory, merely executes the will of others, he or she is by no means passive in the political process. At the very least, his address book will contain plenty of journalists eager to print leaks from "a reliable source" inside the agency. The careful placement of a memo or the details of a meeting may be all that is necessary to nip a proposal in the bud or cause its surprised originator to be summoned up to Capitol Hill for a grilling. An eager young Administration official, intent on rocking the boat by discussing reforms, is usually no match for the skilled and experienced bureaucrat who is threatened by his efforts.

Cornering political officials is by no means the only way in which bureaucrats can thwart attempts to institute reforms that threaten their power or existence. They can also influence to a significant degree the flow of information coming into an agency and the destination of money leaving it. The opinions of career bureaucrats are extremely important in the selection of organizations to undertake research on behalf of the federal government. That can be very important. The public tends to believe, wrongly, that research is a dispassionate activity. The press will portray any study that conforms to its own view of the world as disinterested and factual. But just as a newspaper editor can provide a very subjective picture to his readers simply by his choice of stories, one researcher can produce a very different image of reality from that of another researcher, merely by what he decides to look for and what he considers revelant and significant information. So the selection of a research organization to study a controversial issue is a critical element in the politics of policymaking, and the bureaucrats make every effort to ensure that only acceptable researchers are chosen.

Careerists can have a decisive impact on the choice of who is to receive discretionary federal grant money under human service programs. That influence can be crucial to determining which new approaches will receive federal backing and which will not, regardless of the philosophical disposition of the government in power. One of the authors saw that from the inside in the Reagan Administration's first term as a reviewer of applications for grants from the remnants of the Community Action Agency, by then a small discretionary fund disbursed by the Secretary of Health and Human Services. Like most such discretionary funds, the procedure was that applications were first to be examined by panels of reviewers, who evaluated each application on the basis of the published departmental criteria. The applications were then to be reviewed by professionals within the department, with the Secretary making the final selection on the basis of the evaluations.

Normally the panels of reviewers for such grants tend to be made up of people with a good working knowledge of the programs. Not surprisingly, that usually means individuals who have a strong sympathy with the original objectives of the program. In this particular case, however, the Reagan Administration wanted to alter the thrust of the grant program away from simply sustaining existing organizations that typically were former community action groups, channeling money instead to help establish the development-oriented self-help groups that symbolized the Administration's philosophy. Reagan Administration officials reasoned that simply rounding up the usual suspects from around the Washington beltway would mean panels that would tend to favor continuing grants to the old-style groups instead of making the break wanted by the Administration. Their solution was to bring in from all over the country a wide range of reviewers who were sympathetic to the change in policy.

The panels duly met and sent in their evaluations. As the published criteria required, new self-help groups were favored over those who had relied on federal money for years. But the old guard moved swiftly to turn up the heat. A half-page story in the *Washington Post* carried bitter criticisms from some of the panelists traditionally used to conduct reviews—but passed over this time. The new reviewers were attacked for their supposed lack of expertise and ignorance of the program—and, of course, their "bias." Why would the Reagan Administration turn to such people and spend valuable taxpayers' money to bring them in from all over the country, one critic asked, when close at hand were people who had worked with the program for years? (Precisely to avoid using people with that close a connection, knowing they would resist change.) Telephone calls also began to pour into the department from congressional supporters expressing concern that this or that group in their district appeared likely to lose its funding. The professional evaluators within the department dutifully pointed out how the groups favored by the outside panelists could show little evidence of having successfully handled federal money. (Of course! The idea was to foster *new* organizations, not to keep shoveling cash to old ones.)

It did not take long for the pressure to yield results. Political officials realized that if they persisted in pushing the claims of applicants favored by the outside review panels, they would face an acrimonious and uphill battle within the agency itself and no doubt in the press and in Congress. The bad feeling would be likely to spill over to affect other proposals of the department. If they chose instead to give grants only to a small number of the groups they wished to support while continuing the flow to the groups with friends in the bureaucracy and Congress, legislation and initiatives that were more important to the Administration would face smoother sailing. The easier option prevailed, and the author learned a little more about the realities of government.

The tight relationships among bureaucrats, service providers, program advocates, and beneficiaries act like a political ratchet against change. The ratchet allows only for the expansion of a program. Indeed, program coalitions are always looking for opportunities to increase spending. But when the program is threatened with a change in the direction of reduced spending, the ratchet begins to bite, erecting massive political obstacles against would-be reformers. So while certain underlying trends make this a period of opportunity for fundamental welfare reform, we should not be naive. The institutions created as part of the War on Poverty have a strong interest in seeing the basic structure of today's welfare state left intact. If reform is to be achieved, we must apply some political entrepreneurship and must find ways to limit the power of the ratchet by shifting the political balance of advantage toward those who favor basic reform.

Building a Coalition for Reform

The easiest way to do that might seem to be to adopt Lyndon Johnson's own approach—a sort of "presidential steamroller" strategy in which new constituencies are created, financed and energized, and the opposition is either bought off with compromises or simply rolled over with superior political power. That approach has certainly worked from time to time. President Roosevelt went to Congress with his sweeping Social Security Act, demanding nothing less then the passage of every segment of the bill, which provided for social insurance, public assistance, and a range of new social services. His "all or nothing" strategy worked like a charm. Johnson's Great Society steamroller was even more successful, given its breathtaking scope. President Reagan has had similar successes. His 1981 package of budget and tax cuts steamed through Congress, confounding both his Democratic opponents and the political pundits. His rugged determination to see tax reform completed led to the radical reform of the tax code in 1986.

The presidential steamroller, however, is not something that can be used at will. If it were, every president would win passage of every piece of legislation he sent to Capitol Hill. Besides a president with an iron will and a strong presence—either on the airwaves or when making a political deal—the steamroller usually needs help from many sources. One is the electorate. A crushing election victory, like Johnson's in 1964 and Reagan's in 1980, can change the balance of power in Congress and give the president a popular mandate that lawmakers ignore only at their own political peril. Similarly, a great crisis or national trauma, such as the Depression, an assassination, or a war (even a peaceful one against poverty), can rally the country at least temporarily behind a presidential initiative. In addition, it is generally much easier for a president to win congressional support for spending money on a new program—particularly one seeming to address a social need— than to find the votes to kill or significantly alter a program. Voters may grumble about spending levels and taxes, but no individual voter feels any direct burden when a new program is launched. Besides, there are plenty of people who gain from the program who will demonstrate their gratitude to lawmakers at election time. When reform consists of picking a fight with the ratchet, on the other hand, most taxpaying voters will have little to gain either way, whereas beneficiaries who are directly affected will not forget who in Congress voted for and who against.

Although it is not impossible, it seems improbable that structural welfare reform will occur in the late 1980s in the same way it did in the mid-1960s. Even if Lyndon Johnson were reincarnated, this time as a president who believed in decentralization and a greater reliance on market solutions, it is unlikely that he could mount the kind of onslaught on Congress that gave him victory in 1964 and 1965. For one thing, the American people are still confused about welfare. They know the current system works badly, but they still seem to be wedded to the notion that the answer is somehow tied up with federal funding. The alternatives are not obvious to them. Moreover, it is not good politics to say that we simply do not have the answer and that we must adopt a trial-and-error strategy based on experiments at the state and neighborhood level. If a president is to force change through Congress, he must have clear-cut solutions advanced with the aura of absolute confidence that they, and nothing else, can succeed. Another problem, of course, is the massive bureaucracy now in place, thanks to Johnson's success, and the industry that provides welfare. Taking on that coalition requires careful planning and, usually, a strategy of indirect approach. Charging the machine guns is always heroic but usually suicidal.

So building on the foundation of emerging consensus among many academics and politicians will be no easy task. While forceful leadership from the top will always be essential, it will also be necessary to develop a strategy that builds up coalitions in favor of reform while eroding the power of those who will resist it.

Several tactics have to be used to construct and consolidate a coalition for reform. First, the message of economic empowerment must be carried into America's poor neighborhoods. It is a potent and popular message. Many communities have grown tired of the third-rate services they receive and the paternalistic attitude of the welfare bureaucrats dispensing them. On the other hand, they have also witnessed the remarkable transformation of neighborhoods by tenant management groups, church-based development associations, independent schools, and dozens of other community organizations that decided to take action themselves instead of waiting for others to act. Instead of mushy talk about "consultation" or "public-private partnerships" and the like, which means nothing to the typical welfare mother or street-corner youth, it is time to talk more directly of ideas that would put real power into their hands. Ideas like public housing tenant management, where the residents call the shots. Ideas like education vouchers, so that poor families no longer have to put up with schools that seem to be run in the interests of the teachers' unions, not the children. Ideas like switching service contracts from outsiders to groups from within the community, who are more in tune with community needs. Ideas like changing day care rules so that Mrs. Smith is no longer a lawbreaker if she looks after the kids of mothers who want to work.

Proposals like that are tangible responses to the problems of poor communities, relying on the self-interested motivation of the poor. They do not treat poor Americans as though they are incapable of improving their own condition if given the means and opportunity to do so. They are understandably popular in poor areas. And politically they are dynamite, because they drive a wedge between the poor and the self-righteous politicians and the service providers who talk incessantly about how they are helping the poor, yet keep them dependent on the welfare industry. Poor neighborhoods, in fact, are the soft underbelly of traditional liberalism. When conservatives actually make the effort to go into these areas and talk to the poor, they usually discover to their intense surprise that residents are remarkably receptive to many of their ideas. When a group of conservative Republican Congressmen held a field hearing on tenant management in the Kenilworth public housing project, they received such an enthusiastic reaction that the liberals began to fall all over themselves to endorse the proposal. Democratic politicians at all levels have been shaken by the warm receptions given to conservatives who talk directly to the poor, rather than allow their message to be filtered and distorted by the social welfarists.

Conservatives need to turn up the heat by carrying the battle into poor neighborhoods. They need to force a discussion of welfare in the very communities that have been hurt most by it. Conservatives need to work with the community groups, low-income parents, and black organizations they have ignored. If they do that, and shrug off the initial blasts from liberals on the sidelines, they will rattle the social welfare establishment more effectively than by any other tactic, by cutting away at its base of passive support.

The second tactic flows from the first. If the coalitions supporting the *status quo* are to be challenged effectively, then other coalitions have to be mobilized and raised to prominence. That means they must be identified, energized, and organized. Take education vouchers: There is a wide constituency for the proposal, but the elements likely to be most effective politically are not organized or known to the public—or even to each other, in many cases. Few Americans, for instance, are aware of the independent minority schools in the inner cities, because they have no formal network or spokesman. No official issues press releases to air their positions on educational affairs, because no such official exists. Nor is there a national conference of such schools to attract press attention. In short, the schools are not even part of the debate. So advocates of vouchers do not confront congressional hearings with black inner-city school principals to speak for the proposal or a low-income parent who would no longer have to scrimp and save to send her child to a better school if vouchers were available. Meanwhile, the teacher unions, seeking to preserve their educationally bankrupt monopoly, have a field day talking about their deep concern for the poor.

Contrast that with the growing momentum for tenant management in public housing. A few years ago tenant management was a mildly interesting and controversial curiosity. Today tenant managers are regularly featured in newspaper articles, in national news magazines, and at congressional hearings. The reason? The Washington-based National Center for Neighborhood Enterprise started to work closely with a number of management groups. Reporters eager for a good story were directed to showcase projects by the National Center's president, Robert Woodson. Together with Kimi Gray, the charismatic leader of the tenant group in Washington's Kenilworth project, Woodson became a tireless advocate for tenant management. He and Gray began to appear regularly on television talk shows and at urban conferences. A national conference of tenant managers was organized to introduce managers to each other so that they could share each other's enthusiasm and experience, and so that the press and politicians could see that tenant management was a national phenomenon on the move. The study of the Kenilworth tenant-managed project by Coopers & Lybrand, which found enormous cost savings, service improvements, and job creation attributable to resident control, gave weight to Woodson's arguments and silenced many critics. Woodson even organized a national satellite teleconference, beamed to public housing projects in a dozen cities. That added to the excitement among the groups themselves and led to countless "public housing tenants go hi-tech" stories.

A brilliant political entrepreneur, Woodson helped the tenant managers to build on that strong base by introducing them to officials of the Reagan Administration, to Ronald Reagan himself, to congressional advocates of self-help as politically different as Republican Jack Kemp and the Black Caucus, and to influential research and policy groups, such as the Heritage Foundation. Soon, bipartisan legislation was drawn up to make it much easier for public housing tenants to form management groups.

By drawing such attention to the tenant management movement and welding together a wide coalition, Woodson was able to put the opponents of tenant management—chiefly public housing officials and inefficient service contractors—on the defensive. The bootstrap, self-help successes appealed to the public and to politicians sensitive to the public; housing officials complaining about unorthodox management methods did not. When legislation cosponsored by Kemp and the Black Caucus Democrat Walter Fauntroy came to a vote in the House, it passed unanimously with liberal Democrats making sure that they did not vote "against the poor."

The successes of the tenant management movement shows just what can be done with a little creativity and persistence. Had Ronald Reagan taken the lead in the issue and gone to Congress to demand that the management of public housing be handed over to the tenants, he would no doubt have met with derision. Liberals and public housing officials would certainly have attacked it as a cruel hoax against the poor, and no doubt public housing tenants would have been produced to denounce the idea. But by constructing a network and publicizing it, a small band of political entrepreneurs created what now seems to be an unstoppable movement toward that same objective.

Structural reform of welfare will require more entrepreneurs like Woodson and neighborhood leaders like Kimi Gray. Such people are not easily found, but they can be discovered and aided by those within government and by supporters of reform outside government. A firm start can be made by the Reagan Administration during its final year. As a top priority, studies financed by agencies and private institutions are needed to find the present extent of innovative local efforts to deal with social problems. Technical assistance must be provided so that the techniques of one successful organization can be shared by others. Efforts to develop formal networks must be encouraged, and such networks must receive public recognition as legitimate spokesmen. A cadre of political entrepreneurs outside government should be financed and assisted to mobilize support for alternative approaches to welfare and social services and to confront the welfare industry. If that is done, the chances of political success in Washington and in state legislatures will increase significantly.

A third way to construct and strengthen a coalition for change is to press for small-scale demonstration programs if the votes for more sweeping reforms cannot be amassed. For supporters of large federal programs, the small pilot project or demonstration is routinely seen as the first step toward the ultimate goal. It is hard to oppose a small project to test an approach. Once such a demonstration is in place, however, it acts as the focus for the buildup of political pressure for a much larger program. A bureaucracy is created, which can begin to work on behalf of the program. Potential beneficiaries clamor to be included. The public does not have to take the word of program advocates on trust. Those engaged in providing services in the demonstration have a clear goal to push for.

A similar strategy can be applied in the case of proposals to change or reduce the federal role, if enactment of complete reform is impossible. That enables the reformer to get his foot in the door. It is difficult for politicians to object to small projects to test self-help approaches, for instance, and in many cases such projects are within the discretion of an agency. When launched, however, they can become the rallying point for a coalition and a demonstration to the public that the approach does work. That, in turn, increases the chances of larger-scale projects, or a national program, at a later time. That is one reason why it is important to win support for "welfare opportunity zones" in the states. Novel tactics that would be blocked by the supporters of existing programs could be introduced within the zones in an effort to build up support before a head-to-head confrontation in Congress.

A fourth way of building support for reform is to try and draw potential opponents, as well as supporters, into some form of official or semiofficial working group on the issue. A common form of such a group is the presidential commission or task force. A bipartisan commission can create strong momentum for a particular plan of action.[1] Commissions are ideal for defusing a political dispute and building support for a solution. In particular, a commission can be a springboard for legislative action by putting forward "independent" proposals, or it can introduce radical ideas into the mainstream and thereby prepare the ground for later action. It was President Truman's Committee on Civil Rights, for example, that provided the initial impetus for Johnson's civil rights legislation. By requiring individuals who represent different interests to reach a consensus, commissions can produce a plan of action on controversial issues where nobody is prepared to take the first step.

But there are pitfalls. Commissions can be creative, but they can also block creativity. They can be used to provide momentum for a prearranged strategy, but they can also take on a life of their own. How they will turn out depends very much on the skill with which their members are selected. Obviously a president can pack a commission with his own loyalists, but that invites Congress and the public to discount its views, so its impact is lost. Thus President Reagan's task force on pornography, which consisted mainly of conservatives, did little more than provide a little ammunition to Reagan loyalists and a juicy target to Administration foes. Far more effective is a bipartisan task force that spans the spectrum of reasonable positions on an issue. But even that can run into problems. If members are too set in their positions, there is little likelihood of creativity. The 1982 Social Security Commission chaired by Alan Greenspan, for instance, included a former senior official of the Social Security Administration and several strong congressional advocates of the system. Not surprisingly, the commission failed to develop any innovative proposals to solve the long-run problems of Social Security. The 1983 Kissinger Commission on Central America, on the other hand, contained several respected and open-minded Democrats, such as San Antonio's Mayor Henry Cisneros and AFL-CIO President Lane Kirkland. Under the careful chairmanship of the veteran negotiator Henry Kissinger, the commission broadly endorsed Reagan's tough approach to the region, bolstering the Administration's position in Congress.

Now is the perfect time for a commission on welfare. Although Ronald Reagan might not be in office long enough to see its recommendations reach legislative fruition, he could establish the political template for reform through a carefully chosen commission. But he has to be careful. A commission on welfare must not be a talking shop. Its purpose should be to consolidate support for a particular approach. The commission would need a clear vision, and its members must be drawn from the ranks of those who already acknowledge the importance of decentralization, self-help, and incentives. In particular, there should be strong representation from state government, where the greatest degree of innovation now resides. It is no good appointing zealots to such a commission; zealots from only one side would mean the commission's recommendations will be ignored, and zealots from different sides would mean the necessary consensus is impossible to achieve. Similarly, its members must have a good nose for political reality, but they must be free of close ties to the agencies and programs they are to reform. Lyndon Johnson deliberately kept agency officials off task forces to avoid special pleading. Ronald Reagan ignored that golden rule in the case of the Greenspan Commission.

Such a commission could get the ball rolling and could strengthen the effectiveness of the coalitions developed through the steps discussed earlier. Whereas the American people might not trust a welfare reform package put forward by a conservative Republican President, Reagan might make considerable progress if he were to press for enactment of the recommendations of a distinguished bipartisan panel. Moreover, even if liberal legislators were not willing to give Reagan an opportunity to reform the welfare system himself, the commission could lay down firm political foundations for the next Administration.

Successful reform of the welfare system will require a pincer attack. In addition to building and strengthening a coalition for reform, steps will have to be taken to weaken those who are opposed to change. Of course, the creation of networks supporting change helps to do that by challenging established interest groups in political debate. But other tactics can also be used to undermine the opposition.

One tactic used effectively by the Reagan Administration is simply to hold the lid on federal spending while reducing regulation, so that bureaucracies and the welfare service industry cannot grow, and agencies are pushed into trying alternative approaches. The Administration has had only limited success, for instance, in its attempts to restructure federalism in a formal, legislated way. By squeezing federal support to the states while cutting red tape and allowing them greater flexibility, however, Reagan has managed to outmaneuver the opposition to decentralization. He has done so essentially by holding the budget line and then giving the states an alternative they could not refuse. The budget strategy has also been effective in the case of welfare services. By holding down federal support, Reagan has forced cities and states to look for ways to stretch the federal dollar. The critical need to do that has encouraged them to consider turning away from traditional service providers.

Another method, more direct, would be to take a leaf out of the liberals' book. Ralph Nader has been remarkably successful at creating the conditions for political change through the carefully targeted lawsuit. Nader recognized that even if he ultimately lost the suit, simply dragging a large corporation into court allowed his organizations to engage in legal and public relations hand-to-hand combat with the corporation. Like David against Goliath, Nader could count on the large private bureaucracy to blunder into trap after trap. By forcing the corporation to expose its own deficiencies to the public, Nader was able to damage its effectiveness as a lobbyist and to generate public demand for his proposed reforms.

A similar tactic should be used against the various interest groups that prosper from programs designed to help the poor and disadvantaged. Conservative litigating foundations, which have grown in number in recent years in response to the successes of Ralph Nader, should take cases on behalf of the poor and bring organizations into court. The campaign for education vouchers, for instance, might be boosted by making public school administrators and teachers try to defend their monopoly in court against a welfare mother seeking only a better education for her child. If a suit charging discrimination or antitrust violations were slapped on some of the credentialling bodies that protect professional service providers from neighborhood competition, public anger would soon be aroused. It is not necessary to win such cases. It is necessary only to force organizations to defend the indefensible in the full glare of courtroom publicity.

Moving Beyond the Great Society

Visitors to America from lands far less wealthy find it hard not to be puzzled and dismayed by the poverty that persists beside such affluence. How can the South Bronx exist next to the wealth of New York's Upper East Side? How can destitute farm workers live so close to Beverly Hills? To some, of course, it constitutes evidence that, deep down, Americans do not really care about the poor, only about themselves. But that is nonsense. More than any other nation, Americans help one another in times of distress.

Poverty continues in America not because we allow it to or because we lack the money. It continues because we do not know how to eliminate it. We have tried to spend our way out of poverty, using the immense resources of the federal government, and we have not solved the problem—we may even have made it much worse. We could probably reduce welfare dependency significantly if we simply withheld help from all but the disabled, but we cannot bring ourselves to do it despite the seeming logic of such a strategy, and that is a tribute to our civilization.

The way to deal with poverty in America is not to seek some bold new comprehensive federal plan, another War on Poverty. It is to recognize that America's successful experiment, along with the ability of its people to deal with both great crises and wonderful opportunities, has depended on the inherent strengths of its most basic institutions of community and family and on the political freedom to experiment. Family and community are the cornerstones of America; they hold individuals together. When those institutions crumble, individuals are set adrift. The freedom to experiment has allowed Americans to act on their hunches, using trial and error to make progress and solve problems.

We have entrenched poverty in America because we have allowed—even encouraged—the values of family and community to deteriorate among the poor. We thought it was more important to be generous to poor people than to keep poor families together. We assumed that poor communities bred poverty and that if we rebuilt them, or moved the poor to another place, their condition would improve. We thought that decentralization, competition, and pluralism were good for everything except fighting poverty, and that uniformity and central planning was bad for everyone except the poor. That is why the War on Poverty failed and why the subsequent programs that build on its foundations have also failed. Probably, deep down, many of those poverty warriors who gathered together in 1985 at the Johnson ranch now realize that. But the reunion, twenty years after those heady days in Washington, was an occasion for nostalgia and pride, not a time for self-examination and recrimination. The veterans of the Great Society had every reason to be proud. After all, they had the vision to start the job. Their generation asked the right questions about poverty in America and tried its best to find the right answers. It is now up to the new generation, who have been able to learn from those bold efforts, to finish the job.

NOTES

Chapter 1: Why the War on Poverty Is Being Lost *(pp. 1–27)*

1. For instance, see *The Public Interest*, no. 34, Winter 1974.
2. Mark Lilla, "What Is the Civic Interest?" *The Public Interest*, no. 81, Fall 1985, p. 71.
3. Thomas Sowell, *Ethnic America* (New York: Basic Books, 1981).
4. Charles Murray, *Losing Ground* (New York: Basic Books, 1984).
5. *Ibid*, pp. 64, 65.
6. Charles Murray, "Welfare: Promoting Poverty or Progress?" *Wall Street Journal*, May 15, 1985.
7. Murray, *Losing Ground*, p. 236.
8. Council of Economic Advisers, *Economic Report to the President*, 1964 (Washington, D.C.: U.S. Government Printing Office, 1964).
9. U.S. Office of Economic Opportunity, *The Quiet Revolution*, 2d Annual Report, Office of Economic Opportunity, 1966 (Washington, D.C.: U.S. Government Printing Office, 1967), p. 94.
10. Doris Kearns Goodwin, *Lyndon Johnson and the American Dream* (New York: Harper Row, 1976), p. 218.
11. Joseph A. Califano, Jr., *America's Health Care Revolution* (New York: Random House, 1986), p. 52.
12. Frank D. Campion, *The AMA and U.S. Health Policy* (Chicago: Chicago Review Press, 1984), pp. 263, 264.
13. Lawrence M. Friedman, "The Social and Political Context of the War on Poverty: An Overview," in Robert H. Haveman, ed., *A*

Decade of Federal Antipoverty Programs (New York: Academic Press, 1977), p. 37.

14. Figures from John C. Weicher, ed., *Maintaining the Safety Net* (Washington, D.C.: American Enterprise Institute, 1984), p. 4, based on various editions of the *Budget of the United States Government*.

15. Michael K. Brown and Stephen P. Erie, "Blacks and the Legacy of the Great Society: The Economic and Political Impact of Federal Social Policy," *Public Policy*, vol. 12, Summer 1981, quoted in Murray, *Losing Ground*, p. 87.

16. Friedman, "Social and Political Context," p. 40.

17. George Orwell, *Down and Out in Paris and London* (London: Penguin Books, 1986 edition), p. 186.

18. John McKnight of the Center for Urban Affairs and Policy Research, Northwestern University, in conversation with the authors.

19. National Center for Health Statistics, Washington, D.C.

20. Anna Kondratas, "Poverty in America: What the Data Reveal," *Backgrounder*, no. 475 (Heritage Foundation, Washington, D.C.), December 26, 1985, pp. 7, 10.

21. See David T. Ellwood and Mary Jo Bane, "The Impact of AFDC on Family Structure and Living Arrangements," unpublished report, U.S. Department of Health and Human Services, Washington, D.C., March 1984.

22. Glenn C. Loury, "The Moral Quandary of the Black Community," *The Public Interest*, no. 79, Spring 1985.

23. Irving Kristol, "Skepticism, Meliorism, and *The Public Interest*," *The Public Interest*, no. 81, Fall 1985, p. 37.

24. Paul E. Peterson and J. David Greenstone, "Racial Change and Citizen Participation: The Mobilization of Low-Income Communities Through Community Action," in Haveman, *Decade of Federal Antipoverty Programs*, p. 241.

25. Milton Kotler, discussing Peterson and Greenstone's paper, in *ibid.*, p. 283.

26. Daniel Patrick Moynihan, "The Professionalization of Reform," *The Public Interest*, no. 1, Fall 1965. See also *idem, Maximum Feasible Misunderstanding* (New York: Free Press, 1969), pp. 22–23.

27. Martha Derthick, *Policymaking for Social Security* (Washington, D.C.: Brookings Institution, 1979), p. 25.

28. Lester Salamon and Alan Abramson, *The Federal Budget and the Nonprofit Sector* (Washington, D.C.: Urban Institute, 1982), p.44.

29. Robert L. Woodson, "Helping the Poor Help Themselves," *Policy Review*, no. 21, Summer 1982, pp. 85–86.

30. *Ibid.*, p. 74.

Chapter 2: The Foundations of a Conservative Welfare System
(pp. 28–62)

1. Alexis de Tocqueville, "Memoir on Pauperism" reprinted in *The Public Interest*, no. 70, Winter 1983, p. 108.

2. Richard Hofstadter, *The Age of Reform: From Bryan to FDR* (New York: Alfred A. Knopf, 1955), p. 134.

3. See, for example, the views of the historians George E. Mowry and Alfred D. Chandler, Jr., as summarized in Arthur S. Linle and Richard L. McCormick, *Progressivism* (Arlington Heights, Ill.: Harlan Davidson, 1983), p. 5.

4. Hofstadter, *Age of Reform*, p. 314.

5. Josephine Lowell, *Public Relief and Private Charity* (New York and London: G. P. Putnam's Sons, 1884), p. 1. Emphasis added.

6. Jacob Riis, *The Children of the Poor* (New York: C. Scribner's Sons, 1892), pp. 277–78.

7. William Clinton Heffner, *History of Poor Relief Legislation in Pennsylvania 1682–1913* (Cleona, Pa.: Holzapfel Publishing Co., 1913), p. 172.

8. *Ibid.*, p. 219.

9. *Louisville Courier Journal*, October 27, 1985.

10. Sindlinger Co., Media, Pa., 1985.

11. *Los Angeles Times*, April 20–25, 1985. Data summarized in *Public Opinion*, June/July 1985, pp. 25–31.

12. *Christian Science Monitor*, April 4, 1985.

13. Lyndon B. Johnson, remarks at a Democratic Party fundraising dinner, Detroit, June 26, 1964, reprinted in Marvin E. Gettleman and David Mermelstein, *The Great Society Reader* (New York: Random House, 1967), p. 21.

14. Daniel Patrick Moynihan, *Family and Nation* (New York: Harcourt Brace Jovanovich, 1986), pp. 82–83.

15. Michael Harrington, *The Other America: Poverty in the United States* (New York: Macmillan, 1964).

16. Cited in James Bovard, "Feeding Everybody: How Federal Food Programs Grew and Grew," *Policy Review*, no. 26, Fall 1983, p. 45.

17. Harrington, *Other America*, pp. 12, 18.

18. Rose Friedman, *Poverty: Definition and Perspective* (Washington, D.C.: American Enterprise Institute, 1965).

19. See, for instance, the 1977 report of the Department of Health, Education, and Welfare, and Victor R. Fuchs, *How We Live* (Cambridge, Mass.: Harvard University Press, 1983), pp. 65–66.

20. U.S. Bureau of the Census, Current Population Reports, Series P-60, no. 154, *Money, Income and Poverty Status of Persons in the U.S.: 1985* (Washington, D.C.: U.S. Government Printing Office, 1986), p.38.

21. Greg J. Duncan *et al.*, *Years of Poverty, Years of Plenty* (Ann Arbor: University of Michigan, Institute for Social Research, 1984), pp. 40–41.

22. U.S. Bureau of the Census, Current Population Reports, Series P-60, no. 150, *Characteristics of Households and Persons Receiving Selected Noncash Benefits, 1984* (Washington, D.C.: U.S. Government Printing Office, 1985), table 10.

23. Harrington, *Other America*, p. 170.

24. William A. Schambra, "From Self-Interest to Social Obligation: Local Communities v. the National Community," in Jack A. Meyer, ed., *Meeting Human Needs* (Washington, D.C.: American Enterprise Institute, 1982), p. 38.

25. Ellen Goodman, "United We Stand—Briefly," *Washington Post*, July 1, 1986, p. A15.

26. William A. Schambra, "Progressive Liberalism and American 'Community'," *The Public Interest*, no.80, Summer 1985, p. 34.

27. U.S. Congressional Budget Office, *Reducing Poverty Among Children*, May 1985, p. 12.

28. Study by Martha Burt for Center for Population Options, reported in the *Washington Post*, February 19, 1986.

29. Marshall Ingwerson, *Christian Science Monitor,* March 15, 1985, cited in *The Journal of the Institute for Socioeconomic Studies*, Spring 1985, p. 35.

30. See Arthur Laffer, "The Tightening Grip of the Poverty Trap," Cato Institute Policy Analysis, no. 41, August 30, 1984.

Chapter 3: Reactivating Federalism *(pp. 63–101)*

1. Terry Sanford, *Storm over the States*, quoted in Denis P. Doyle and Terry W. Hartle, "The States Are Leading as Washington Wallows," *Washington Post*, September 8, 1985, p. C1.

2. *Ibid.*

3. See *The Question of State Government Capability* (Washington, D.C.: Advisory Commission on Intergovernmental Relations, 1985), p. 9.

4. Carl W. Stenberg, "Federalism in Transition: 1959–79," *Intergovernmental Perspective,* vol. 6, Winter 1980, p. 4.

5. Catherine Lovell, "Effects of Regulatory Changes on States and Localities," in Richard P. Nathan, Fred C. Doolittle, and Associates eds., *The Consequences of Cuts* (Princeton, N.J.: Princeton Urban and Regional Research Center, 1983), p. 170.

6. Stenberg, "Federalism in Transition."

7. Paul E. Peterson, "When Federalism Works," in Donald W. Lief, ed., *Emerging Issues in American Federalism* (Washington, D.C.: Advisory Commission on Intergovernmental Relations, 1985), p. 22.

8. Randall G. Holcombe and Asghar Zardkoohi, "The Determinants of Federal Grants," *Southern Economic Journal*, October 1981, p. 399.

9. *Troubled Local Economies and the Distribution of Federal Dollars* (Washington, D.C.: Congressional Budget Office, 1977).

10. Aaron Wildavsky, "Birthday Cake Federalism," in Robert B. Hawkins, Jr., ed. *American Federalism: A New Partnership for the Republic* (San Francisco: Institute for Contemporary Studies, 1982), p. 182.

11. Committee on Federalism and National Purpose, *To Form a More Perfect Union* (Washington, D.C.: National Conference on Social Welfare, 1985), p. 19.

12. Peter L. Berger and Richard J. Neuhaus, *To Empower People: The Role of Mediating Structures in Public Policy* (Washington, D.C.: American Enterprise Institute, 1977), p. 2.

13. Neal R. Peirce, "Comments," in Lief, *Emerging Issues*, p. 82.

14. Berger and Neuhaus, *To Empower People*, p. 7.

15. John Herbers, "Cities Turn to Private Groups to Administer Local Services," *New York Times*, May 23, 1983, p. A1

16. Robert L. Woodson, "Helping the Poor Help Themselves," *Policy Review*, no. 21, Summer 1982, p. 78.

17. *Ibid.*, pp. 80, 81.

18. Peter L. Berger, "Toward an Alternative Vision of the Welfare State," *Catholicism in Crisis*, November 1983, p. 22.

19. Gallup poll conducted in September 1981, *Opinion Outlook*, February 12, 1982.

20. Poll by Louis Harris Associates, June–July 1979, *State Legislatures*, November 1979, p. 23.

21. Quoted in Neal Peirce, "The States Can Do It, but Is There the Will?" *National Journal*, February 27, 1982, p. 375.

22. John Herbers, "The States Learn to Rely on Their Own Devices," *New York Times*, October 13, 1985, p. E4.

23. Peirce, "States Can Do It."

24. Robert Pear, "States Are Found More Responsive on Social Issues," *New York Times*, May 19, 1985, p. A32.

25. *Ibid.*

26. George E. Peterson, "Federalism and the States," in John L. Palmer and Isabel V. Sawhill, eds, *The Reagan Record* (Washington, D.C.: Urban Institute, 1984), pp. 244-46.

27. *Ibid.*, p.244.

28. *Block Grants Brought Funding Changes and Adjustments to Program Priorities* (Washington, D.C.: General Accounting Office, 1985).

29. Richard P. Nathan, Fred C. Doolittle, and Associates, *The Consequences of Cuts* (Princeton, N.J.: Princeton Urban and Regional Research Center, 1983), pp. 192, 193.

30. *Ibid.*, p. 201.

31. Peterson, "Federalism and the States," p. 227.

32. *Hodel* v. *Virginia Surface Mining and Reclamation Association, Inc.*, 425 U.S. 264 (1980).

33. Richard P. Nathan, "Reagan and the Cities: How to Meet the Challenge," *Challenge*, September–October 1985, p.6.

34. Committee on Federalism and National Purpose, *To Form a More Perfect Union*, p. 21.

Chapter 4: Rebuilding America's Communities *(pp. 102–136)*

1. See Jill Jonnes, *We're Still Here* (Boston: Atlantic Monthly Press, 1986).

2. Ivan H. Light, *Ethnic Enterprise in America* (Berkeley: University of California Press, 1972), p. 7.

3. *Ibid.*, p. 63.

4. *Ibid.*, p. 59.

5. Jane Jacobs, *The Death and Life of Great American Cities* (New York: Vintage Books, 1961).

6. Robert K. Yin, *Conserving America's Neighborhoods* (New York: Plenum Press, 1982), pp.74, 75.

7. Daniel P. Moynihan, *Maximum Feasible Misunderstanding* (New York: Free Press, 1969), p. 98.

8. William A. Schambra, *"Is New Federalism the Wave of the Future?"* unpublished remarks to the "Great Society Revisited" Conference, Boulder, Colorado, June 10–12, 1984.

9. Marc Lipsitz, ed., *Revitalizing Our Cities* (Washington, D.C.: Fund for an American Renaissance, 1986), p. 101.

10. Peter L. Berger and Richard J. Neuhaus, *To Empower People* (Washington, D.C.: American Enterprise Institute, 1977), p. 35.

11. Lester M. Salamon, "Nonprofit Organizations and the Rise of Third-Party Government," paper presented to the Independent Sector Research Forum, May 1983.

12. Eugene Meehan, *Public Housing: Convention Versus Reality* (New Brunswick, N.J.: Center for Urban Policy Research, 1975), p.77.

13. David Birch, *The Job Generation Process* (Cambridge, Mass.: Center on Neighborhood and Regional Change, 1979).

14. See Thomas Sowell, *Ethnic America* (New York: Basic Books, 1981), ch. 8.

15. *Cato Policy Report*, vol. 8, no. 1, January/February 1986, Cato Institute, Washington, D.C.

16. See, for example, Albert Shapero, "Some Social Dimensions of Entrepreneurship," unpublished paper, Ohio State University, 1979.

17. *Black Enterprise*, August 1981, p. 37.

18. Anne Allen, "Never Say Never," *Foundation News*, September/October 1982, p.19.

19. "Kenilworth Parkside Cost-Benefit Analysis," unpublished study for the National Center for Neighborhood Enterprise by Coopers & Lybrand, Washington, D.C., May 9, 1986.

20. Landrum R. Bolling, "Volunteerism: The President and Sister Fattah," *Saturday Evening Post*, January/February 1982, pp. 18, 20, 88. See also Robert L. Woodson, *A Summons to Life* (Cambridge, Mass.: Ballinger, 1981), ch. 3 and 4.

21. See John C. Weicher, "Halfway to a Housing Allowance?" in John C. Weicher, ed., *Maintaining the Safety Net* (Washington D.C.: American Enterprise Institute, 1984), ch. 5.

22. Lipsitz, *Revitalizing Our Cities*, p. 102.

23. William Raspberry, "Self-Help Overruled?" *Washington Post*, June 6, 1980, p. A17.

24. *NAN Bulletin*, National Association of Neighborhoods, Washington, D.C., Spring 1986, pp. 5, 8.

25. See comments by Carol Steinbach in Stuart M. Butler and William J. Dennis, Jr., ed., *Entrepreneurship* (Washington D.C.: Heritage Foundation, 1986), pp. 22, 29.

26. See Stuart M. Butler, *Enterprise Zones: Greenlining the Inner Cities* New York: Universe Books, 1981).

27. Morton J. Sussheim, "Selling Public Housing: How Feasible?" un-

published report by the Congressional Research Service, 1984; figures updated by letter to Representative Jack Kemp, April 24, 1986.

Chapter 5: Welfare and the Family *(pp. 137–159)*

1. Vee Burke, "The History of American Social Welfare Policy: 1930–1980," *Policy Forum*, vol. 2, no. 2 (March 1985), p. 4.
2. *CBS Reports*, "The Vanishing Family: Crisis in Black America," aired on January 25, 1986.
3. Burke, "History of Social Welfare Policy," p. 5.
4. Speech by William J. Bennett, U.S. Secretary of Education, to the fourth annual meeting of Networking Community-Based Services, Washington, D.C., June 10, 1986.
5. 1985 Sindlinger Poll commissioned by the Heritage Foundation.
6. A national poll conducted by Decision/Making/Information in 1983 showed that about half of all working women described themselves as working out of necessity and not by choice.
7. Joseph Ball *et al.*, *Interim Findings on the West Virginia Community Work Experience Demonstrations* (New York: Manpower Demonstration Research Corporation, November 1984), p. xvii.
8. Nicholas Lemann, "The Origins of the Underclass," *Atlantic Monthly*, June and July, 1986.
9. *Ibid.*, Part II (July 1986), p. 66.
10. *Ibid.*, p. 68.
11. Mickey Kaus, "The Work Ethic State," *New Republic*, July 7, 1986, p. 30.
12. Ibid., p. 33.
13. Eugene Steuerle, "The Tax Treatment of Households of Different Size," in Rudolph G. Penner, ed., *Taxing the Family* (Washington, D.C.: American Enterprise Institute, 1983), p. 75.
14. Rebecca M. Blank and Alan S. Blinder, "Macroeconomic Income Distribution and Poverty," *Working Paper*, no. 1567 (National Bureau of Economic Research), Cambridge, Mass. February 1985, p. 35.
15. Catherine England and Robert J. Valero, "Working Women: Is Uncle Sam the Solution . . . or the Problem?" *Backgrounder*, no. 263 (Heritage Foundation, Washington, D.C.), May 2, 1983, p. 7.
16. Social Policy Task Force, U.S. House of Representatives, *The Road to Independence, Strengthening America's Families in Need* (Washington, D.C.: National Legislative Education Foundation, 1986), p. 12.

Chapter 6: Better Education for the Poor *(pp. 160–191)*

1. Ernest L. Boyer, *High School: A Report on Secondary Education in America* (New York: Harper & Row, 1983), p. 16.
2. Cited in Carl Sommer, *Schools in Crisis: Training for Success or Failure?* (Houston: Cahill Publishing, 1984), p. 6.
3. National Commission on Excellence in Education, *A Nation at Risk* (Washington, D.C.: U.S. Government Printing Office, 1983).
4. Reported in *Time*, May 5, 1986, p. 68.
5. Kenneth B. Clark, "Full Educational Opportunity," in Marvin E. Gettleman and David Mermelstein, eds., *The Great Society Reader* (New York: Random House, 1967), pp. 186, 187.
6. *Ibid.*, pp. 190–91.
7. Stephen P. Mullen and Anita A. Summers, "Is More Better? The Effectiveness of Spending on Compensatory Education," *Phi Delta Kappan*, January 1983, p. 339.
8. Diane Ravitch, *The Troubled Crusade* (New York: Basic Books, 1983), pp. 267–68.
9. Milton Friedman and Rose Friedman, *Free to Choose* (New York: Harcourt Brace Jovanovich, 1979), p. 156.
10. National Commission on Excellence in Education, *Nation at Risk*.
11. Edwin G. West, "Are American Schools Working?" *Cato Institute Policy Analysis*, Cato Institute, Washington, D.C., August 3, 1983.
12. John E. Chubb and Terry M. Moe, "Politics, Markets and the Organization of Schools," *Brookings Discussion Papers in Governmental Studies* (Washington, D.C.: Brookings Institution, 1986), abstract.
13. *Ibid.*, pp. 44–45.
14. Statement of William J. Gainer, Associate Director, Human Resources Divisions, U.S. General Accounting Office, before the Subcommittee on Elementary, Secondary, and Vocational Education, House Committee on Education and Labor, on the school dropout problem, May 20, 1986.
15. *Investing in Our Children, Business and the Public Schools*, statement by Research and Policy Committee of the Committee for Economic Development, Washington, D.C., 1985, p. 2.
16. "Labor Letter," *Wall Street Journal*, June 24, 1986.
17. *Investing in Our Children*, p. 2.
18. *High Schools and the Changing Workplace: The Employers' View*, report of the Panel on Secondary School Education for the Changing

Workplace, National Academy of Sciences (Washington, D.C.: National Academy Press, 1984), p. 19.

19. Cited in Janet Hook, "Vocational Education Act Due for Overhaul," *Congressional Quarterly*, February 18, 1984, p. 318.
20. *Ibid.*
21. Charles L. Betsey, Robinson G. Hollister, Jr., and Mary R. Papageorgiou, ed., *Youth Employment and Training Programs: The YEDPA Years* (Washington, D.C.: National Academy Press, 1985), p. 2.
22. *Ibid.*, p. 24.
23. Robert E. Taylor, Howard Rosen, and Frank C. Pratzner, eds., *Job Training for Youth* (Columbus: National Center for Research in Vocational Education, Ohio State University, 1982), p.161.
24. It is important to realize, of course, that cost-benefit analyses of social programs often contain speculative or arbitrary measures of "social benefits."
25. Denis P. Doyle and Terry W. Hartle, *Excellence in Education: The States Take Charge*, (Washington D.C.: American Enterprise Institute, 1985), p. 1.
26. Peter Skerry, "The Charmed Life of Head Start," *The Public Interest*, no. 73, Fall 1983, pp. 35, 36.
27. Daniel Patrick Moynihan, "Government vs. Private Education," *Paidea*, Spring 1978, p.1, reprinted from *Harper's Magazine*, April 1978.
28. Based on Katharine Davis Fishman, "The Middle-Class Parents' Guide to the Public Schools," *New York*, January 13, 1986, p. 28.
29. Northwest Ordinance, cited in Ralph W. Tyler, "The Federal Role in Education," Eli Ginzberg and Robert M. Solow, eds., *The Great Society* (New York: Basic Books, 1974), p. 164.
30. Alec M. Gallup, "The 18th Annual Gallup Poll of the Public's Attitudes Toward the Public Schools," *Phi Delta Kappan*, September 1986, pp. 58, 59.
31. Quoted in "Notable and Quotable," *Wall Street Journal*, June 23, 1986.

Chapter 7: Making America Healthy *(pp. 192–225)*

1. Regina E. Herzlinger and Jeffrey Schwartz, "How Companies Tackle Health Care Costs: Part I," *Harvard Business Review*, July–August 1985, p. 69.

2. Joseph A. Califano, Jr., *America's Health Care Revolution* (New York: Random House, 1986), p. 12.

3. Michael Harrington, *The Other America* (New York: Macmillan, 1962), p. 188.

4. Karen Davis, "A Decade of Policy Developments in Providing Health Care for Low-Income Families," in Robert H. Haveman, ed., *A Decade of Federal Antipoverty Programs* (New York: Academic Press, 1977), p. 213.

5. *Ibid.*, p. 204.

6. Califano, *Health Care Revolution*, p. 53

7. John R. Wirts and George W. Wilson, "The Determinants of Rising Health Care Costs: Some Empirical Assessments," in Jack A. Meyer, ed., *Incentives vs. Controls in Health Policy* (Washington, D.C.: American Enterprise Institute, 1985), p. 70.

8. *Ibid.*, p.73.

9. Califano, *Health Care Revolution*, p. 101.

10. Karen Davis and Diane Rowland, "Uninsured and Underserved: Inequities in Health Care in the United States," *Health and Society*, vol.61, no. 2, 1983.

11. William J. Dennis, Jr., *Small Business Employee Benefits* (Washington, D.C.: National Federation of Independent Business, 1985), p. 14.

12. Pamela J. Farley, "Who Are the Underinsured?" *Health and Society*, Summer 1985, vol. 63, no. 3.

13. *Ibid.*

14. Clark C. Havighurst, "The Debate over Health Care Cost-Containment Regulation: The Issues and the Interests," in Meyer, *Incentives vs. Controls*, pp. 9, 10.

15. Barbara Yondorf, Nancy H. Shanks, and Robert Pierce, *Hospital Cost Containment* (Denver: National Conference of State Legislatures, 1985), p. xi.

16. U.S. Chamber of Commerce, Bureau of National Affairs, *Health Care Costs: Where's the Bottom Line?* (Washington, D.C.: Bureau of National Affairs, 1986), p. 3.

17. *Wall Street Journal*, April 4, 1986, p. 23.

18. "Company Expenses for Retirees Soar," *New York Times*, September 9, 1985, p. Al.

19. Health Service Institute, *Health Care Cost Containment* (Walnut Creek, Calif.: Health Research Institute, 1986).

20. Bureau of National Affairs, *Health Care Costs*, pp. 13, 14.

21. "Hospitals Moving to Prepaid Care," *New York Times*, December 2, 1985, p. Al.

22. "HMO Insurance Plans Face Some Threats to Own Good Health," *Wall Street Journal*, January 16, 1986, p. 1.

23. See Peter Ferrara, John C. Goodman, Gerald Musgrave, and Richard Rahn, *Solving the Problem of Medicare* (Dallas: National Center for Policy Analysis, 1984).

24. *Washington Post*, April 8, 1986, p. D2.

Chapter 8: Advancing the Agenda *(pp. 226–243)*

1. See Anna Kondratas and Stephen Moore, "Breaking the Entitlements Deadlock with a Presidential Commission," *Backgrounder*, no. 469 (Heritage Foundation, Washington, D.C., November 13, 1985).

Index

Index